Myrick — Thank you
Sue — For

To Sue Myrick who has charm and
gumption and gallantry — and totes
her own load

Margaret Mitchell

Atlanta, Ga.
Jan. 22, 1937   Laura Hope Crews,

Thomas Mitchell

Leslie Howard.

Carroll Nye

To
Lovely Miss Myrick
whom I have
been so happy to know
I trust we can get our
Southern dinner — before
she says adieu —
"Mammy —"
Hattie McDaniel.

Reggie Callow
to one who
appreciates the
value of laughter

White Columns in Hollywood
Reports from the GWTW Sets

BOOKS BY RICHARD HARWELL

Confederate Belles-Lettres (1941)
Confederate Music (1950)
Songs of the Confederacy (1951)
The Confederate Reader (1957)
The Union Reader (1958)
The Confederate Hundred (1964)
Brief Candle: The Confederate Theatre (1972)
The Mint Julep (1975)
In Tall Cotton (1978)

BOOKS EDITED BY RICHARD HARWELL

Destruction and Reconstruction,
by Richard Taylor (1955)
Cities and Camps of the Confederate States,
by FitzGerald Ross (1958)
Kate: The Journal of a Confederate Nurse,
by Kate Cumming (1959)
Lee, by Douglas S. Freeman
(1961; a one-volume abridgment)
Washington, by Douglas S. Freeman
(1968; a one-volume abridgment)
Tiger-Lilies, by Sidney Lanier (1969)
Georgia Scenes, by A. B. Longstreet (1975)
*Margaret Mitchell's "Gone With the Wind" Letters:
1936—1949* (1976)
GWTW: The Screenplay, by Sidney Howard (1980)

To Miss Nonie

for Sue,
who brought all
the warmth of
the South to
Culver City,

with appreciation
of her charm,
her good nature,
and her help,
        David O. Selznick
                1939.

White Columns in Hollywood

Reports from the GWTW Sets

by SUSAN MYRICK

edited with an introduction by RICHARD HARWELL

Mercer University Press

Macon, Ga. 31207

ISBN 0-86554-044-6

All books published by Mercer University Press are produced
on acid-free paper that exceeds the minimum standards set by the
National Historical Publications and Records Commission.

Library of Congress Cataloging in Publication Data

Myrick, Susan.
    White columns in Hollywood.

    Bibliography: p. 319.
    Includes index.
    1. Gone with the wind (Motion picture)
I. Harwell, Richard Barksdale. II. Title.
PN1997.G59M9 1982   791.43′72   82-18881
ISBN 0-86554-044-6

TABLE OF CONTENTS

PREFACE

As HISTORY Susan Myrick's reports from Hollywood are a fragile record. I hope my introduction and notes strengthen that record, for hers are delightful accounts of the movie capital in the last days of its golden years. If Miss Myrick's record is a fragile one, it is somehow particularly fitting that this is so; for Hollywood's reputation in those days was no stronger than the bubble of illusion it produced. Her record of wonderment at Hollywood and its ways is as much the record of a typical movie fan turned loose on studio sets as it is of the making of a particular film, big though the particular film she helped to make and wrote about happened to be. The year before Sue went to Hollywood a former secretary of David O. Selznick published a humorous exposé of moviedom called *I Lost My Girlish Laughter*. Susan Myrick never lost hers.

There are other fine accounts of the making of *Gone With the Wind*—Gavin Lambert's, Roland Flamini's, William Pratt's, Ron Haver's, to name the best—but there is none that reflects any better than Sue's the excitement and the fun of making the biggest film of the thirties, perhaps the biggest film of all time. She worked hard in California—in Hollywood and on location—and loved every minute of it. Her enthusiasm for her work is evident in the columns she sent back to be published in the *Macon Telegraph*, the *Macon Telegraph and News*, the *Atlanta Georgian*, and the *Atlanta Sunday American*.

I have edited Sue's columns lightly, very lightly indeed. Nothing has been omitted. Her newspaper-style paragraphing has been retained. Her individualized hyphenation of words has been retained except where the meaning might not be clear to a reader in the 1980s. She was very good, as a newspaperwoman should be, at getting names right, but not quite so good on geography. But I have let her versions stand without remark in the text. A few corrections have been made in spelling. These, I think, are largely to correct typographical errors in the newspaper originals.

The movie people are mostly identified within the text of Sue's columns. I have noted the jobs of a few of the members of Selznick's organization. Among outsiders only the famous have been identified. The very famous (such as Al Smith) and the host of Maconites and other Georgians who visited the *Gone With the Wind* sets are left without notations that would burden without embellishing the text.

It was a privilege to know Sue Myrick. It has been a privilege to prepare her "Straight from Hollywood" columns for publication by her neighbor across Tattnall Square. In my work in doing so I am deeply indebted to her sister, Mrs. Allie M. Bowden of Austin, Texas; and to her nieces, Dr. Lil James of Macon and Miss Susan Lindsley of Atlanta—especially to Miss Lindsley for permission to use and to quote the Susan Myrick Papers in the Robert W. Woodruff Research Library at Emory University, and also the valuable private papers in her own collection. I am also indebted to Miss Lindsley for permission to use the snapshots taken by Miss Myrick on the *GWTW* sets and to reproduce the autographed endpapers from the copy of the novel presented to the Macon journalist by Margaret Mitchell.

As many times before, I am grateful to Mr. Stephens Mitchell for permission to quote from letters written by Margaret Mitchell. Likewise I thank Mr. Walter Howard for his generous cooperation, this time for permitting me to quote from the letters of his father in the Sidney Coe Howard Collection in the Bancroft Library of the University of California, Berkeley. For generous help in making possible my use of the Howard Collection I thank especially Anthony Bliss and Peter Hamff. I once again thank Mrs. Annie Pye Kurtz for letting me delve in the Wilbur G. Kurtz Memorial Collection at the Atlanta Historical Society. And it is a special pleasure to acknowledge the interest and industry of Mr. Robert T. Summer of the Mercer University Press.

My thanks are due also to Messrs. David Bishop, Robert M. Willingham, Larry Gulley, Marvin Sexton, Mrs. Dot Shackelford, and others of my former colleagues at the University of Georgia Libraries; to Mrs. Linda Matthews and Miss Diane Windham at Emory; to Kay Brown, veteran of *GWTW*'s fortunes as book and film since 1936; to Mrs. Margaret Branson; to Mr. Joseph R. Mitchell; to the Atlanta Historical Society (especially Mrs. Ann E. Woodall); and to Mr. Tom Dietz and Mrs. Patty Leard. Very special thanks go to Mr. Tom Fletcher of Emory University's Department of Medical Illustration. His fine work in making the photographs for the endpapers of this volume has made them more easily decipherable than the originals.

Richard Harwell
Washington, Georgia
1 March 1982

INTRODUCTION

FROM the moment that screen rights to *Gone With the Wind* were purchased by Selznick International Pictures in July 1936, every amateur (and professional) Southern historian of the Civil War and Reconstruction had lightning rods raised high and pointing towards Hollywood. Each was waiting for lightning to strike and signal his or her selection as a technical adviser for producer David O. Selznick. Eventually it struck Wilbur G. Kurtz and Susan Myrick.

Sending Susan Myrick to Hollywood to work on *Gone With the Wind* compares with Bre'r Fox's throwing Bre'r Rabbit into the Briar Patch. That is just what novelist Margaret Mitchell did for her Macon newspaper friend. Of course Miss Myrick wasn't born and bred in that briar patch, but—to mix metaphors and use one of Miss Mitchell's favorites—she took to Hollywood like "a duck on a June bug."

The storm that had been gathering since the decision to film *Gone With the Wind* was first announced reached the first of several peaks when the Selznick organization sent Kay Brown and Tony Bundsman to Atlanta in December 1936. Margaret Mitchell wrote Sidney Howard, then working on his screenplay of *Gone With the Wind*, 4 January 1937:

> In the early part of December, the Selznick company sent down a crew to Atlanta to "audition" people with the possible hope of picking up a new face for the cast of "GWTW." As I wrote you before, I have nothing to do with the filming of the book. I didn't want to have anything to do with it as I know that everyone in the U. S. except me is movie crazed and yearns to act. And I

knew if I had any connection with the film, life would be more of a
burden than it has already been for six months. But, of course,
when the audition crew arrived, the populace of six states descended on me, demanding that I endorse each and every one of
them for the role of Scarlett, etc. The phone went every minute and
wires and special deliveries deviled me and shoals of people
camped on the door step and clutched me if I went out. No one
seems to believe that I have nothing to do with the movie as it
seems to be beyond human comprehension that any mortal does
not yearn to be connected with the movies. . . . Alas where has my
quiet peaceful life gone? I will be so glad when the picture goes into
production, then perhaps some of my problems will be over.[1]

While Kay Brown was in Atlanta she reiterated Selznick's wish
that Margaret Mitchell come to California and oversee aspects of the
filming of her novel. The author's response must have been much the
same as she had written Miss Brown on 1 October: "Will you please
thank Mr. Selznick for me for his renewed invitation for me to go to
California. I just do not think it will be possible. But I am appreciative
of the invitation just the same."

The storm stirred up by the visit of "the Selznickers" (as Miss
Mitchell called them) had two happy by-products. Mr. W. T. Ander-
son, the veteran editor and publisher of the *Macon Telegraph*, wrote
Margaret Mitchell on 9 December:

Sue tells me about Hollywood wanting you to come out there
and see that your book is properly filmed, and that you won't go. . . .
If you don't think of anything better I should like to see Sue
Myrick deputized to supervise. She has studied stage business,
knows Southern dialect, has Southern background and understands the characters and the qualities every foot of the way. I
think you would do the best job, and think Sue would do the
second best. She'd fight to keep the picture off the rocks. If you are
asked what to do about the job you don't want, keep this idea in
mind.

---

[1]Margaret Mitchell to Sidney Coe Howard, Atlanta, 4 January 1937, typed letter
(copy), Margaret Mitchell Marsh Papers, University of Georgia Libraries. All manuscripts quoted in this introduction are, except as otherwise noted, part of these Margaret Mitchell Marsh Papers.

Margaret Mitchell had met Susan Myrick at the first Georgia Press Institute, held in Macon in 1928.[2] The two women formed an immediate friendship and were good friends indeed by the time *Gone With the Wind* was published eight years later. Miss Mitchell liked Mr. W. T.'s idea and told him so when she replied to his letter on 12 December. "I will certainly beat the drum for her," she promised. She undertook the drum beating two months later, after she had spent some time with Sue while visiting Macon for the funeral of their mutual friend Aaron Bernd on 13 February 1937.

The day after the funeral she wrote Kay Brown, who had met both Myrick and Bernd during her visit to Georgia, praising her friend and, wisely, omitting Mr. W. T.'s reference to Sue's having "studied stage business." (It might well have been a kiss of death to mention that.) She said:

> We fell to talking about the coming production of *G. W. T. W.* (as you probably know wherever two or more of ye are gathered together these days, the two or more talk about the movie). As I listened to Susan Myrick talking an idea dawned on me that made me wonder why I had not thought about it before. I spent the night with her and encouraged her far into the night to talk about the picture. She had such good ideas (at least I thought them good) that I came home determined to write you.
>
> You know what my attitude has been all along in the matter of not making any suggestions to any of you Selznick folks about the film. You know the fight I have put up against the general public who wanted to get in the picture as actors, script assistants, costumers, advisers, etc. Half of my fight has been, frankly, because I didn't want any more grief than I already had. The other half was because I sincerely believe that you people know your business far better than I'll ever know it and I did not want to hamper or embarrass you with suggestions that were useless or

---

[2]Myrick wrote on 9 October 1937, after one of many quick visits with the Marshes in Atlanta: "Peggy telephoned to come up and I was delighted of course. She is always kind. And she is more fun than anybody in the world I guess. The only person alive who could take what she has taken and be completely unchanged. I knew her nearly eight years before she wrote *GWTW* and she is just the same girl now she was then, unspoiled, unchanged in every way. I couldn't have helped wallowing in excitement and riches and fame and I'd have accepted all the literary teas and probably have made a perfect ass of myself." From the diary of Susan Myrick in the possession of Susan Lindsley.

impractical. I've even refused as much as five hundred dollars to name the cast *I'd* like because I thought it might embarrass y'all in some way. So this is my first suggestion and for Heaven's sake, if it sounds foolish to you, don't mind telling me because it won't hurt my feelings and no one else except John will ever know about it.

My suggestion is why not take Susan Myrick out to the Coast in some capacity while the picture is being made? (I say "in some capacity" for I do not know just what sort of title such a job would carry.) You said that you'd like to have me there to pass on the authenticity and rightness of this and that, the accents of the white actors, the dialect of the colored ones, the minor matters of dress and deportment, the small touches of color, etc.

Well, I can't go and you know why. But I thought if you really wanted a Georgian for the job there wouldn't be anyone better than Sue. In fact, she'd be a better person for the job than I would because she knows more about such matters than I do. I hope you will not gag when I explain why. I know you are sick and tired of people who want to get into the picture "because of their lovely Southern background." I know I am. But I have to drag in Sue's background for explanation.

Her Grandpa, old General Myrick, had the biggest and whitest colyumed house in Georgia, at Milledgeville. It's still there, a lovely place but no longer in Myrick hands. The family lost it due to hard times. Sue is the youngest child of a Confederate soldier and God knows she's heard enough about the old days. Being poor as Job's turkey, she was raised up in the country and she knows good times and bad, quality folks and poor whites, Crackers and town folks. And good grief, what she doesn't know about negroes! She was raised up with them. And she loves and understands them. Since going on the paper, she has been the paper's official representative at most of the negro affairs of her section. Mr. W. T. Anderson, owner of her paper (I wish you could have met him), is strong for the colored folks and tries to get a square deal for them and the saying among the colored folks in the district is that "De Race is got two friends in dis County, sweet Jesus and de *Macon Telegraph*." So whenever there's a colored graduation if Mr. W. T. can't be there to make a speech, Sue goes and if the colored P. T. A. wants to be addressed by Mr. Anderson and he can't make it, Sue does the addressing—the same holds for funerals and awarding of prizes.

Moreover Sue is as competent a newspaper woman as we have in this section. She can—and does—do every thing from advice to the lovelorn and the cooking page to book reviews and politics and hangings. But the main thing that recommends her to me is her common sense and her utter lack of sentimentality about what is tearfully known as "The Old South." She knows its good points and she doesn't slur over its bad points. She knows her section and its people and she loves them both but she is not unaware of either the faults or the charm of both people and section. In other words she's a commonsense, hardheaded person with an awful lot of knowledge about Georgia people and Georgia ways, not only of this time but of times past. So I'm handing the idea on to you of using her on the picture.

Now, Katharine, please don't think you've got to consider her seriously just because I suggested her or just because she's a friend of mine. If the idea doesn't seem good to you, just tell me so. It won't bother me and Sue will never know that I've written you so there'll be no skin off anyone's nose.

Another by-product of the visit of the Selznickers was the emergence of Atlantan Wilbur G. Kurtz as a possible adviser for *Gone With the Wind*. In October, when Margaret Mitchell had expected a fall visit from Director George Cukor and his staff, the novelist told Miss Brown of Mr. Kurtz's special qualifications as an expert to show Cukor around Atlanta. "I want to render any aid possible to Mr. Cukor," she said. She wrote further: "Mr. Wilbur Kurtz of Atlanta is a well-known architect and painter. More than that, he is our greatest authority on the Civil War in this section. He has studied every campaign, been over every battlefield, mapped out the position of the troops. He also has a fine collection of early Atlanta pictures. He would be the proper man to show Mr. Cukor around. Of course, I would go too but Mr. Kurtz is the real authority."

Kurtz pushed his candidacy in a letter written 7 December 1936 to the Atlanta Chamber of Commerce. He wrote Chamber president Eugene Harrison: "I'd like very much to go to Hollywood and direct the historical setting for this picture. I have all the information, the maps, etc. . . . The possibilities are great! The book is unique! The producers should see that if they preserve the historical part of the story as the author wrote it, they will have a picture as different from other pictures as the book is from the average novel."[3] In a letter to Kay Brown on 8 March 1937 Margaret Mitchell reinforced her endorsement of Kurtz as an authority on the Civil War and added: "As a matter of fact, if you wanted an honest to God expert on the War part

---

[3]Wilbur G. Kurtz, "Technical Adviser: The Making of Gone With the Wind—The Hollywood Journals of Wilbur G. Kurtz," ed. Richard Harwell, *Atlanta Historical Journal* 22:2 (Summer 1978): 9.

of the picture you couldn't do better than kidnap Mr. Kurtz and take him to Hollywood."

Things moved along as intended. Kurtz was hired by Selznick as historian and went to Hollywood in late January 1938 for three weeks. The movie people were pleased with his preliminary work and he returned in November. His wife, Annie Laurie Fuller Kurtz, was brought out to work with him shortly before Christmas. The Selznick studio already had on its staff as "dialect coach," Will Price, a Mississippian who had worked in Atlanta as a member of the WPA Federal Theater project. Mrs. Kurtz was also regarded as an expert on rural Georgia accent, but the possibility of a job for Sue Myrick was still very much alive.

Kurtz reported on 8 December, in the journal-letter that he periodically sent home, that Daniel O'Shea, Selznick's legal officer, had broached the subject of her "coming out here, as arbiter of manners and customs—and of Negro and white dialect." Kurtz added: "I was thrilled to hear this matter brought up and listened with both ears. When my time came to speak, I pulled for Sue with all my might."[4] O'Shea asked Kurtz for Myrick's address and said he would wire her that day. The plan was to have Miss Myrick and Mrs. Kurtz make the trip to Hollywood together. Sue, however, delayed accepting a contract.

Kay Brown had written to Sue in May 1937: "On other pictures of similar magnitude, the director and producer have engaged persons whose qualities fitted them to serve in a capacity similar to yours and these services have been at the approximate weekly salary of between $125 and $150 per week. We want very much to have you on this job and I regret that I am not in a position to make an offer comparable to our discussions, but I am hopeful you will see your way clear to accept this assignment at $150 per week." She added: "Mr. Selznick asked me to tell you that he would be delighted to have you write daily stories from the set and do anything of that nature which might be of interest to Mr. W. T."[5]

---

[4]Ibid., pp. 94-95.

[5]Katharine Brown to Susan Myrick, New York, 26 May 1937, typed letter signed, Susan Myrick Papers, Emory University Library.

It was little wonder that after waiting for the call to Hollywood for more than a year and a half, Sue was disappointed that O'Shea's telegram of 9 December offered "not more than one hundred dollars week."[6] She wired back stating her surprise at terms less than mentioned in the May 1937 letter.[7] O'Shea answered on 12 December that Selznick International would meet the minimum salary mentioned in Miss Brown's letter and would guarantee five weeks employment.[8] No copy of Myrick's reply survives but in his telegram of 13 December O'Shea said: "IT'S A DEAL. HOPE TO WIRE YOU NEXT WEEK DATE FOR YOUR ARRIVAL HERE. BARELY POSSIBLE YOU WILL NOT BE CALLED UNTIL AFTER HOLIDAYS."[9]

Mrs. Kurtz left Atlanta for Los Angeles by train and arrived in California on 23 December. Sue flew out, not leaving Atlanta until 6 January. On her first day there she signed her formal contract with Selznick International Pictures, Inc. The first clause of her contract sets forth her duties:

> FIRST: Producer hereby employs Employee to render her services exclusively to Producer (1) as an expert consultant and adviser on the speech, manners, and customs of the period and localities depicted in the novel entitled GONE WITH THE WIND; (2) as a coach and tutor of the pronunciations and accent characteristics of each social class and locality depicted in said novel for the members of the cast (both white and negro) of Producer's photoplay now entitled GONE WITH THE WIND and (3) in such other capacities in connection with the production of said photoplay as Producer may determine befit Employee's capabilities.[10]

[6]Daniel T. O'Shea to Myrick, Los Angeles, 9 December 1938, telegram (night letter), Myrick Papers.

[7]Myrick to O'Shea, Macon, 10 December 1938(?), telegram (typed copy), Myrick Papers.

[8]O'Shea to Myrick, Los Angeles, 12 December 1938, telegram (typed copy), Myrick Papers.

[9]O'Shea to Myrick, Culver City CA, 13 December 1938, telegram (night letter), Myrick Papers.

[10]Selznick International Pictures, Inc. contract with Susan Myrick, Culver City CA, 7 January 1939, typed copy.

It was a standard contract. There was no mention of Miss Myrick's intention to write stories for the *Telegraph* while on the *Gone With the Wind* set. But, as that had been part of the understanding with her as early as May 1937, approval was most likely given now as a simple oral agreement.

Margaret Mitchell later (23 January 1939) wrote Kay Brown of Sue's departure from Atlanta.

> John [John Marsh, her husband] and I went out to the airport to tell her good-bye, thinking she might be a little lonely. Good Heavens, half of Macon was there and the staffs of the two Macon papers. The airport restaurant was so jammed with them that other travelers could get nothing to eat. I asked who was getting out the *Macon Telegraph* that night and they replied that it was in the hands of the office boy, the antique colored porter and Mr. W. T. Anderson, owner and publisher. Practically everyone burst into tears when the plane took off, all because Sue was going to be away from Macon for a few weeks. Believe it or not, the Mayor of Macon issued a public statement to the press proclaiming "a period of mourning" during her absence.

Sue Myrick arrived in Hollywood on 7 January. Miss Mitchell now had three of her own people in place on the *Gone With the Wind* set. With what she heard from the Kurtzes and from Myrick, plus what she learned from calls and letters from Kay Brown and occasional communications from Selznick himself, Miss Mitchell was kept very well informed of the progress on the film.

The Atlantan had cooperated more than was ever publicly acknowledged in the months of preparation for filming. She had made extensive arrangements for the visit of Kay Brown and Tony Bundsman in December 1936. The next year she had gone all out to make George Cukor's visit in early April a success. Of that trip by the Selznickers she wrote her friend Herschel Brickell, book critic for the *New York Post*, on 8 April:

> Mr. Cukor, who is to direct "Gone With the Wind," has been here with his technical staff, and I took them over all the red rutted roads of Clayton County. The dogwood was just coming out and the flowering crabs blooming like mad. The movie people wanted to see old houses that were built before Sherman got here and I obligingly showed them. While they were polite, I am sure they were dreadfully disappointed, for they had been expecting architecture such as appeared in the screen version of "So Red the

Rose." I had tried to prepare them by reiterating that this section of North Georgia was new and crude compared with other sections of the South, and white columns were the exception rather than the rule. I besought them to please leave Tara ugly, sprawling, columnless, and they agreed. I imagine, however, that when it comes to Twelve Oaks they will put columns all around the house and make it as large as our new city auditorium.

As the date for beginning work on the film approached, Margaret Mitchell received queries from Selznick's Research Department, which she carefully answered, and telephoned questions from Kay Brown (acting for Selznick himself) concerning difficult passages in the ever-changing screenplay. Just two days before filming began Selznick himself wrote her a long plea for help—specifically a request to write a new scene in which Melanie Hamilton's and Ashley Wilkes's traits of character would be fully apparent in their first introduction to screen audiences.

Miss Mitchell answered that she saw and understood the problem but could not help. She explained that she knew nothing about writing for films.

No matter how much I might wish to help you [she wrote], by writing the dialogue or sketching the scene, it would be impossible. I am a slow writer and writing takes time, uninterrupted time. For nearly three years I have had no time for writing of any kind. With hundreds of letters coming in, with the telephone constantly ringing, with people clamoring for "introductions to Mr. Selznick" and newspapers bedeviling me for statements on subjects that do not concern me, I have had no time even to think about creative writing, much less to attempt it.... So I must ask to be excused but not without regret that I am in no position to help. I am proud that you wish to keep the whole film true to the book and I would help if I could.

Assistant Director Eric Stacey wrote a series of questions about *Gone With the Wind* on 15 November 1938. These were dutifully referred by Ruth Leone, research assistant, to Miss Mitchell. They demonstrate both the detail exercised in planning the movie and exactly the kinds of questions Miss Myrick would later be called upon to answer:

1. House servants at Tara; how many unnamed in story? For example, number of people who would be seen at prayer, and nature of the group.

2. Plantation slaves at Tara; how many would be seen at one time; how many visible around the house?

3. At the barbecue at Twelve Oaks, how many people did Miss Mitchell visualize? Proportion of adults and children? Proportion of old and young? Were colored children and white children playing together? How many barbecue pits?

4. At Belle Watling's establishment, what type of small orchestra, trio, quartet? What instruments? What type of music would they play?

5. Servants at Aunt Pitty's; how many other than the named ones, Uncle Peter, cook and Prissy?

6. Hospital in Atlanta in war time; could it be pictured in a church which had been converted into a makeshift hospital?

7. Negro labor battalion, passing Aunt Pitty's, with Big Sam as one of the group; how many in round numbers, 10 or 100? Also how dressed; uniforms or ragged clothes?

8. Artillery battalion, how many men in one?

9. Convicts working at Scarlett's mill; how dressed, ragged clothes or uniforms?

10. Sheep on lawns of some of the big houses, such as Tara or Twelve Oaks; (want to show these, primarily for pictorial value, but ostensibly to keep grass clipped short) may they be shown?

11. Did they use the symbol of the Red Cross on ambulances in the Civil War?[11]

Miss Mitchell answered some, but not all, of the questions referred to her. Then came the back-breaking straw. Shortly after Kurtz arrived in California he and Marian Dabney, a former Atlantan by then in charge of women's costumes in Selznick's Wardrobe Department, wrote asking if Mammy's headkerchief should be tied with knots showing or folded under. Miss Mitchell later said she refused to go out on a limb over a head-rag. Her immediate reaction was a long letter (16 December) to Kurtz reiterating her position vis-à-vis the film.

I'm returning the sketches of the head rag, and you will note that I have not ok-ed them. My reasons for not o k-ing are two in number. The first is that I am not connected with the film and I do not think it my place to pass upon anything of this nature. During the past year or more I have received several letters from the Selznick offices asking for information of one kind or another. I

---

[11]Memo by Eric Stacey, Culver City CA, 15 November 1938, Selznick International Pictures, Inc. Research Papers, University of Georgia Libraries.

have answered some of the questions and have been glad to do it if the information was readily available. I was also glad to assist the Selznick people in getting a list of books and people they might consult in their research work. However, I am not a technical adviser on this job. I have given some pretty broad hints of my attitude in several of my previous letters, but now I think I had better state my position more directly. I haven't minded discussing certain matters informally, as I have done in some of the previous letters, but I don't intend to give official o k's on any part of the film. That would put on me a responsibility I don't wish to have.

It would also be directly in conflict with the position I have taken for the past two and a half years. From the minute I sold the film rights, I said that the picture was Mr. Selznick's and I did not wish to have anything to do with it. You know how the public has hammered on me, trying to get me to take a hand in the selection of the cast, trying to get me to make Mr. Selznick do this or do that, trying to get me to mix myself into something that is none of my business. You also know how stubbornly I have resisted all of this pressure on me. Having withstood it all of this time, I certainly don't intend to reverse myself at this late date and actually take a hand in the production as an adviser, officially or unofficially. That just isn't my job.

My second reason is that, even if I were inclined to act as an adviser, I haven't the time to do it. As you know, I am no authority on the period covered by my book, and I do not carry a lot of details in my head. Whenever I want to know something I sit down and check all my references, no matter how minor the point may be—and no matter whether I have looked it up just the week before. I do not like to give offhand judgments, even on head rags. When I was writing my book I remember having seen several pictures of head rags that were tied the way they ought to be tied, and there was one in particular that I thought would be helpful to you. This morning I went through the twenty or more memoirs of ladies of the sixties I have here at home and did not find the photograph I wanted. . . . The news that the picture is actually going into production has stirred a number of people to fresh frenzies—would-be Scarletts are arriving at my door again and people who want to be technical advisers, dialect experts, or who want me to get them on the Selznick lot "just for a look around" are bedeviling me. So, you can see I wouldn't have the time for any research work, even if my life depended on it.

In other words, I don't mind being obliging and I am hopeful that the picture will be accurate as to the background, costumes, etc., but I can't and won't take on the responsibilities of serving as an adviser and we might as well understand each other on that point before we go any further.

> When Sue Myrick and Annie Laurie get there you three ought
> to be able to handle the situation without needing any help from
> me and much better than I could.

Margaret Mitchell expected the turmoil in her life to subside once
the filming of *Gone With the Wind* began. There was, however, one
more storm on her horizon, the announcement of definite casting of
the major roles. Clark Gable had been signed for the part of Rhett
Butler for months. It was the time at which Metro-Goldwyn-Mayer
could make him available that controlled the schedule of the film. But
the parts of Scarlett, Melanie, and Ashley had not been assigned. In
December Mr. Kurtz thought Ashley's role would go to Douglas
Montgomery. Paulette Goddard was still front-runner for Scarlett's
role at the time of the studio Christmas party on 24 December. By the
time Sue Myrick arrived on the set, it was strongly rumored that Vivien
Leigh had cinched the part but was still unsigned. The casting of Leslie
Howard, Olivia de Havilland, and Leigh was announced on 13 January and did indeed stir up the author's life again. Margaret Mitchell
wrote in a long letter to Selznick the next day:

> Yesterday afternoon (Friday) the *Journal*, one of our after-
> noon papers, carried a copyrighted UP story about Miss Leigh,
> which I am enclosing. It bore the marks of being an "official
> release" but, on second reading appeared to be a news leak. None
> of our three papers queried me about it. Around nine o'clock your
> first wire came and the Western Union girl told me that a long wire
> was on the way and segments of it would arrive at fifteen minute
> intervals. It seemed sensible to avoid delay in delivery by going to
> the Western Union office, so John and I did this. Three sheets
> telling about Miss Leigh had arrived by the time we reached the
> office; I knew our morning paper was going to press and of course
> I wanted the hometown papers to have the break on this story, so I
> left John at the Western Union office to wait for the remainder and
> I went to the *Constitution* office. By good luck, they had a photo-
> graph of Miss Leigh and they tore out part of the front page, put
> her picture in, and began setting your wire. At intervals the rest of
> the wire came in. It was all very exciting and reminded John and
> me of our newspaper days.

The selection of an English actress to play the part of Scarlett
created new furor. Even Sue Myrick was disturbed that three of the
leading parts would be played by Britishers. There were protests from
the United Daughters of the Confederacy that the news services built

into a national story. In an effort to deflect some of the reaction Miss Mitchell wrote Kay Brown (21 January) suggesting that the Selznick organization publicize the work of Southerners Myrick and Wilbur and Annie Laurie Kurtz. "Your publicity department," she wrote, "has done nothing with them in the way of dramatizing them and showing just what good assistants Mr. Selznick has."

She described to Miss Brown the situation the casting announcement had brought about. "The Associated Press," she said, "had me on the phone for nearly an hour last night. . . . In fact, everyone in creation has had me on the phone for hours during the last two days. Things were never this bad, even when GWTW was selling around a million. Newspapers make up part of the calls; others come from people who wish to sell me old fashioned beds and bowl and pitcher sets (and matching chambers, for all I know) to be used in Mr. Selznick's film; numbers of the calls are from people who are being 'just neighborly.' "

When Sue Myrick arrived in California she dived immediately into her work at the SIP studio. On that first day Cukor (whom she had met when he visited Georgia in 1937) took her in tow. She met Selznick and various staff and cast members, watched actual screen tests for the Gerald and Belle Watling parts, and had screened for her tests of Vivien Leigh acting Scarlett's role opposite both Leslie Howard and Douglas Montgomery. In January 1939 Miss Myrick was already forty-five and would reach her forty-sixth birthday on 20 February, but she had the energy and vivacity of one half her age. Better yet, she sparkled with enthusiasm. Her genuine interest in everyone and everything on the sets for *Gone With the Wind* lights up the columns she wrote for the *Macon Telegraph* and the *Atlanta Georgian* and shines even more brightly in the frank and open letters she wrote to Margaret Mitchell and in the private record she kept of her months in Hollywood.

That record is not a diary in the usual sense. It varies widely in the extent of its entries, probably according to how tired its author was after a given day's work. It is spasmodic in its entries and hurried in its style, but it is informative and entertaining. Before her first night's rest in California she wrote in it: "My head is buzzing and my eyes are sticking out and my brain is whirling from the fast way things have happened today." She had been pleased at Cukor's "greeting me like a long lost friend." She noted her first impression of the producer: "I met David and he is charming, big, lanky, slightly Jewish, glasses, slouchy looking—everybody here wears flannels and looks as if he slept in them—fine good natured grin and completely disarming."

Sue's first column was sent from Culver City on 8 January and published in the *Telegraph* on 12 January. Her initial column reports on Vivien Leigh (Miss X) only by mentioning her screen test. In her first letter to the novelist and her husband (11 January) Sue wrote:

> Gosh, but I wish you were here so I could talk for about seventeen hours. There ain't strength in my fingers to write all I'd like to say. And to your ears alone can I say the following. I have not written it to a soul and the studio is so secretive about it all I'm almost afraid to write it to y'all. But I have seen the gal who is to do Scarlett. I am even yet afraid to say her name aloud. Will Price (who used to be with Fed Theater in Atl) and I speak of her in hushed tones as "That Woman" or as "Miss X" and we have spent several mornings with her, talking Southern just for her stage-taught ears. She is charming, very beautiful, black hair and magnolia petal skin and in the movie tests I have seen, she moved me greatly. They did the paddock scene, for a test, and it is marvelous business the way she makes you cry when she is "making Ashley." I understand she is not signed but far as I can tell from George et al, she is the gal.

That first letter back to Atlanta is typical, and delightfully full of gossip. It is in that letter she tells her classic story of how screenplays are made.

> Story told me by chap here [Will Price] is a honey [she wrote]. Producers and what they do with scripts is like a chef making soup. The chef gets an idea from a soup he ate. He spends days making a stock that is just right. He tastes, adds seasonings, tastes again, adds again. Then he does more things to it until he has the finest soup in the universe. Whereupon, he calls in other chefs and they all stand around and pee in it! And this, the treasonable ones of us seem to agree is what happened about GWTW.

The state of the script was one of several continuing topics in Miss Myrick's letters. Others were the architecture (and other points of exaggeration) of the sets, George Cukor's parting with Selznick, the accents of the actors and, of course, Miss Myrick's day-to-day efforts to keep the film true to her and Miss Mitchell's ideas of the South in the days of Scarlett and Rhett.

Margaret Mitchell had been immensely impressed by George Cukor when he visited Atlanta in the spring of 1937. When in the summer of 1938 it was rumored that Cukor would be displaced as director of *Gone With the Wind*, she wrote Kay Brown (7 July 1938): "Do, please, tell me if it is true that George Cukor is out of the picture. I have very little interest in who will act in the picture, but I am sorry if George will not direct. I thought him a grand person and a brilliant one." After the Cukor-Selznick split she wrote Sue Myrick (15 February 1939): "We can't help feeling bad about George quitting the picture. You know how much we liked him personally and how impressed we were with his mind and his ability and his lovely simplicity. And we don't like many people." To this Sue replied in her letter of 23 February:

> Cukor came in the other day (Monday, I think) for a moment and told me to tell you he is sorry not to finish this production because he liked you and the book so much but he just couldn't go on with the thing when he felt it wasn't as good as it should be. I had told him you had written you were sorry for him to leave the pic. I miss him a lot for he was so gay and full of pep. But I think Fleming is going to be a good director though I'll never like him personally as I did George.

Myrick and Kurtz waged a losing battle to keep *Gone With the Wind* sets from being too grand. It was determined very early that Tara should be dressed up with columns and Margaret Mitchell's description of Twelve Oaks as looking like a Greek temple was interpreted as license to make it look as impressive as the Parthenon. It was all decided, really, as early as 15 February 1938 in a conference among Selznick, Cukor, and Kurtz. Kurtz wrote:

> Cukor was inclined to think Twelve Oaks should be a rich-looking place, should have a lot of that favorite soup known as "glamour." . . . Since the house *is*, after all, pure fiction, and since 'tis our only chance to spread on the Old South, it was deemed by both Mr. S. and Mr. C. that something really nice is here indicated. As for Tara, they listened closely to my explanation of rural architecture in North Georgia and Clayton County, in particular. They admitted that what I said was true . . . , but since Tara was also on the fictional side, they indicated that the house should be warmed up a bit . . . with a quiet elegance that would do no real violence to the spirit of the story. "After all," said Mr. Selznick, addressing me, "the Atlanta and Clayton County audiences are a very small percentage."[12]

---

[12]Kurtz, "Technical Adviser," p. 60.

After Margaret Mitchell saw the first stills from *Gone With the Wind* the *Atlanta Constitution* proclaimed in the headline for its story about them "Margaret Mitchell Puts Okay on First Screen Stills of Novel." Writing to her friend Col. Telamon Cuyler on 17 February 1939, the author commented that "the headline was completely at variance with the story" and went on to say:

> Far from "okaying" the pictures, I cried "Godalmighty" in horror before I caught myself. My eye had lighted on Scarlett's widow's bonnet and long veil in the midst of the decollete gowns of the Atlanta belles. I cannot imagine even Scarlett having such bad taste as to wear a hat at an evening party, and my heart sank at the sight of it. Probably the reporter mistook my exclamation for one of pleasure. A quick view of the uniforms showed not a one that looked as if it had seen active service. Nor was there a wounded man to be found even with a microscope. The Armory looked vaguely like Versailles and not like the rough room in which drills were held. However, it was not my place to remark on these things, as the *Constitution* had only requested that I identify the chapters from which the scenes were taken. Should I be asked at some later date if these scenes were correct in detail, I will be in an embarrassing position for I will have to *tell the truth*. I have an idea that Mr. Kurtz and Susan were overridden on these points. After all, they can only suggest and can do nothing if their suggestions are not followed.

Despite Hollywood's triumph in making the South of *Gone With the Wind* a never-never land of its own creation, Margaret Mitchell was grateful indeed to Kurtz and Myrick for what Hollywood did not do to her novel. She was especially grateful to Myrick for her work with the accents of the players. Like many Southerners, Miss Mitchell was very sensitive about how the movies consistently treated Southern accents.

When Vivien Leigh's casting as Scarlett was announced Miss Mitchell was misquoted as saying that she thought the actress could easily be taught to talk like a Southerner. She wrote in a long letter to Selznick on 30 January 1939:

> I did not attempt to get the misquotation corrected because I know how futile it is to try to get statements like that changed after they have been published, but I do not wish you to be left under the misapprehension that I think Miss Leigh or any of the others should try to "talk Southern." . . . The misquotation forces me to state what my real attitude is.

Good quality stage voices are not distinctively Northern or Southern or Eastern or Western, and natural voices of that kind will be far more acceptable to the South than any artificial, imitation "Southern" talk. Of course, a voice with distinctively un-Southern qualities, a New England twang or a Mid-Western rolling "r", would be out of place in a Southern film, but I don't believe even that would be as offensive as pseudo-Southern talk in the mouth of a person who did not come by it naturally. If Miss Leigh says "bean" for "been" and uses a broad "a", naturally it would be desirable to attempt to eliminate such distinctive British-isms, but I doubt the wisdom of attempting to go much further. Eliminating distinctively un-Southern accents or pronunciations of words will be fine, but attempting to teach her to "talk like a Southerner," as I was misquoted as saying, will probably do more harm than good.

This is partly because Southerners have been made sensitive by the bogus Southern talk they have heard on the stage and screen so often. But it is also due to the fact that there is no one "Southern accent." There are at least five different Southern accents in different sections of Georgia alone, and Georgians talk differently from other Southerners. Virginia people have a very distinctive accent and Charlestonians speak differently from everybody else. Louisiana and Mississippi lie side by side but the people in the two states do not talk alike. And so it goes.

So many Southern people have expressed the wish that your actors will talk in good quality natural stage voices, instead of imitation "Southern," leaving the atmosphere to be built up by the Negroes and other actual Southerners who may be in the cast. I believe this is the dominant public sentiment and it conforms directly with my own ideas. I would be embarrassed if you were given a wrong impression of my attitude by reason of a misquotation in the newspapers.

Much later (23 July 1942) she gratefully wrote Virginius Dabney, a distinguished Richmond editor:

I was so very pleased at the credit you gave Susan for the Southern accent (or rather, for the lack of Southern accent) in the film. I've always felt that she did not get enough credit outside her own section for the truly miraculous job she did. For nearly three years the South rared and pitched and muttered threats about seceding from the Union again if "you all" was used in addressing one person or if any actor spoke as if he had a mouth full of hot buttered okra. Unfortunately for me, who had nothing to do with the film, a great deal of this raring and pitching took place on our doorstep, in our parlor and over our telephone, as embittered

Southerners demanded that I "do something" to keep travesties of
our accent from the film. Susan was the one who "did
something"—and far better than I could have done. I thought the
finest praise she received was this—after the premiere here in
Atlanta, I went to a large party and encountered some of our
dowagers who had been most belligerent about the Southern
accent. I questioned, "And what did you think of the accent of the
picture?" They looked at me and said, rather blankly, "What
accent?"

In that same letter to Mr. Dabney she noted:

Since my novel was published, I have been embarrassed on
many occasions by finding myself included among writers who
pictured the South as a land of white-columned mansions whose
wealthy owners had thousands of slaves and drank thousands of
juleps. I have been surprised, too, for North Georgia certainly was
no such country—if it ever existed anywhere—and I took great
pains to describe North Georgia as it was. But people believe what
they like to believe and the mythical Old South has too strong a
hold on their imaginations to be altered by a mere reading of a
1,037 page book. So I have made no effort to defend myself against
the accusation but it was a great satisfaction to me that a man of
your perceptiveness knew that my South was not "The South That
Never Was." I thank you for your understanding and for what you
wrote.

Sue Myrick and Wilbur Kurtz tried very hard to keep Hollywood
from making Miss Mitchell's South a "South That Never Was." They
succeeded only partially. Their accounts of their work in Hollywood
are records of their efforts. (Mr. Kurtz's accounts of his work on *Gone
With the Wind* were published as an issue of *The Atlanta Historical
Journal* [22:2 Summer 1978] under the title "Technical Adviser: The
Making of Gone With the Wind—The Hollywood Journals of Wilbur
G. Kurtz.") The accounts are also a great deal more. They are a record
of Hollywood in a high moment of its glory days. They are part of the
documentation of a film that typifies the Hollywood of its time. And
they are interesting and entertaining in their own right. Particularly is
this true of Sue Myrick's "Straight from Hollywood" columns. She
had long experience in writing to entertain the readers of the *Macon
Telegraph and News*. Her Hollywood columns are written in the same
neighborly, gossipy spirit as her "Fannie Squeers" columns and other
Macon pieces. She was thrilled to be in Hollywood and to be working
on *Gone With the Wind*, but not so impressed with what she was doing

as to take herself too seriously. She remarked in her diary on 10 January that she was "feeling very important with one of me and laughing at myself with the other one of me." She elaborated: "There are two of me. One feels important and proud and puffed up and the other laughs her head off at the puffed [up] one and pinches her now and then to see if it [is] real." Sue was always real, always herself—her vivacious, ebullient, effervescent self.

Back in Georgia Sue's columns were an immediate hit. Margaret Mitchell herself praised the columns, writing, on 10 February 1939: "Dearie, your *Georgian* articles are fine. Not long ago my barber, who does not know I know you, talked about them during an entire hair-setting. Everybody enjoys them so much." Two weeks later (23 February) she wrote:

> This letter is just a bouquet for Miss Myrick.
> Of course John and I have thought your articles for the *Georgian* the best things that ever came out of Hollywood. Generally Hollywood stuff is the dreariest drivel in the world and only fit to be read while sitting under a drier in a beauty parlor. It is so press agentish that I do not understand how even the ten-year-old mind can tolerate it. Your stuff is so fresh and interesting and, in other words, dearie, we think it's swell.
> Tuesday I heaved my flu-ridden carcass from the bed to attend a party given by Medora Perkerson for the Atlanta Women's Press Club. Medora has just been elected president. There are about forty-five members and I believe every last one rushed up to me and, completely unprovoked, cried, "Susan Myrick's stuff is simply marvelous!" When you get such enthusiasm from your fellow-professionals you are indeed good. Furthermore, I heard no note of envy nor of criticism; everybody seemed pleased and proud that "one of our girls" was in the game pitching and being a credit to her State. Lib Whitman, society editress of the *Georgian*, said proudly, "You've been sick so I guess you haven't seen the *Georgian* trucks recently. For the last two weeks all *Georgian* trucks have had enormous banners on them screaming, 'Read Susan Myrick's Hollywood Stories—Exclusive in the *Georgian*.'" The *Journal* and the *Constitution* girls looked as though their vitals were being gnawed. Of course, I swole up as if you were my daughter or something and I had everything to do with each word you put down.

Later in the same letter she added:

> I wish you could get your stuff syndicated in the North. Ellen Wolff, formerly of the *Journal* staff, is just back from New York

and she found herself the center of attention because she quoted from your stories. She told everyone she saw that she could not understand why the New York papers were not running them.

Kay Brown wrote Miss Mitchell on 26 January: "I think Sue is doing a perfectly wonderful job on her material and I wish it were being widely syndicated." Victor M. Shapiro, Selznick's publicity director, wrote Publisher W. T. Anderson a letter that was quoted in the *Telegraph* on 21 February: "We here in the department are of the opinion that her stuff is so good that it might even be syndicated to a great number of Southern papers."

Shapiro had recently succeeded Russell Birdwell. Birdwell had long been Margaret Mitchell's pet peeve on Selznick's staff. He had repeatedly overstepped himself in using her name in connection with publicity for *Gone With the Wind* and she had just as repeatedly let him know her displeasure. In the beginning it looked as if he might be Sue Myrick's special nemesis too; he held up the dispatch of her second column (published on 17 January). Sue wasted no time in doing something about it. She described the incident in her letter to Margaret Mitchell on 15 January:

> I have had a fine encounter with Pappy Selznick. I wrote you about the requirement that I send publicity to Birdwell. Well, Birdwell is the revolving bastard if there ever was one. (The Revolving Bastard, in case you don't know, is a bastard any way you turn him.) He kept my copy four days and edited the hell out of it. Pappy, because George [Cukor] brought it up with him, asked me about it and I told him the whole story, being as gentle about it as I could be and taking care not to sound uppity and accusatory. David went up in the air, told me to send the copy to his office in future. I did and he oked it, noted that he found it very interesting and did not edit out a single word. Left in all the Birdwell gang had taken out![13]

---

[13]Birdwell may not have censored her copy as extensively as Myrick implies. Her annoyance at his editing was doubtless compounded by the delay that submission of copy to his office caused. In her diary Myrick states that Publicity "cut—of all things—my saying 'Only God could make a tree.'" After Selznick intervened on that column, Birdwell wrote Myrick that he was acting on a principle generally held by moviemakers of the 1930s that fans would be disenchanted with films if the techniques by which their illusions were produced were exposed to public view. (For such passages as were deleted from Myrick's copy, see notes 10 and 11 to section 1, p. 48.)

Sue had no further trouble with censorship. She simply used her own good judgment, knowing very well what information was to be kept on the sets and what could go public. In his letter to Mr. W. T., Shapiro wrote: "I am also of the opinion that you will find Miss Myrick to be one of the first to tell you that we have no restrictions on what she writes, that we, of our own volition, have told her to go ahead as she sees, hears and observes."

Towards the end of the filming Sue apparently (her letter is missing from her files and from Miss Mitchell's) wrote to her friend, at the instigation of Selznick's publicity people, asking the novelist for permission to use what she had said about Miss Myrick's columns in their promotion of the film. In a letter of 10 June Miss Mitchell answered:

Please tell Mr. Selznick and the Publicity Department that under no circumstances will I permit them to quote my remarks about your newspaper articles in their promotion program. I haven't the time to tell you all the difficulties it would cause me but here is one of them. During the past three years whenever I have voiced an honest and enthusiastic opinion about anybody's writing I have been in danger of immediately getting a request to use my statement for advertising, and I have had frequent experiences of this kind about newspaper stories. I'm not exaggerating when I tell you that requests for statements about books, magazine articles and newspaper stories have run into the thousands. I've had to turn them all down, even at the risk of appearing most ungenerous and ungracious, but I did not intend to have my name appearing six times a day in newspapers recommending this or that. I might as well go ahead and endorse Pond's cold cream and get it over with, and I have no intention of doing that sort of thing. To make matters worse, there would be the unavoidable suspicion that Mr. Selznick had paid me for the use of my name. This would give a number of people a chance to say that as long as I got paid for the use of my name I did not care how it was used. Of course our friends in Georgia would understand that I am very sincere in liking your articles, but you understand better than most people that I have got to take into consideration what people in other parts of the country would think. So, caution them not to use my commendation of your stuff in any way, shape or form, directly or indirectly.

I hate to write you this because I honestly do like your stuff a lot, but I can't break my rule on this matter. It has reached the point where I'm afraid to open my mouth in any words of praise about anything because, with very few exceptions, I get an immediate request for my words to be used for advertising purposes.

Moreover, your stuff does not need any recommendation from me or anyone else. It is good stuff and it can stand on its own feet.

Sue Myrick completed her work in Hollywood early in July and made a vacation trip home to Macon. But she did not immediately go back to full-time work on the Macon papers. She was hired by Metro-Goldwyn-Mayer, who were to distribute *Gone With the Wind*, and spent the next four months speaking to civic clubs in Georgia and neighboring states, telling them what a great picture *Gone With the Wind* was going to be.

She had her doubts along the way. There were good days and bad. She was repeatedly concerned about the cuts made in the story and about the endless efforts to come up with a satisfactory screenplay. She was a partisan of Sidney Howard and wished from the beginning that no other scenarist had ever tinkered with his work. Similarly, she loved Cukor and his work. But she, grudgingly, became an admirer of Victor Fleming, Cukor's replacement, too.

She felt the scenes at Twelve Oaks were ridiculously overdone and made fun of the chic mourning bonnet John Frederics designed for Scarlett. "But," she wrote on 9 April, "the stuff they've shot in the Atlanta streets is very thrilling. The daily rushes are perfectly beautiful. The red earth looks just right and the people fleeing the city are very exciting. . . . One day I think this pix is going to be a grand mess. Next day I am thrilled over it and think the thing is a *Birth of a Nation*."

As late as 28 May, after a trip to Northern California for scenes made "on location," she said: "I wore a play suit and loafed in the sun and rested to beat the band. If I hadn't I should have been throwing things by now." Since 8 January there had been six-day weeks of twelve-hour days for her. No wonder she complained. "The whole company is so damn tired of the picture they are ready to cut each other's throats at any moment."

But she did not lose her faith in Selznick or in her conviction that *Gone With the Wind* would be a great film. Of Selznick she said years later (in an interview published in the *Atlanta Journal* on 25 March 1976)[14]: "He was not content with half-done anything. We would do

---

[14]By Ron Taylor.

things over and over to please him. But he was always right. He had a feeling for pageantry, a good, overall feeling for everything." And as her work at the "Forty Acres" (as the main *GWTW* filming site—Selznick's "back lot"—was referred to) drew to a close she wrote: "When I get back I'll promise to tell you all you want to know about *Gone With the Wind.* I hope you will forgive me if I constantly rave about what a marvelous picture it is going to be."

Miss Myrick lived until the late summer of 1978.[15] For most of her life after *Gone With the Wind* she worked for the *Macon Telegraph and News*, writing an occasional column or feature article until just a short time before her death. She acted in the Macon Little Theater for many years, but finally gave that up. From time to time she traveled, usually with one or more of her sisters. In her spare time she painted, and painted quite well. "The difference between me and Grandma Moses," she said, "is that she got paid for what she did."[16]

She never tired of talking of her friend Margaret Mitchell and of her own days in Hollywood—to historians, reporters, and just plain fans. Recalling how Prissy told of birthing Melanie's baby, she loved to tell how she went to California to make *Gone With the Wind* and how Mr. Selznick—"well, he helped."

---

[15]Susan Myrick was born in Baldwin County, Georgia, on 20 February 1893; she died in Macon on 4 September 1978, and was buried in Milledgeville, Georgia.

[16]*Atlanta Journal*, 25 March 1976.

ONE
12 January—27 January 1939

Macon Telegraph, 12 January 1939

Straight From HOLLYWOOD

Miss Myrick Finds Plenty Going On in Movie Capitol

CULVER CITY, Calif., Jan. 8—The noise of the plane motors and the eight-thousand-feet-height we flew from El Paso to Los Angeles have got my head still buzzing but that is nothing at all to the way things at Selznick International Pictures Studio have got my brain whirling. I have met dozens of fascinating persons, looked at everything from plans for Tara to costumes for Scarlett and try-outs for Carreen and Suellen (in the flesh) and private showings of screenings of Miss X (who may play Scarlett) and someone who will probably play Aunt Pitty Pat.

(Ya-a-h! don't you all wish you knew who Miss X is?)

It is Sunday and I have slept twelve hours since things started happening at Culver City; I have had two cups of coffee and a scrambled egg and maybe you'd like to know that out here they put hashed brown potatoes and a canned peach on the breakfast plate just as we put hominy grits on all plates down South.

Leaping backward nimbly about twenty-four hours, I go back to my arrival here at 9:35 Saturday (an hour late) to find Mrs. Wilbur Kurtz of Atlanta (whose husband is technical adviser on historical background) waiting for me in a studio car. Mr. Daniel T. O'Shea, who telephoned me to come on out "right now," had sent Mrs. Kurtz because he thought it would make me feel good to have someone I knew at the plane.

Which is typical of everything that has happened since I got here. Everybody is so kind, so gracious and so considerate that it is overwhelming. And that includes the Kurtzes, whose daughter Annie Laurie (by the way) is a student at Wesleyan.

Mrs. Kurtz brought me to the hotel where she and Mr. K. are stopping.[1]* (And I am temporarily at Hotel Washington but any of you who want to write me can send letters to me care Selznick International Studios, Culver City, Calif.)

After I repowdered my face and got a fresh hanky we trucked on over to the studios which are only three blocks away. I was still so excited over the plane ride I could scarcely be thrilled over the studio. For the sleeper plane was a new experience and when the first rays of the morning sun crept inside my berth window I got up to watch the scenery. It was about Tucson that I waked and, from there on, the mountains were indescribably lovely.

Some of the time we flew above the clouds and mountain tops pushed through, all stark and bare and awesome. Some of the time the ceiling above was limitless and bright shafts of sunlight painted mountain sides in gold, while purple and smoky shadows sulked deep in crevices.

An Englishman, who occupied the berth across from me, was also an early riser and we exclaimed at each other about the beauty of this or that scene. He grumbled because there was no way for an Englishman to shave on a plane and muttered something about Americans who use electric razors when an Englishman cawn't manage the things. Then his wife, across in the upper, called:

"Chawles, er—do help me get my skirt on."

You see, one has to dress in the berth on a sleeper plane and it is a trial. Charles replied to the wife that he still had his pajama trousers on because it was "the only way I could decently dress in the aisle." And I wished for James Shelburne, who knows how to take a man's vest off

---

*Editor's Notes. Many of the explanatory and illustrative editor's notes to Susan Myrick's columns are necessarily long. In order not to interrupt the flow of the columns by the imposition of lengthy footnotes, the editor's notes are gathered at the end of each section of the columns.—Editor, MUP.

without taking off his coat. I bet he could have taken off the English-man's pajama trousers without removing the outer garments.

I had managed very nicely to get my clothes on in the berth and was quite well-dressed when I got off the plane. And I got one of the thrills of my life when I found a telegram waiting for me at the air port. A group of friends had wired:

"Social life died in Macon last night. Light of the party went out. No barbecue today, turnip greens and chitlings." And they signed it, "Belles (not Watling) and Colonels of your set."

That wire bucked me up so I didn't tremble as I went up Scarlett Walk, leading to the studios. Mrs. Kurtz took me at once to the office of Mr. O'Shea, who it turns out is business manager of the organiza-tion. She left me in the hands of a secretary who took me to another secretary who telephoned Mr. O'Shea (in the next room) I was here and he said, "Bring her right in," which she did.

Mr. O'Shea was boomingly glad to see me, asked how I slept and if the plane ride was pleasant and did I have any trouble about transpor-tation and seemed happy that his wire to the airport in Atlanta had fixed everything up.

He had his secretary phone Mr. George Cukor, director of *Gone With the Wind*, that I was here and Mr. Cukor said bring me right over.

We walked about three blocks (all inside the lot) to Mr. Cukor's office, where more secretaries phoned more secretaries and some one ushered us into Mr. Cukor's office.

He came to meet me with both hands outstretched and greeted me like an old friend and warmed the cockles of my heart with his welcome.[2]

Well—in order that this story may not go on forever, I'd better skip down to where he told me he thought I'd be given an office right near his own where I'd be available for quick conferences and now would I like to go over to meet the art department for he thought maybe I really belonged to them.

At that moment some one telephoned that the Misses Somebody were outside, according to appointment with him, and he said:

"Sue, wouldn't you just as soon see these tests?"

Of course, I'd just as soon; so I did. Two lovely young things rehearsed a scene for Suellen and Carreen and did it about six times. The way Cukor directed them was something to remember for a life time. He is so patient, explains so well what the scene means, shows them just how it should be done, walks up and down the room, stops the girls, makes them do it again and again but never is impatient and always is understanding.

(Memo—to Mrs. Piercy Chestney: Maybe we can get Cukor for the Macon Little Theater next year if Harry Schofield resigns).

Rehearsal over, we started once more to the art department, to be stopped again by someone who said Mr. Somebody was outside by appointment. Mr. Somebody is a famous movie actor whose name I dare not tell. He, too, was trying for a part in *Gone With the Wind* and patiently Mr. Cukor rehearsed the scene with him.[3] It was funny to see Mr. Cukor, a big, dynamic sort of man, clad in loose flannels, playing the role of Scarlett O'Hara for the try-out. But he could do the role on the screen and get away with it!

Anyway, it was almost lunch time and Mr. Cukor had the secretary telephone the art department to have lunch with us. We went to a dining room on the lot that was marked Private, (Everything out here is marked Private, even the Ladies' Rest Rooms) where I met Mr. Platt, head-man for the *GWTW* sets, and his assistant, Mr. Wheeler.[4] We had lunch (a good one, too) with much idle chatter and again I found the strangers affable and gracious.

At last we moved on across the lot to the art department headquarters though Mr. Cukor returned to his office. With the two art-men I climbed miles of stairs and then they brought out sketches of Tara and of Aunt Pitty-Pat's house to show me. But before we got started a secretary said Mr. Cukor had phoned, would we please bring the sketches to Mr. Selznick's office.

Three more men joined us. I daresay they'd be shocked to know I haven't the faintest notion who they are; for I judged they were important by the manner in which various secretaries bowed down before them. Anyway, we got to the office of David O. Selznick—head man of the studios.

He is a big, loose-jointed, pleasant and rather handsome, sort of like a huge, friendly Saint Bernard, and his smile is the friendliest in the world. He wore flannels, loosely fitting his big frame. (Most of the big shots here seem to wear flannels which look like they'd been slept in!)

We looked at sketches and argued about various points and Mr. Selznick ordered some changes and sent the art department away while he sat down on the sofa with me and talked about the picture and his plans for it.

Both Selznick and Cukor are determined to make the production the best in the world and they are aiming to make the Southern feeling as right as is humanly possible.

Not only do they say so; they give definite evidence in many ways. They are deferential to a marked degree to the opinions of Kurtz and of me and though I have spent only one day on the lot I am convinced that they mean it when they say they want a real Southern background and they want the Southerners to like the picture.

We talked on and on; then Mr. Cukor deferentially asked if I were too tired to see Miss Somebody read a scene for Belle Watling.[5] I was so tired my knees were crumbling but I'd have died before I'd have admitted it: so we went again to Cukor's office where a real Southerner rehearsed a scene for us, over and over. She was blonde and lovely but she had frowsled her hair and wore an enormous hoop skirt thing of red and gold brocade, cut very low, and she made a fine impression in a scene between Belle and Melanie.

Presently we were summoned to a set to see the floor plans for Tara and after those were done Mr. Cukor sent me back with his assistant, Mr. Stacey, to Selznick's office. Mr. Selznick, it seemed, wanted me to see some screen tests for Miss X,[6] and others.

And believe it or not (Mr. Glogauer) the tests were shown me on Set. No. 3. I sat all alone in a small theater while two men put on the shows just for me. I was so amused at the idea I could scarcely get the thrill I should have got at seeing Miss X.

It seems the people on the Selznick lot refer to any Scarlett candidate as Miss X. And there aren't many who have any idea who IS Miss X.

Back once more to Mr. Selznick's office for more discussion and finally the Big Boss said goodnight and he hoped I'd have a fine Sunday rest.

So, tomorrow I report to Mr. Cukor again. Maybe I'll find out what I am to do. As I said in my last Fannie Squeers column, I still don't know much about anything!

Straight From HOLLYWOOD

Miss Susan Myrick Becomes Part of the Hollywood Beehive

T HINGS, have happened so fast since I got to Culver City, Calif., that my head is still swirling. But one thing is sure: All you scoffers who think *Gone With the Wind* will never be made into a picture had better call off your bets. At the Selznick International Studios things are moving so fast toward production that a Florida hurricane would look like a gentle breeze by comparison.

For instance, last Saturday afternoon Director George Cukor and Producer David O. Selznick OK'd the plans for Tara and on Monday afternoon Mr. Cukor took me out to see the grounds so I might consult with Miss Florence Yoch,[7] a distinguished California landscape artist, about the plantings around the grounds.

To my amazement, when we drove out to Forty Acres, there stood the rambling country house that has made Jonesboro and Margaret Mitchell famous.

We drove down "Peachtree Street" and I saw the Atlanta railroad station, under construction, already beginning to look exactly as it did during the early days of De Wah, when Uncle Peter carried Scarlett in his arms from the car shed to Aunt Pitty Pat's carriage so her feet wouldn't get muddy. I could almost see Prissy following with little Wade Hampton in her arms! Wilbur Kurtz whose attractive daughter,

Annie Laurie, is a student at Wesleyan, is technical adviser on structures (among other things) and he had advised with the Selznick architects on how the old station looked.

Well, to my complete astonishment I found that the art department had about a half-dozen persons on the grounds and there were two or three assistants and assistants-to-assistants busy about the place.

Everybody was considering what should be planted in the Tara grounds so the place would look just as Miss Mitchell meant it to look. My own soul had shivered within me, fearing lest there should be Spanish moss somewhere or the trees would look like those of California (which don't look like anything that grows in Georgia): but I found Miss Yoch knows her stuff.

She began talking about dogwood trees and boxwood and post oaks and mimosa and cape jessamine and spoke of the hospitable air of a Southern home over which branches arch and of the casual aspect of Tara—and won my Georgia heart at once.

Mr. Cukor listened with grave attention: then spoke:

"Look now, remember there is a real lady in the house. What might Ellen have brought from the coast with her—something that gives the feeling that a cultured lady is mistress of Tara?"

And he seemed satisfied with the talk of Maréchal Neil roses and cape jessamine.

Then came the most astonishing thing of the afternoon. Miss Yoch began to tell one of the landscape men what to get to make boxwood and what to find that would look like oak leaves.

And all these years you and I have been thinking "Only God can make a tree!"

But Miss Yoch shows pictures of bark and limbs and foliage to the men in charge of plantings and before you can say "Katie Scarlett O'Hara," they've manufactured trees that the camera can't tell from the kind Nature grows.

Today I saw men working on the trees. Poles about as large as telephone poles were placed on the spots selected by the art department and then the men applied ribs to make the diameter larger. Over this they put chicken wire and then make the bark of plaster.

But seeing men make trees is nothing to the big thrill I had when I went on Stage No. 11 to see some tests made. Eric G. Stacey, assistant to Mr. Cukor, wanted me to go along to watch for certain things. (It seems that is part of the technical adviser's job. And every day I am finding out more things that are part of my job!)

At ten, promptly, we were on the stage, a gigantic, barn-like room. A camera on wheels rested quietly on its track but it somehow gave me a feeling that it was rearing to go; for a half dozen men were doing various things to it. Six or eight more men were fooling with lights and altogether there were about twenty men working, testing equipment, arranging positions, measuring things from here to there and busily getting everything ready.

And up on the cat-walk! Whew! Macon's Little Theater helpers would die with envy if they could see those lights and the men who work them.

Somebody gave me a cup of coffee and got me a chair. Maybe I looked bewildered! But probably it is just a part of the usual day's work; for at the Selznick Studio everybody is so kind it is almost embarrassing. From the Big Boss, Mr. Selznick, down to the boy who comes to get an inter-office communication off your desk, everybody is courteous, considerate, polite and sincerely kind.

"Mr. Cukor, I'm due at such-and-such a place at one. Will I be through by then?" asked one of the actors who was on stage for a test.

Cukor shrugged his shoulders and smiled: "Well, if you're bright you may get through by one."

"It's a little late for me to start being bright," the actor laughed back. And that's the sort of camaraderie that I find on all sides.

Mr. Cukor went over the scene with the man several times; then while the director took a phone call (the telephone rings every-other-second on the lot, no matter where you are!) the actor and the stand-in began rehearsing. The actor was putting all he had into the scene. Mr. Cukor was talking to me about a certain plan for doing the scene and the actor stopped, wiped his brow and said:

"Teacher! PLEASE look at me. Here I am acting all over the place and you aren't looking!"

So, with bantering and pleasantries the work went on until Cukor was satisfied. Then he called, "OK, boys, let's make it."

A bell rang. The camera was focused on the proper spot, the long armed microphone reached out to hang just over the head of the actors, a man ran out with a two-foot-square board that bore numbers of the test and names of the actors and he held it for a few seconds in front of the camera. Then he snapped down a piece of wood on the board and somebody yelled:

"Quiet!"

And I worked so hard, trying to help that actor do the best job he ever did, I was weak all over when the test was finished and Cukor called:

"Fine! You did that nicely Mr. Umph!" Then, "Print it, boys."

More tests and more of them through the day. Now and then when ladies were being tested, a half dozen persons from the wardrobe would be about the stage. Somebody would run out and freshen up the lipstick or smooth down the powder on an actress and another girl would stick in hair pins and arrange coiffures to the proper degree of perfection.

Once Cukor suggested that the timing was a bit slow and snapping his fingers said: "Don't let it bother you if I do like this. I am reminding the artists."

Once in a while during the rehearsals a tall man, clad in an old sweater and gray trousers, would call out:

"Rest your arcs, boys!" and a battery of lights would dim. It took me several minutes to figure what he said, I thought he was saying "Rest your dogs" and expected everybody to sit down for a minute.

So somewhere about four in the afternoon, I "rested my dogs" back in my office (which is known as the Melanie room. Not because I look or act like Melanie but because the room has a sort of spine-of-steel look to it.).

Two or three actors or would-be actors were assigned for me to hear their Southern accents and we practiced on such words as "girl" and "bird" and "mother" and other things that must sound right if Maconites are to think of the photodrama as Southern.

Then at six I got a car, picked up my belongings at the hotel where I'd been staying and started for my new home. I'm living now in Santa Monica, which is about ten miles from Culver City, and is only about twenty minutes away by inter-urban trolley.

I am getting plenty of kidding because I am living now at—of all places—the Georgian Hotel Apartments. Well, when I'm for Georgia, I'm for Georgia!

The ocean (the Pacific, mind you) is about as far from my apartment as from the Telegraph Building to the Dempsey Hotel and the mountains rise up to the east and the north and the city of Santa Monica is lovely.

And don't let anybody fool you; the climate IS divine.

Straight From HOLLYWOOD

Novice in Studios Learns Still More Tricks of Trade

Culver City, Calif.—"Seven men to make a pin"; so says the old nursery rhyme. But seven times seventy are scarcely enough to make *Gone With the Wind*, not to mention the women.

And naturally, I make much of the women concerned with the picture, particularly one woman who is a technical adviser and is finding out every day more things that a technical adviser must do.

Today, for instance, I discovered I am to check with the man who dresses the sets on knick-knacks for making the halls of Tara as well as its parlors and bedrooms look as they should look to represent a Southern home of the sixties—a home in Clayton County, Ga., where the earthy and homey spirit prevailed and life was not so esthetic as it was in Charleston and Savannah.

And Tara is only one of the four houses that are being built for the picture. Twelve Oaks, gracious, beautiful and much grander than Tara, is designed to represent the finest of Georgia tradition in antebellum homes. The house which Rhett and Scarlett built in Atlanta is to look just as Margaret Mitchell described it. And Aunt Pitty Pat's house is a plumb honey with more doo-dads and knick-knacks than you ever saw, and everything in perfect keeping with the fussy character that is Scarlett's maiden aunt.

It was fun riding with a gentleman from the art department to shops that rent or sell objects to the studios and helping in the selection of lamps, candlesticks, mirrors, bric-a-brac and so on for Aunt Pitty's home. The shops are marvels and I no longer doubt the statement that everything on earth anybody could possibly want can be found in the vicinity of Hollywood. It may cost a pretty price but it can be had.

And speaking of Aunt Pitty, I met Laura Hope Crews the other day and as Aunt Pitty she is perfection. She is delightful to talk to and after she had chatted with me for a short while she declared she expected to "hant me from now on" in order that she might sound exactly as Southern as I do. For, she said, she adores Aunt Pitty Pat and is thrilled at doing the role and hopes everybody is going to like her interpretation.

Of course they will. Laura Hope Crews has been a star too long to do a role any way but just as it should be done.

But the time for shooting the Aunt Pitty scenes is not close at hand. The first shooting will be scenes at Tara and then, of course, the barbecue at Twelve Oaks.

You may know more about the inside workings of a studio than I did, but I am constantly astonished at things like discovering that there are two separate Taras built for the picture.

One handsome exterior stands on Forty Acres, with columns over which tiny ivy climbs, with sanded walks through which the red clay soil shows (they are using two thousand loads of brick dust to make the grounds look the right color), with flowers blooming along the walks and giant trees growing near and a green lawn of Bermuda grass and everything that you'd expect about a house.[10]

And, yes, there is the shelf with the bucket of water, the gourd and the washpan, not far from the well.

That Tara is only for exterior shots. The other Tara is inside a huge building. I walked into the wide hall with its simple stairway, exclaimed over the parlor with its green velvet curtains from which Scarlett makes her dress when she goes to call on Rhett, and then looked at the little room which Ellen used as an office.[11]

I went over to Stage 11 where some test shots were under way. Two boys whose hair had been dyed red were being tested for the Tarleton twins. One of them, George Bessolo, is from New Orleans; the other, Fred Crane, is from Kentucky and they both are born Tarletons! They act like screwballs all the time they aren't working.

While they waited for the test they played at duelling, standing back to back, advancing ten paces, turning quickly and pretending to fire, using their riding crops as guns.

Meanwhile, I watched a test shot of the probable Frank Kennedy, who was costumed in the approved style of the sixties and wore a "ginger-colored beard" and acted like an "old maid in britches."[12]

A beautiful girl from Shreveport, La., Marcella Martin, is doing the part of Scarlett for the tests; because of course the real Scarlett can't be on hand for test shots of others.[13]

Everybody on the lot kids Marcella because she takes it so good naturedly. The other day in a test Marcella had to rise from a stooping posture outside a carriage and get into the conveyance with Belle Watling. As Marcella rose she moved too fast and bumped her pretty head on one of the heavy lamps that lighted the set.

Without batting an eye, George Cukor, director, said:

"Now, Marcella, quit knocking our lamps around. First thing you know you'll break one and have to pay for it."

And Marcella just stuck out her tongue and went on with the scene.

And that story somehow reminds me of the joke on myself. It is too good to keep, though I am embarrassed to tell it.

With Mr. David O. Selznick and Mr. Cukor, I was in a projection room waiting to see some tests when a gentleman walked in the door and said "Good morning" in a quiet voice. He was wearing a baggy suit with an old sweater and his demeanor was very modest and I guessed him to be one of the men from the projection booth, maybe, or perhaps a property man.

Mr. Cukor introduced us, calling the man Mr. Fitzgerald. But I paid no attention to the name. A minute or so later, Mr. Cukor turned to the man and said "Sit down Scott!"

"Oh Mr. Cukor!" I gurgled, "That's so cute for you to call him 'Scott'."

And I laughed gaily.

"But he IS Scott Fitzgerald," said Mr. Cukor.

Then everybody laughed except me. I blushed! But Mr. Selznick saved my embarrassment by telling a story. It seems that Selznick said something about Scott Fitzgerald to someone the evening before and the friend said, "Who is he?" Selznick, amazed that everybody should not know the author, looked incredulous and said:

"You mean you really don't know who Scott Fitzgerald is?"

"Oh, yes," replied the friend, hastily covering up. "Of course I do. You mean the actor!"[14]

Macon Telegraph, 27 January 1939

Straight From HOLLYWOOD

Miss Myrick Entertained at Home of Actor Leslie Howard

HOLLYWOOD, Calif., Jan 26—A day which started off mournfully, with everything awry, turned out to be ripping—if you know what I mean.

It rained as it does in the movies. Probably there have been so many photodramas made in this state that even the weather man has been influenced by sunny Californians, who like the Hawaiians speak of the rain as "liquid sunshine," and are fooling themselves. There was so much rain that the trolley which runs from Santa Monica to Culver City (where Selznick International Pictures have their studio) was washed out and it took me an hour to detour with two changes of trolley cars.

Looking bedraggled and feeling very damp, I arrived at the studio at ten, to find I was expected to go at once to the home of Leslie Howard for work on Southern accent. I went.

The house, in Beverly Hills, is modest and unpretentious and I had expected a glamorous, imposing residence that looked like a movie set. But once inside, I was charmed.

The living room which is two steps down from the hallway, was decidedly English in appearance, with its beamed ceiling, ivory walls and masculine furnishings. A log fire warmed the room and made it the

cozier. On the walls were etchings and prints in natural wood frames
and books which looked as if they had often been read filled a recessed
book case opposite the fireplace; a baby grand piano stood open and
the whole room had an air of good taste and modest luxury that was
heart-warming.

A soft-cushioned couch upholstered in cream faille stood near the
fireplace and before it was a black-walnut table with cigarette boxes,
two pipes, matches and two bowls of smoking tobacco.

The rug was a pale green and there was a large easy chair in darker
green, while the dull colors of the room were complemented by the
black and henna design on the taupe draperies at the windows.

Mr. Howard's maid explained that he would be down in a moment
and she brought me a cup of coffee while I waited. She pulled aside the
brass fender and urged me to warm my feet; then she stood and talked
to me of *Gone With the Wind.*

She is Scotch, she explained, and to her *Gone With the Wind* had a
peculiar appeal; for she lost a brother in the World War in 1916.
Another brother is in the hospital in Edinburgh as a result of shell
shock and many cousins and uncles were killed in the war. Therefore,
she felt a vast sympathy for the South and the trials the Southern
people suffered after the War Between the States.

She expressed, also, great pleasure that Mr. Howard is to play
Ashley for she thinks Ashley was a gentleman and she is sure Mr.
Howard is one. In fact, she is a complete refutation of the old statement
that a man cannot be perfect in the eyes of a valet, for she thinks Mr.
Howard is the finest gentleman in the world.

Presently Mr. Howard came in, apologized for having kept me
waiting and we began a lesson in pronunciation of those words that are
most likely to show differences between British and Southern American accent. To anyone listening in, it must have been very funny.

"I love you," Mr. Howard would say. Then turning to me: "How
do you say that, my dear?"

And I'd repeat the word "love" and he'd say it again.

Then we'd come to the word "Georgia" and we'd try that a half
dozen times and so on.

When we had finished a scene (after some four or five readings) he
would say "Let us rest a bit on this. Won't you just talk to me so I can
get the sound of your voice and the manner of your pronunciation in
my mind?"

And we talked—of his performance in *Petrified Forest*, of things Hollywoodish, of England and again of the production of *Gone With the Wind*.

"I've never bean in—" he'd begin.

"'Been,' Mr. Howard," I would interrupt.

Smilingly, he would correct himself, then musingly:

"Been is the old-English way of saying it. I am sure it was be'n—the pawst particle of be—"

"Not 'pawst,'—'past,' Mr. Howard," I'd interrupt again.

And so on, until I wonder he didn't throw the whole edition of the works of Galsworthy at my head.

But he never showed any impatience whatever. In fact, he refutes everything you ever heard about the temperamental antics of actors.

Mr. Howard is upset over his hair. To make him more like Ashley Wilkes, make-up lightened his ash blonde locks several shades. And the actor doesn't like his looks much.

"Can't I put some oil or something on it?" he asked make-up. For the very fine hair which is Howard's was trying to stand on end after the treatment.

Make-up shook his head. "If you do," he said, "you'll wake up tomorrow with green hair."

So, after a pleasant two hours of work, I returned to the studios to have lunch with Miss Marian Dabney, who works in wardrobe (I have learned not to speak of "the wardrobe" or "the make-up department," but to say "wardrobe" and "make-up"). Miss Dabney and I talked about the various styles of arranging head rags for Mammy and presently we were joined by E. P. Lambert, who is head of wardrobe.

Mr. Lambert is such a human being that he is delightful. He talked of his books (and Miss Dabney confided to me he has the finest collection she ever saw—he reads the books too). By strange coincidence I asked if he [had] read Don Marquis' *Master of the Revels* and he said that only last night he spoke of that play of the life of Henry the Eighth, walked to the book shelves to pick it up and found it missing.

After a lunch of mushrooms on toast and a fine green salad of endive (which they call chicory, here) I went with Miss Dabney to see some tests made of various types of head-rag tyings for Mammy.

You probably know that Hattie McDaniel is to play the role of Mammy and she says "Yessum" and "No'm" to me in a way that makes me mighty homesick for my Mary Brown back in Macon.[15]

The Negroes for the show, besides Hattie McDaniel, are Oscar Polk, who played Gabriel in the movie version of *Green Pastures*, and Butterfly McQueen, who has had considerable stage and movie experience.[16]

Mr. Lambert reported that he spoke to his colored cook about Butterfly McQueen, asking if she ever heard of the actress and the cook replied:

"Nawsuh, I never heard uv 'er, but that show is a pretty name."

Butterfly is Prissy and Polk is Pork. And all of them take to Southern Negro dialect like a co-ed takes to frat dances.

That matter of "talking Southern" has caused a funny situation in my office. From time to time a dozen young men have been in to have me go over lines with them suggesting proper accent and cutting them down when they over-do it. It has got so now the people passing the door pay no attention when they hear coming from my office in an impassioned tone:

"I love you. You are the most beautiful girl in the world. Dare I hope—?"

Clark Gable has not been in for much practice so far because he is finishing another picture and he hasn't much spare time right now. But Southern accent is duck soup for him.

Anyway, I doubt if it matters what he says—the ladies will be swooning at his manly beauty; for the costumes which Walter Plunkett has designed for him enhance the good looks of even Mr. Gable. Frilled shirts, wing collars, and frock coats give an air, you know.

Harry Davenport, who comes of an unbroken lineage of stars and heads the ninth generation of actors, will play the role of Dr. Meade in *Gone With the Wind*. His son, Edward L. Davenport, who will be his stand-in for the production, carries the tradition forward into the tenth generation.[17]

I talked to Mr. Davenport yesterday and he sounds as much like a Southerner as I do. In addition to his pleasing voice Mr. Davenport has back of him sixty-seven years' work as an actor. He has starred on the New York Stage and in many movies.

I worked yesterday on accent with Miss Barbara O'Neil, the screen's youngest character actress who has been signed by David O. Selznick to play the part of Ellen in *Gone With the Wind*.

Miss O'Neil is but twenty-eight years old but this is in strict accordance with the character of Ellen O'Hara drawn by Margaret

Mitchell in her best seller novel of the War Between the States. Scarlett's mother married at fifteen and at sixteen she became the mother of Scarlett. Thus when her daughter had grown to marriageable age, Ellen was still a young woman.

Miss O'Neil is a delightful young woman and I feel quite happy about her as the choice for Ellen.

[1]"Mrs. Kurtz and Wilbur brought me here to Hotel Washington and I am grateful but the place is dreary. And there is not a place where you can get even the first bite of decent food and you know I am a nut about my eating. So, while I am very sorry to leave them I can't stand it here any more and tomorrow I am moving to Santa Monica, to an apt with tiny kitchenette where I can get my own coffee, an apt with maid service, roll-away bed, bath and enormous closet. It is about a block from the Pacific and is very nice and reasonable, too." Susan Myrick to Mr. and Mrs. John R. Marsh, Santa Monica, Calif., 11 January 1939, Margaret Mitchell Marsh Papers, University of Georgia Libraries.

[2]Cukor had met Myrick on a visit to Macon in the spring of 1937.

[3]"Also, have worked with William Farnum who is, I think to be Gerald. I liked his work very much. Saw him rehearse with George." Myrick to Mr. and Mrs. Marsh, 11 January.

[4]Here Myrick inverted the studio pecking order. Lyle Wheeler was Art Director for *Gone With the Wind*. Joseph B. Platt designed the interiors.

[5]This was Gertrude Michael of Talladega, Alabama. Myrick noted in her diary entry for 7 January: "She is blonde, hussyish looking, beautiful and wore the damnedest frock, all red and gold brocade and bosom showing. She was good." Marla Shelton and Peggy Shannon tested for the Belle Watling part on 11 January. The part did not have to be assigned immediately. Myrick wrote on 17 February that Nancy Carroll tested for the role. According to Ronald Haver, Betty Compson and Marjorie Rambeau were considered for it before the part was awarded to Ona Munson. *David O. Selznick's Hollywood* (New York: Alfred A. Knopf, 1980), p. 275.

[6]Vivien Leigh.

[7]"Miss Yoch who is landscaper is a fine old sister, hard featured and looks like Calvin Coolidge, but she is smart as hell. In fact, everybody out here is smart. I have found out there is no place for lack of efficiency at the movie making business and I am scared to death I'll not do something I should do." Myrick to Margaret Mitchell, Santa Monica, 15 January 1939.

Kurtz recorded on 12 January: "The tree expert was on the lot today, Miss Yoch. She has been in Georgia and her job is to take California trees, shrubs and vines and do tricks with them so as to make passable likenesses to Georgia trees, shrubs and vines. I saw her at work today on the Forty Acres, where Tara is abuilding. She was superintending the planting of certain trees around Tara, which had been hauled—roots and all—on trucks. Two real magnolia trees had been secured, and some very creditable bushes and vines were being emplaced. As for dogwood, some sort of tree that had the right lines was set up, and for blossoms, the skillful fingers of the Property Department had fabricated hundreds of amazing replicas which they tie on greenery as shooting requirements demand. A gang of laborers and plaster artists were making oak trees, huge affairs built of wooden framing, chicken wire and plaster, all around tall telephone poles—the upper ends of which show as poles and serve as anchorage for guy wires running to the top of the house." Wilbur G. Kurtz, "Technical Adviser: The Making of Gone With the Wind," *Atlanta Historical Journal* 22:2 (Summer 1978): 124.

[8]Margaret Mitchell wrote Myrick on 10 February: "Laughs have been few and far between recently, as I have been laid up with a cold and a persistent fever. But your letter had a laugh in every line. I must admit some of my laughter was on the wry side—especially when you described Twelve Oaks. I had feared, of course, that it would end up looking like the Grand Central Station, and your description confirms my worst apprehensions. I did not know whether to laugh or to throw up at the *two* staircases. Probably the Twelve Oaks hall will be worse than the one in 'So Red the Rose.' People here in Atlanta got up and left the theatre in herds when that hall was shown. And I will never forget the pungent remarks about the level of Hollywood brains. God help me when the reporters get me after I've seen the picture. I will have to tell the truth, and if Tara has columns and Twelve Oaks is such an elegant affair I will have to say that nothing like that was ever seen in Clayton County, or, for that matter, on land or sea. This would be somewhat embarrassing to me and perhaps to the Selznick company, but I am not going on record as telling a lie just to be polite. When I think of the healthy, hardy, country and somewhat crude civilization I depicted and then of the elegance that is to be presented, I cannot help yelping with laughter. . . .

"God forbid that Scarlett's Reconstruction house should be a poem of good taste. That would throw out of balance the whole characterization of the woman. Hurrah for George and Mr. Platt for standing up for a bad-taste house. Hobe Erwin [who had been succeeded as Interior Decorator by Edward G. Boyle] had some swell ideas on that house and we had a hot correspondence on wallpaper and many other details, including a perfectly ghastly gas lamp fixture which stood at the bottom of the stairs (my own idea), a large brass nymph, discreetly draped and bearing aloft the gas fixture."

[9]"Just about the nicest person I know here is Miss Laura Hope Crews, who is to take the part of Aunt Pittypat. When I first met her and heard her natural soft voice, I wondered why anyone would want to change it. But she

insisted she wanted to talk as I talk for the picture. For a while I just sat and conversed with her; then I read; when I had finished, she said, 'Come, I want to have a record made of your voice so that I may study its tones.' We drove first to the Brown Derby, where we had lunch, then to a broadcasting station in Hollywood. Here I sat before a 'mike' and read five pages of script. We made three records before we got satisfactory results; guess I was a little bit scared, being somewhat of a novice.

"Yesterday I saw this particular scene filmed; Miss Crews is adorable in her hoop-skirted black lace and frilled lace cap. She said her lines like a native, but I hope my coaching will not ruin her accent, for I would not mind if she gave me a few lessons and taught me to speak as she does." Annie Laurie Fuller Kurtz, *Atlanta Constitution*, 19 February 1939.

"I adore Laura Hope Crews. She is cute as hell and more fun than anybody except you and John. She thinks Annie Laurie Kurtz is the most marvelous thing she ever encountered and doesn't believe she is real. Says nobody could really be that sweet and gentle and naive and innocent and Southern. While she makes fun of Annie Laurie, in the same breath she thinks she is adorable." Myrick to Mitchell, Hollywood, 10 April 1939.

"The picture of you and Miss Crews was so good and she looks too cute to be true. She sounds as if she'd be so much fun. Confidentially, we have been expecting to see upon the screen Miss Pittypat with the face and form of Miss Crews and the voice of Annie Laurie. I knew Annie Laurie was so fond of Miss Crews and had been with her so much and I did not see how Miss Crews could resist annexing for her own use a Clayton County voice." Mitchell to Myrick, Atlanta, 17 April 1939.

[10]Here Russell Birdwell deleted from Myrick's original copy: "But only the front and one corner of the house exists. The back is wide open, except one end where there will be some back-yard shots made. That is where the well stands and where fig trees grow and a clean-swept yard looks like any Georgia country yard." From Myrick's original typescript in the collection of Susan Lindsley.

[11]Following this paragraph Birdwell deleted the following passage:

"Across from the parlor is the other parlor but only a small part of it is made—just enough to look like a room when shots are made that would show through an open door a portion of the adjoining room. But even that didn't prepare me.

"Down the long hall, which has a back door with a small fan light, I noticed a door leading to a room back of the office.

"'I must see that room' I told myself, walked on down the hall, peeped in, and found only space.

"It made me a little unhappy to see such a beautiful door with its well-executed panels, leading nowhere at all.

"But you can't stay unhappy long around this place."

[12]Conrad Nagel, Alan Baxter and Frank Morgan also tested for the part of Frank Kennedy.

[13]Marcella Martin was one of the positive results of Selznick's talent search for a new girl to play Scarlett. She was brought to Hollywood and twice tested for the Scarlett part. In addition to reading Scarlett's part in testing other actresses, she did Melanie's role in some tests. She played Kathleen Calvert in the film. After *Gone With the Wind* she did no further work in films.

[14]"I wish you'd write something about Scott Fitzgerald when you get the time. If anyone had told me ten or more years ago that he would be working on a book of mine I would have been stricken speechless with pellagra or hardening of the arteries or something. I dearly loved his books and still do and re-read them ever so often. 'This Side of Paradise' is the most perfect crystallization of an era in all American fiction. It makes me feel sad when I think how utterly past that era is now. I'm sure Mother picked him up in our car one day when he was at Camp Gordon during the war. The streetcar tracks had not been laid that far at that time and we usually hauled twelve soldiers to town every time we went out to see Stephens. After he got famous and I saw his picture I remembered him." Mitchell to Myrick, 10 February 1939.

[15]"George [Cukor] agrees with me that Hattie McDaniel (who is signed but not announced I understand) is not the right Mammy and he is still looking. He agrees with me she lacks dignity, age, nobility and so on and that she just hasn't the right face for it. God knows where they will find an actress who looks right and talks right." Myrick to Mr. and Mrs. Marsh, 11 January 1939.

"I suppose you saw the newspapers that Hattie McDaniel is going to play Mammy. She's an excellent actress so I suppose this is all right, but I was hoping for a new face in the part." Kay Brown to Margaret Mitchell, New York, 24 January 1939.

Hattie Noel had been tested as Mammy in December. It may be that Pearl Adams, who served as McDaniel's stand-in and double, was also tested. McDaniel won an Oscar for her performance as Mammy.

[16]"Eddie Anderson, who was Noah in Green Pastures, is to be Uncle Peter, you may know, and I think he is excellent so far as accent goes and his looks are pretty near right, too. I could like him to be a mite thinner and less well-fed looking but he is not bad. I aint quite so happy about Pork who is to be done by a man named Polk who played in Green Pastures. His accent is rotten but maybe I can teach him." Myrick to Mr. and Mrs. Marsh, 11 January 1939. McQueen had not arrived on the scene when this was written. Kay Brown wrote Miss Mitchell on 16 January from New York: "We shipped Butterfly McQueen for the part of Prissy on Sunday night [15 January]."

The blacks posed special problems to Myrick in coaching for Southern-sounding speech and she was amused enough by Cukor's comment on that situation to record it in her diary on 17 February: "George laughs about me teaching accent to Hattie, Polk and Butterfly. Says it reminds him of time when he was complaining of having to work so hard directing Dinner at Eight. Friend replied 'Yes, it must be difficult, directing John Barrymore in the role of a worn-out actor, Marie Dressler in the role of an old lady who had a mind of her own, Jean Harlow as a hussy and so on.' And, says George, my hard time is just about the same, teaching Negro talk to Hattie McDaniel."

[17]"Harry Davenport, who is Dr. Meade, is divine. He makes all manner of fun of the movies in general and Pappy's tactics in particular and he keeps his mouth shut so I can giggle with him about things. He is the cutest old man in the world. He is about 75 and is a marvelous Dr. Meade. Sounds just like a Confederate Decoration Day orator when he talks." Myrick to Mitchell, Hollywood, 9 April 1939.

"On April 20, Mr. Harry Davenport . . . celebrated the 68th anniversary of his debut on the stage. Everyone on the set offered this distinguished thespian congratulations and best wishes for many more successful years in the profession.

"Mr. Davenport comes of a gifted family, the members of which have been prominent on the American stage for nearly a century. . . . Harry Davenport, the youngest of nine, made his stage debut when only five years old in his father's company. . . .

"In the role of Dr. Meade, Mr. Davenport seems to have stepped right out of the pages of Margaret Mitchell's book. When you see him on the screen you are going to be quite as charmed with his characterization of this part as we here at the Selznick International studios are. Mr. Davenport's son, Ned, is his stand-in. Ned, following the tradition of the family, is also an actor, both on the screen and on the vaudeville stage." A. L. F. Kurtz, *Atlanta Constitution*, 14 May 1939.

TWO
1 February—8 February 1939

Macon Telegraph, 1 February 1939

Straight From HOLLYWOOD

GWTW Shooting Begins under Watchful Eyes of Miss Myrick

HOLLYWOOD, Cal., JAN. 31.—Bright sunlight streamed over Forty Acres to glisten on the windows of Tara and glitter on a score of reflectors and take a little of the frostiness out of the air so that we, who worked at making the first shot of *Gone With the Wind*, might stop shivering for a while.

It was three minutes past nine Thursday morning that the first "Roll 'em boys," was heard and the camera swung slowly to take a long shot of the exterior of Tara, home of the O'Hara family.

We had been on the set since eight. I don't know how many of us. There seemed to me to be more men required to shoot the scene than there were soldiers in the Confederate army. And many of those had been at work since long before daylight. Only the "white collar workers," such as Director George Cukor and I arrived at the late hour of eight in the morning.

Even Miss Vivien Leigh, star of the production, had to report at make-up at six o'clock. And nobody knows what time the poor girls and boys in make-up got out of bed in order to be ready for Miss Leigh and a half dozen other characters when six o'clock came.

When I arrived at the edge of the scene at 7:45 I found a regular platoon of men working, running about, fixing cameras, setting up screens of leaves and grass to cast proper shadows, putting more brick dust on the walks to make them look like Georgia clay, finishing the opening of the dogwood blossoms, raking stray leaves from the lawn, testing arc lights and spot lights and goodness knows what else. And there were a dozen men giving orders and errand boys scooting about and script girls finding a place to sit and Reggie Callow, assistant to Eric Stacey, who in turn is assistant to Mr. Cukor, were the busiest men in the world.

And there stood Mr. Cukor chatting gaily with Miss Leigh who had two girls from wardrobe holding up her lovely skirts and helping to keep a heavy shawl wrapped about her shoulders. For the early morning air was cold.

Nobody looked grouchy and nobody grumbled at getting out of bed before sunup. The atmosphere was gay and there was much bantering in spite of the rapidity with which everybody worked.

The scene reminded me of a bunch getting up early to go on a dove shoot—everybody was in such good spirits.

Everybody on the set laughs when I say "G'mawning," because they all say "Good mor-rning"; so by the time I had spoken to a half dozen folks questions began pouring at me from Stacey and Callow and Cukor and make-up men and everybody else. Or, so it appeared to my sleepy brain.

"Will you please look at this little colored boy and tell me if his clothes are right?"

"Miss Myrick, do you think the dogwoods are the right shape and color?"

"Is this dirt red enough, Miss Myrick?"

"When you can spare a minute, please come tell me if this ivy is thick enough."

"Do you think this colored man's shoes are right?"

"Sue, now tell me, would Scarlett do thus and so?"

On and on they went. I demanded that the little boy who was holding the horse should have his shoes off because the scene is in the spring; told somebody that the plantation bell could NOT be in the front yard; got some holes cut in the shoes of the yard man; told somebody to put more sand in the brick dust for the walks about the house; suggested that the groom might be in this clump of bushes; answered some questions from Mr. Cukor about what the colored groom could say that would sound more like a colored boy; and did about fifteen dozen more things.

Then I sat down in a chair (it didn't have my name on it but it looked like the chair that Fred and Betty New gave me for a going-away present at the Rozars' party before Christmas), and listened to the accents of the Tarleton twins and Miss Leigh.

George Bessolo is one twin and Fred Crane is the other, but nobody knows which is who. They both have mops of red hair and though they are not exactly alike, they are both so funny that we didn't bother to remember one from t'other.

By this time, I was almost frozen and somebody thrust a cup of steaming coffee in my hands and I drank. Right after that Mr. Cukor asked me where the horses would be and if the little boy could sit down to hold them and there was much scurrying about and Eric Stacey said they were ready to roll 'em.

Stacey talked into a microphone and he announced to all in hearing (and anybody on the Forty Acres was in hearing) that when the siren blew there must be no starting of cars nor any other sound. And policemen took their stands on the roads and there was some more talk. Then Eric said:

"Ready boys?"

The boys were ready and Eric yelled:

"Clear the set. Everybody off. This is a long shot."

A few persons scurried out of sight. Eric looked about again and said:

"Whistle."

A whistle blew, the siren screamed, and the man held the inevitable little board in front of the camera to indicate that this was "Take One," long shot of Tara for *Gone With the Wind*.

The shooting of the long-awaited film was begun.

Slowly the camera turned to take in the beauties of the O'Hara home. On the front porch sat the Tarleton twins and Scarlett and as the camera caught her, Scarlett rose and ran down the steps and down the walk.

"Cut," yelled somebody. Then we started rehearsal for the closer view of the twins and Scarlett.

Over and over the scene was rehearsed until Cukor considered it just right. The camera men had measured the exact distance from Scarlett's pretty ears to the lens and there had been much shifting of boughs to set the right flicker of shadow and there had been much changing of reflectors and lights.

"Ready when you are, Eric," called Mr. Cukor.

"Ready to roll 'em, boys?" said Stacey.

Then there would be a brief delay while somebody in a distant field was shoo-ed out of the picture or something was adjusted about a costume.

Then I'd hear the strange admonition from the chief electrician:

"Rest your arcs, boys," which was followed by:

"Save that broad over there!"

(I still don't know what the man meant but I hope to find out. I only know it means something about lights that get too hot and smoke for I discovered that when I saw a man fanning a huge light during a long retake.)

Finally all was ready and the familiar "Rolling 'em" came, followed by "Quiet! Speech!" and again, louder than before:

"Quiet."

Then Mr. Cukor's gentle voice saying:

"Camera."

And the first sound-take for the production was done.[1]

I was hungry enough to eat two lunches, looked at my watch and discovered it was only eleven. There were several repeats on the scene and finally Mr. Cukor had told the boys to "print two of them" and we moved on to rehearse the next shot.

But before we could make it, the fog came rolling in and outdoor shots for the day were over. Only we didn't know it and we sat around waiting for the sun to come back and finally (after about seven hours it seemed) Eric said we could go to lunch.

Nobody objected, for even with extra service of coffee, there is plenty of time to get hungry before eleven if you've eaten breakfast at 5:30 or six.

By the time we had finished lunch Eric had decided the weather would not clear so we started work on an interior set, Scarlett's bedroom at Tara.

It is enough to say that I left the studio at 7:30 that evening, rode the car home, drank a glass of milk and fell into bed. I realized then that the thing I had heard all day was true—"Sit down. You'll be so tired tonight if you stand so much with the running around you have to do."

So the next day I sat down every moment I could snatch. I walked up and down the same place about forty times, while Mr. Cukor rehearsed a scene between Scarlett and her father (Tom Mitchell is playing Gerald) but I managed to sneak in considerable sitting down.[2]

The weather man helped me because about nine the fog came in and Mr. Cukor sent me to Miss Leigh's dressing room to talk Southern talk for her and Mr. Mitchell while the crew waited for the sun.

At eleven there was a bright sun and we had the rehearsal all over again. And again and again, for scenes where animals are used are always difficult. The horse managed to spoil a half-dozen takes by moving out of the camera's vision and it seemed we'd never get the thing done. Then up came another fog and we took out for the morning once more.

During the afternoon, we shot again on interiors at Tara and tomorrow we shoot interiors again. And that is nice. For we do not have to be on set until 8:45.

Hope you all are getting plenty of sleep!

Macon Telegraph, 6 February 1939

Straight From HOLLYWOOD

Progress Being Made in Shooting Bazaar Scene for Movie

HOLLYWOOD, Calif.,—The rebel yell resounds over the studios of Selznick International Pictures and Confederates are all over the place: for we are shooting the bazaar scene for *GWTW*.

Booths at the old armory in Atlanta are gaily decorated in smilax, pine boughs and bunting with faithful following of the details given by Margaret Mitchell in her famous novel. The official flag of the Confederacy and the battle flag of the Southern states fly all over the set. Gentlemen (about a hundred of them) in gray with red or gold sashes stroll about in the uniforms of navy, home guards, Atlanta firemen, militia, infantry and so on—every costume accurate as to detail, thanks to the careful supervision of Wilbur Kurtz, Atlanta authority on historical matters, who is here as technical director.

A hundred young ladies, in hoop skirts and tight basques wear flowers in their hair and the curls bob as they trip through the gay steps of the polka. To the tune of "Dixie," they dance the Virginia reel and all the while, from the chaperones' corner come whispered comments on the scandalous behavior of Scarlett O'Hara, so lately widowed, and dancing with the arch scoundrel Rhett Butler!

What the property department can't do on a movie set just can't be done. Those boys have supplied for the booths at the bazaar just what Wilbur Kurtz ordered. There are mustache cups, bowls and pitchers, pillows with Confederate flags for tops, mufflers, blankets, tatting, crochet, afghans, hair-receivers, candle sticks, booth-jackets— everything you can imagine.

And even hardened cameramen accustomed to shooting every sort of scene, are smiling as Aunt Pitty Pat, Mrs. Merriwether and Mrs. Elsing have their little tiff near the booth where Scarlett and Melanie are standing.

Jane Darwell, who plays Mrs. Merriwether, wears rusty black taffeta with a shiny little jacket and as she moves across the floor of the armory to speak to Aunt Pitty about the misbehavior of Scarlett, Mrs. Merriwether gives the impression of the *Queen Mary* steaming into port.

Laura Hope Crews flutters just as Aunt Pitty should with her tight curls bobbing under her lace cap and her little hands showing indecision as she starts to faint.

Mary Young is a sweet Mrs. Elsing,[3] echoing the stern remarks of Mrs. Merriwether and somehow the scene with these three is funny every time, though I've seen it rehearsed again and again.

For George Cukor has the infinite patience that bespeaks genius. Over and over and over a scene must be done until it is exactly right. A lesser director might be satisfied with any one of a dozen "takes," but not Cukor.

"That's fine, girls," he says, "but I'd like to take one more."

Then he goes over some little part of the scene carefully, explaining just what he wants. There is another take and Cukor says:

"Hold that one boys. Don't print it. That was good, Laura, Jane, Mary. It was good but I want to do one more."

And one more there is—and one more—and maybe one more a dozen times until all is perfection.

I am constantly surprised at the number of shots required for a scene, anyway. The camera boys shoot from up in the rafters to get the dancers whirling about the floor of the bazaar; they shoot from the front of the hall, toward the musicians' platform; they shoot from the platform-end of the room toward the front entrance. Then they move the camera again and shoot halfway down the hall, first pointing front, then back.

Then it's time to shoot close-ups.

Stand-ins for Miss Vivien Leigh and Clark Gable take their places. The director calls for the music, the cameraman says, "quiet" and the waltz begins. The stand-ins practice just as the director and the camera-man direct, taking care to dance in a circle of such dimensions as the cameraman indicates.

A prop man makes little marks on the floor for the places where Rhett Butler and Scarlett O'Hara should be turning and where they should be swaying so that the camera can best catch the expressions on their faces.

After this is rehearsed a half dozen times or more, a call boy goes to the stars' dressing rooms and brings them to the set. They take their places to watch just what the stand-ins are doing and the rehearsal is done again. Then Miss Leigh and Mr. Gable have a rehearsal along with the hundred other dancers.

Finally it is all set and the takes begin.

Part of the time I stand near Mr. Cukor for "ready reference." In fact, I am beginning to feel like a thesaurus or a set of encyclopedias or a dictionary for I must be available for reference at any moment.

"Sue," Mr. Cukor, will say, (for instance) "come look at this line. It does not sound distinctly Southern to me. What could she say instead of this?"

Sometimes he calls to me: "I need a line to use right here because this is a bit abrupt. What can she say that indicates so and so?"

I'll make a suggestion and he will say:

"No, now quit going Hollywood on me. Get on back down to the Georgia plantation. I want a line that sounds Southern. What would your grandfather, General Myrick, have said?"

Cukor is always quick with his wit and humor. The other day he told a prop man to move a huge candlestick to the other side of the booth and before the man could pick it up, Cukor tried to lift the heavy candelabra.

"Whew," he laughed, "they might have used this to kill General Sherman."

Matter of fact, there is lots of fun on the set, though hours are long and players and technicians and dancers and directors work hard.

For a delightful interlude one afternoon I sat for an hour in the dressing room with Laura Hope Crews. The dancers were rehearsing and there was no need for me to remain on the set and Miss Crews had invited me in to talk about her costume. That finished, she asked me to sit down and just talk. She told of her early days on the stage; for she played her first role at the age of four. And remarkably enough, she played in a show with Harry Davenport, who takes the part of Dr. Meade in *GWTW*.

Of all the shows in which she played, Miss Crews says, the one that stands out brightest in her memory is *Peter Ibbetson*, in which she played with John and Lionel Barrymore and Maude Adams. As she talked of John Drew, of Booth, of Miller, of Otis Skinner and Corneila Otis Skinner, of Agna Enters, Ruth Draper and many other great ones of the stage, her puckish face lighted with the love of the dream which is so great a part of her being.

As we talked, George Cukor came in to invite us to join him in eating a present he had just received. Miss Marlene Dietrich had sent him a cake, made with her own hands and he wanted to share it with us. The prop man brought a knife. I cut the cake and we all complimented the cookery skill of Miss Dietrich.

Then I had great fun with a Frenchman, Albert Morin, who is technical adviser for another Hollywood studio. He is a language expert, speaking Greek, Latin, Italian, Spanish, German and French with equal fluency. He is playing the role of the Zouave officer in *GWTW* and his English is delightful with its French accent.

He kids me continually, declaring I shall soon be obliged to return to Georgia in order to regain my Southern speech after association with Californians and French, as well as British folks.

There are, however, plenty of Southerners around. Pretty Miss Bebe Anderson of Birmingham,[4] who is playing Maybelle Merriwether, and her mother, Mrs. J. O. Anderson, speak in distinctly Southern tones and there is handsome young Bruce Lane, who was born in Brunswick and has lived for many years in Montgomery.[5] He is doing the part of Hugh Elsing.

Then there are dozens of extras who can give the rebel yell so it sounds like a cross between Memorial Day in Georgia and a Tech-Georgia football cheer. They are all Southerners.

One man, named Revel Freeman, told me he was in the 151st Machine Gun Battalion and he asked about Boyce Miller, Julian and Charlie Peacock. He is a former Atlantan.

Macon Telegraph, 8 February 1939

Straight From HOLLYWOOD

Premiere Proves Disappointing because of Lack of Stars

HOLLYWOOD, Calif.,—One evening last week I went to a preview at Grauman's Chinese theater. David O. Selznick sent me an engraved invitation and tickets for the press preview of *Made for Each Other*, starring Carole Lombard and James Stewart.

Well, I'd seen news reels of previews and premieres and I was excited over the prospect. So much so that I wasn't even tired at the end of the day's work on the set which began at 8:45 and lasted until six with much running around and more standing-up.

With a friend I went to Hollywood, ate a hurried bite of supper and rushed to the theater. It was half an hour before time for the show but people were lined up along the sidewalk waiting for the appearance of the stars. Huge lights were trained on the entrance to the theater and cameramen stood about waiting.

We felt very grand as we pushed through the crowd to the door, feeling that we were only a degree less important than the Duchess of Windsor and pitying the poor commoners who could not enter the sacred portals.

"We'll stand around in the lobby and watch for the celebrities," we told each other, thinking to see mink coats, ermine, beautiful ladies on the arms of handsome escorts and plenty of orchids.

We located the right aisle; then wandered about to look at the lobby, which is well worth looking at. Huge round columns of Chinese red stand at the corners of the room; handsome Chinese tapestries hang on the walls, curious Chinese figures decorate elaborately carved bases and Chinese red chairs that might grace the home of the emperor stand close to the walls.

As we stood looking at a tapestry, I had a queer feeling that the Chinaman standing in the corner near me was staring at me.

"That chap never moves," I whispered to my companion. "Isn't it strange?"

"Yes," she murmured back, "and those two girls by the door are motionless."

Then we both burst out laughing; for we discovered that they were wax figures—not real persons.

But the ushers are dressed in Chinese costumes and when they are not ushering they stand motionless in the pose of an Oriental dancer and we thought all the figures in the lobby were alive.

That wasn't the only surprise of the evening, however.

We soon discovered we couldn't loiter in the lobby. Polite ushers told us we were not allowed to wait there, we must go to the ladies' room to wait. We moved to the left of the house and stood back of an enormous vase of flowers until the usher on that side started toward us; then we moved to the middle of the lounge.

After we had stood until our feet hurt and it was almost 8:30, we had seen nary a celebrity and the ushers were so persistent that we went into the theater and found our seats.

"Never mind," we told each other. "The stars will come in presently. They are just avoiding autograph seekers. The lights will come on and the actors and actresses will enter, take their bows and then their seats."

In vain we hoped. The picture began. We whispered to each other that the personal appearance would come after the picture.

It was a delightful comedy we saw, with Carole Lombard and James Stewart having a fine time as a young couple who had mother-in-law and servant problems. Then came tragic moments with, of course a happy ending. (I recommend you see the picture when it arrives in Macon.)

Well, we could scarcely wait for the ending of the show. We wanted to see flash bulbs popping and stars bowing and accepting applause from the multitude.

The lights came up: the people began flowing from the house. Nary a star had showed herself—or himself.

Two very disappointed women left the show. But just as we came out of the lobby we saw a mob of people surrounding somebody. This must be an actor, we thought, so we rubbered.

This time we were not disappointed. He was Robert Montgomery and he had autographed about fifty little books.

There was a rush for the other side of the walk. This time Henry Fonda came out to be mobbed by autograph hunters. Then we began to understand why stars slip out of back doors. I bet those two men had writer's cramp before they got home from signing their names in books for queer-looking people.

I never saw such garbs as people wear out here, anyway. Half the women wear slacks, and some of the women even wear men's clothes—suspenders and standing collars and ties and britches and coats. And most of the autograph seekers were clad in non-descript things that looked like what we'd give the wash-woman in Macon.

We stood around for a few minutes to watch for others who might be coming out of the theater but the wind was biting and we walked away, giggling over our ignorance of things Hollywood.

Today a cameraman told me that I was not such an idiot. They do have just what I expected when they have premieres of pictures that are outstanding. *Gone With the Wind* would have just such a premiere he assured me. Maybe I'll get to see it.

Funny how I always find somebody who looks like somebody else. The girl who leads the dances during practice at the bazaar scenes we are shooting looks enough like Dot (Mrs. Bo) MacEwen to be Dot's twin.

And the head electrician on the set would be a good double for Basil Hall.

Here are some disassociated bits I've been wanting to mention: I had a chat with William Farnum on the set the other day. He remembers playing in Macon many years ago on the legitimate stage. . . . I went to the Hollywood Brown Derby the other day. The most impressive thing about it was the strange costumes of the waitresses. They wear light brown cotton frocks with short sleeves and the skirts—knee length—are boned to stick out so the effect is faintly reminiscent of a hat-box . . . The snapdragons out here are about the size of the chrysanthemums sponsors wear at football games. . . . Sweet peas are blooming all over the yards here . . . I had a note from Vance Maree, late of Macon, asking that I give my phone number to him and his wife. . . . I think I shall move from Santa Monica soon: so write me care Selznick International Pictures, Culver City, after this.[6]

Editor's Notes—Two

[1]"The first scene scheduled was also the first scene of the picture, Scarlett and the Tarleton boys talking about the war and the upcoming barbecue at Twelve Oaks. . . . The two Actors playing the Tarleton boys were at worst amateurs and at best adequate. Directing them, for a perfectionist like Cukor, must have been frustrating, for his concentration was on Scarlett and her reactions to them. . . . Cukor had to spend an inordinate amount of time trying to bring the two actors down to the natural unforced kind of work neither of them had been trained in, and Leigh, though a gifted technician, was not above being rattled by having to stop constantly while Cukor tried to make the scene and the actors all blend together. The tension permeated the entire studio." Haver, *David O. Selznick's Hollywood*, p. 264.

By the time *Gone With the Wind* was finished George Bessolo had changed his name to George Reeves. His and Crane's names were reversed in the credits. Actually Crane played Brent Tarleton and Reeves played Stuart Tarleton.

[2]Myrick was immensely impressed, as were all observers of his work, with the directing genius of George Cukor. She was equally impressed by his charm, his patience, and his intelligence. She wrote in her diary on 9 January: "Friday morning, when we started to shoot the scenes with Gerald and Scarlett, right after he has jumped the high fence and she caught him, it was cold as the north pole and we worked with chattering teeth. After rehearsing over and over (George walking up and down and me right after him and trailing also, two script girls) until about nine, Geo said he was ready for a full rehearsal. They said 'Ready,' blew whistle, shrilled siren and yelled 'Speech Quiet.' Then an air plane came over.

"We relaxed. All got set again—yelled 'Cut.' Fog began rolling in. Geo took Vivien and Tommy Mitchell and me up to Vivien's dressing room and he rehearsed the scene. He is amazing. He is vital, compelling, patient and knows how to get perfection from the actor. He talked and talked to the two principals, explaining what the scene meant and analyzing emotion and every movement. . . .

"And so on and on. All the time making gestures and grimaces! But inspiring, just the same. No wonder he is the highest paid of all directors."

³This part was deleted from the script when this scene was reshot by Victor Fleming. Mary Young does not appear in the finished picture.

⁴Like Marcella Martin, Bebe Anderson was a product of the great talent search. She was given a contract, tested for Scarlett, and assigned the part of Maybelle Merriwether. After arriving in Hollywood she called herself Mary Anderson. After *Gone With the Wind* she played in more than a score of films, the last in 1960. Best remembered are *Cheers for Miss Bishop, Bahama Passage, The Song of Bernadette,* and *Lifeboat.* Malcolm Vance, *Tara Revisited* (New York: Award Books, 1976), pp. 160-61.

⁵Bruce Lane's participation in this scene was not repeated in Fleming's refilming of it. His small part was replaced by one played by Harry Davenport, Jr. for which Davenport received no billing. William Pratt, *Scarlett Fever* (New York: Macmillan, 1977), pp. 94, 161. The call sheets for Lane's appearance in the Cukor filming list him under his real name, James Brame.

Myrick wrote in her diary entry for 19 February: "Had a fine visit with Bruce Lane whose real name is James Yancey Brame the Sixth. He is handsome, attractive boy who is here doing bits in movies. Used to be Western star but since singing cowboys came in has only got bits. Trying to get in stock to go to San Francisco and on to Broadway. Also, trying to get in G W T W. Met him when he was doing bit part in bazaar scene."

⁶Myrick found the daily trek from Santa Monica too long a haul. She moved to Hollywood. In her letter of 23 February to Mitchell she said: "Living now at the Stonehaven Apartments I find life more pleasing. Hollywood is more centrally located and shops and things are nearer than they were in Santa Monica. I have a good kitchen, too, where I can fry my own side meat and that is very fine for restaurants as a steady diet make me ill."

THREE
10 February—17 February 1939

Straight From HOLLYWOOD

Scarlett and Rhett Win
Miss Myrick's Enthusiastic Praise

HOLLYWOOD, Calif., Feb. 9.—Vivien Leigh and Clark Gable have spent most of the past week at the bazaar, where the ladies of the Confederacy are raising money for hospital supplies, as Selznick International Pictures shoot *Gone With the Wind.*

If the gentlemen readers of this Hollywood column wish to retire they can leave now for we, the girls, are going to get excited over Clark Gable.

You should have seen him, Ladies, making a grand entrance as Rhett Butler, the blockade runner, arriving at the bazaar! Wearing full evening garb in the mode of the sixties, Rhett was like something from What-The-Well-Dressed-Young-Man-Will-Wear ads of whatever was the pre-war counterpart of the modern *Esquire.*

His shirt front was edged with a tiny ruffle, his wing collar encircled with a wide black tie; the figured vest of off-white was adorned with buttons of the same shade and over his faultless evening clothes he wore an evening cape. A cane, white gloves and a silk hat completed the outfit. And Mr. Gable not only stopped the hearts of the cast; he made the script girls' and a technical adviser's heart flutter as he bowed and smiled in acknowledgement of the tributes of those gathered at the bazaar.[1]

Spot lights, "scoops," "broads" and such (see, I'm learning the vernacular of the electrician!) played on Rhett as the camera did its work. Then the cameramen took shots of the reaction of the crowd to Rhett Butler's entrance; took shots of the bids for ladies to lead the Virginia reel, shots of Rhett's bidding for Scarlett and numberless other shots.

And I watched from a perch on a high stool as they photographed Rhett waltzing with Scarlett and Rhett doing the reel with Scarlett while scores of pretty girls in hoop skirts danced with Confederate soldiers.

Later during the week most of the extras were sent home and closer shots were made of principals.

Mr. Gable stepped over to the booth where Scarlett sat and, following the dialogue and directions of the novel, teased the young widow, while the camera recorded every twinkle of his eye.

And (steady, now, girls!), I sat in an arm chair, marked "Clark Gable," while many of the shots were made. Besides that, I chatted with Mr. Gable between many takes.

"How are you this mawning, Miss Myrick?" he asked with his most charming smile.

"A little chilly, Mr. Gable," I returned; for it had rained and in spite of what the chamber of commerce may say about California weather, it was cold.

"But not so cold as you'd be at home, are you?" continued Mr. Gable.

"Oh! Georgia weather is much nicer than this," I lied, "though of course we do have an occasional chilly day."

Then we talked of how I had imagined a California winter would be about like Daytona Beach and he laughed heartily; then declared this was very unusual weather. Why, when he came to California about fifteen years ago he wore white flannels all through the winter.

Back for another take he went, and then returning he anxiously inquired if his accent sounded right.

"When the Southern women hear you say 'warm' and 'charming' and 'sure,' they'll be eating out of your hands," I assured him, for his accent is decidedly on the side of the Deep South.[2]

And now if the gentlemen will crowd around, I'll tell you how ravishing is Miss Leigh in her widow's garb. I looked through a thesaurus to find a word to describe her and "ravishing" is the nearest right of any word I can find.

As she sat in the little booth where she and Melanie were selling pillows embroidered with the flag of the Confederacy to the soldiers, her blue-green eyes alternately beckoned Rhett Butler and scorned his attempts to tease her. And when he bid her in for his partner in the waltz and she danced with him she was as light as swan's down and as graceful as plumed grass rippling in the wind.

She has, in fact, what Elinor Glyn and I call "It" and what the moderns describe as "Umph." And if she doesn't prove the biggest find in the movies in a decade, Sirius is not a star.

Olivia de Havilland makes a dignified and tender little Melanie, proving she is a good actress; for out of the role, Miss de Havilland is so young and gay and child-like that it is difficult to think of her with the spine of steel that Melanie possesses. When she was working on Southern accent with me in my office one day she asked if she might answer the phone every time it rang.[3]

"This is Miss Myrick's office," she would say in her best Southern manner. Then, with twinkling eyes: "I'll see if Miss Myrick is in. Who's calling, please?"

And all the while I'd be sitting within six inches of the telephone.

But her fun did not end with that. Once when she answered the phone she said: "Just a moment, please, I'll ask Miss Myrick if she has seen Miss de Havilland."

Smothering her laughter, she turned to me and asked: "Miss Myrick, do you have any idea where you can reach Miss de Havilland?"

And back to the phone: "Who's calling, please?"

Finally, she said: "Miss Myrick says she will endeavor to get the message to Miss de Havilland. Will you give it to me, or shall I ask Miss Myrick to come to the phone? . . . Very well. I'll have her tell Miss de Havilland to go over to Wardrobe, if she sees Miss de Havilland."

But I scarcely believe the episode ever took place when I see the actress portraying the role of Melanie and in a dignified fashion explaining to the meddlesome Mrs. Merriwether that whoever critic-izes her sister criticizes her.

People keep telling me that the shooting is going to get monoto-nous to me; but I can hardly see how it is possible. If they shoot the same scene fifteen times there is still something new for me and it is like an exciting game to watch the manner in which Director George Cukor manipulates the actors in order to get perfect results.

Sometimes I think he is three men instead of one; as when he manages to get proper reactions from a hundred extras on the floor and at the same time gives signals for starting and stopping music, watches the closer reactions of the stars in the performance and knows exactly what is right and what is wrong when a take is done.

"That's a good one!" he'll say to the principals. "That's good. We'll make that the first print."

Then to the cutter: "Was that one all right for you, Hal?"

And to his assistant: "We'll make one more, Eric. Will you get ready to make another?"

Carefully, he explains to the person whose action was not quite what he wanted the procedure for next time. The camera clicks again and when Cukor says: "That's perfect," the whole force knows that is the final print.

To me, the funniest thing is the way Cukor says "Perfect" with a southern accent. When the picture began, his voice had a definite "R" in such words as "perfect." Now he pronounces all words containing "R" exactly as a native Georgian would.

The days on the set are long, beginning at 8:45 in the morning and sometimes lasting until 7:30, but there is always something entertaining and somebody always has a good joke to tell. This week, if conversation stops between rehearsals and takes, somebody begins singing:

"When this cruel war is o-over,
Pra-ay that we meet again."

Straight From HOLLYWOOD

Miss Myrick Learns Still More Tricks of Movie Industry

HOLLYWOOD, Calif.,—Today I felt like a loafer. I did not report on the set until nine this morning and was off at six tonight. I did go to my office and dictate some letters later, but I was off the set promptly at six.

When shooting is out of doors, we begin at eight because the morning light is particularly good for Technicolor, it seems, and the sooner we start the more morning light we have. And when shooting begins at eight that means the cameramen, the electrical men, the property men and goodness knows who else must be on the spot about seven to get everything ready for the shooting.

The actors and actresses report at make-up at six to get hair done, make-up on, costumes on properly and then get down to the location on Forty Acres promptly. So the make-up girls and men must be on hand well before six to get ready for those who are reporting at six. On the days when there are two hundred extras (as when we shot the bazaar scenes last week), the make-up department might as well have slept at the studio!

This morning, however, we were shooting indoors—the green bonnet sequence (where Rhett gives the Paris bonnet to Scarlett) and since the camera position had been determined the day before, we did

not have to get there so early. Of course the assistant directors and a
flock of workers reported long before nine, however.

The Army of the Potomac did not have as many men in it as the
Selznick organization employs to make *GWTW*.

Every day I find something new is going on and two or three men I
never saw before are working about the place. Today, for instance, I
saw a man get a little can with a long rubber tube attached to it and he
picked up the hat box in which the Parisian bonnet arrived and sprayed
it thoroughly. The nozzle of the hose turned on a fine stream of
droplets and the stuff that dampened the box was colorless. I asked
what it was and how come and the man said it was because of
Technicolor.

White, it appears, does not take well in Technicolor. It stands out
in too great contrast so the man sprays very light colored objects to
tone them down for proper color effect.

And the men who handle the lights are legion. It is very funny to me
to look up in the loft and see a dozen or more men, roosting like
chickens on a fence, looking after the lighting machinery.

And there are men who spend hours holding little pieces of fine
wire screening in front of lights to get just the right effect. And the head
electrician (named Jimmie Potevin—looks just like Basil Hall) calls
now and then:

"Put a double gauze on that light, Bill."

Or he says, "Watch that silk, Jud!"

And Jud takes off a framed piece of gauze which shows a dark
brown spot in the center where the heat of the light has burned the fine
silk and he thrusts his fist through the burned spot, puts the frame on
the floor and gets a new cover for the light.

The lights are very hot and they smoke and burn the gauze screens.
That's why Jimmie is always calling out: "Save that spot," or "Save 'em
all, boys!"

When Lee Garmes, head cameraman, wants a brighter light on
some particular place, he tells Jimmie and Jimmie calls to some
roosting bird high in the loft:

"Make it about two turns hotter, Hank."

A funny one happened today about that. Mr. Garmes wanted the
sofa where Rhett and Scarlett sat more brightly lighted, passed the
word to Jimmie and Jimmie called:

"Jud! make it hotter where they are sitting!"

Nobody laughed except me. I guess I am just un-sophisticated.

I still am not accustomed to the way things happen. Director George Cukor will rehearse a scene until he thinks it is right. Then the cameraman consults with him on various angles from which to shoot. They rehearse again with the camera following the actors.

And that camera is some Brownie, believe me. It is blue in color, shaped just like the old-time Brownie, is about four feet square and a foot thick and a man told me it costs $75,000 to make one!

Well, a man sits on a stool to the left and back of the camera and sights everything that is being rehearsed. And back of the camera is a platform about six feet high on which sits a man who manipulates the long arm of the microphone. This little piece of machinery is fastened to a sliding steel arm that can stretch out twenty feet long or shorten down to about four or five feet, so that the sound man may follow the movements of the actors with his microphone.

Then Cukor calls out: "Can we make it, gentlemen?"

And Eric Stacey says: "Are you ready, boys?"

"Roll 'em," answers somebody.

Then I get quiet and tense, ready to watch a take. But shucks! They aren't nearly ready.

A flock of girls and men rush out. Someone brushes the dust off the hem of Miss Leigh's long skirt; another girl pushes in recalcitrant hair pins, smoothes down Miss Leigh's curly hair, adjusts the old fashioned snood; another girl arranges the veil or the bonnet or fixes whatever may be a trifle imperfect.

A man brushes Mr. Gable's coat; someone adjusts his scarf carefully; a man touches up the make-up which may have become unsmoothed and so on they go.

Then Jimmie starts calling to men about spots or gauzes or shadows.

Maybe a man brings a leafy branch and fastens it to a standard and adjusts it so a faint shadow of leaves lies across some spot that is not properly lighted. Then, if that is not quite what Mr. Garmes wants, another man holds a piece of wire screen in front of the branch and the light.

Still that is not all!

Somebody calls "Kill the heaters;" for the noise of a gas heater is recorded on the sensitive microphone and if the heater is going when the take is made, the noise spoils the shot.

Then, somebody starts the breezes to blowing so the branches of the trees make dancing shadows. A gigantic canvas tube that reminds me of the "Caterpillar" at the fair, has a tube of air attached to it; the air is turned on and the breeze blows outside Aunt Pitty's windows—inside a barn-like stage.

All this done, we are ready for the take. Then a milliner comes to put the green bonnet on the lovely head of Vivien Leigh so the effect is just as it should be to produce the most chic.

Finally, we take the shot.

When a shot is just right and Mr. Cukor calls: "Print that one in color" and then says: "Thank you," with a little bow toward the actors and the cameramen, we know it is a finished job. Then we hear:

"Bring 'em up for a test!"

For a long time I looked to see what somebody would bring up. It couldn't be the actors because they just stood where they were in the take. It couldn't be the camera, for it remained in exactly the same position.

A man ran out with a card on a stick and held the card with its varied color chart in front of the actors but I hardly thought that was what the man meant by bringing 'em up for a test.

Today, I asked Jimmie. He nearly died laughing but he explained the phrase meant to increase the light slightly so the Technicolor expert could make an examination and find out if all were well with the take.

After the take today, I sat in a chair and went over accents with Butterfly McQueen, who is playing Prissy.[4] But I knew from experience that the camera was moving to a new position, that Mr. Cukor was talking over the next take with cameramen and actors and Eric Stacey was calling:

"Second team in!"

Which, interpreted, is to say: "The stand-ins will now take their places while we plan the lighting for the next scene and get the camera properly set."

Macon Telegraph, 14 February 1939

Straight From HOLLYWOOD

Technicolor Baby Is Lots of Trouble but He Finally Arrives

HOLLYWOOD, Calif.,—Melanie Hamilton Wilkes (Miz Wilkes to you) has been having her baby for three days at Selznick International Pictures. It is more difficult to have a baby in Technicolor, it seems; so the birthing has been long-drawn-out.

Little Beauregard Wilkes is the first baby ever born in Technicolor. Perhaps that accounts for the presence of so many onlookers at the proceedings.

Besides the necessary cameramen, electricians, sound-effects men, script girls, make-up men and women and Technicolor experts, there was a real obstetrician to see that everything was done just as it should be.

Present, too, was I, a technical adviser, whose job was to see that a Technicolor birthing was strictly Dixie.

"Sue," anxiously inquired George Cukor, "would Melanie have her baby on a feather bed?"

I assured him that feather beds at Aunt Pitty's Atlanta house were quite proper and that even if any Southerner had acquired Yankee notions and wanted any other sort of mattress, the excitement and fright and worry, caused by the arrival of the Yankee troops in Atlanta, the refugeeing of the ladies of the city and the attendant circumstances would have made it difficult to get the desired mattress.

"Would the door to Melanie's room be open?" was the next question fired at me.

"Yes, it would,"—for summer weather in Atlanta is hot and there were no men in the house at Aunt Pitty's and the door would have been left open for any possible breeze that might be stirring.

Prissy had run up the stairs, yelling that the Yankees were coming, having just comprehended the import of Scarlett's remark. And Scarlett, coming into Melanie's room to tell her sister-in-law they must pack at once to leave for Tara, had discovered that Melanie was in no condition to leave.

Prissy had been sent for Dr. Meade and had gone switching down the street (I wish you could have seen me teaching Prissy how to "switch"), and Scarlett was left alone with the patient.

No—not alone, really; for there were all of us referred to in the third paragraph above.

There was much discussion of what could be done and what could not be done to show just what was happening.[5]

Melanie turned her pretty head away from the camera so her face would not register anything, but Scarlett was permitted to advise Melly to hold on and yell if she wanted to—there was nobody to hear.

About half way through the scene, Leslie Howard, who is playing Ashley Wilkes, showed up on the set. He was just visiting for he had no lines in today's scene.

Hoots of laughter greeted him.

"It's high time you were showing up, what with your son about to be born," chided Eric Stacey.

"But I'm in Virginia, fighting for my Confederacy," insisted Ashley.

"Well, no birth can be completed unless there is a father hanging around being miserable," insisted various friends.

"How about writing in a scene for Ashley?" I asked George Cukor. "Couldn't we show him pacing up and down on the Confederate breastworks somewhere in Virginia?"

"Yes, that would be good," grinned Cukor. "And we could have the whole regiment behind him, walking up and down and worrying."

All this talk went on while the camera moved in for a closer shot of Scarlett's worried but lovely face.

Then we all whooped with laughter when Prissy advised Miss Scarlett to "put a knife under de bed to cut de pain in two." And then Cukor called to me at the close of the shot:

"How's the take for Dixie?"

Maybe it was the fine quality of Miss de Havilland's performance that got us all keyed up so we laughed for relief. Our laughter was due to the presence of the actual obstetrician. He stood outside camera's range and made motions for the proper moment for Melanie's registering of pain and it was somehow vastly amusing to me when Cukor would call out:

"Is there a doctor in the house?"[6]

Anyway, we finally finished the scenes that show young Beauregard Wilkes had come into being (maybe he should be called Technicolor for short)[7] and tomorrow we are starting on the takes that will show the departure of Scarlett, Rhett, Melanie, the baby and Prissy.

Talking with Miss Vivien Leigh today about the name for young Beauregard, I told her of other famous Georgia names, such as Lavoisier Le Grand Lamar, Lucius Quintus Cincinnatus Lamar and so on. The conversation turned to the names of colored persons and Miss Leigh fairly wept with laughter over the names of Aunt Blue-Gum Tempy's Peruna Pearline's chillun, as they are given in *Aunt Minerva and William Green Hill.*[8] Her favorite of the names was Admiral Farragut Moses the Prophet Esquire.

She is a charming person and we have arrived at that state of camaraderie where she calls me "Sue."

But, then, so does Clark Gable call me "Sue."

The first time he did I almost fell off the high stool on which I was sitting. George Cukor, sitting near Clark, turned to me and said:

"Sue, come tell Clark about the horse you selected for Rhett. I don't know anything about horses."

And Clark said: "Sue, are you a good judge of horse flesh?"

When I had recovered from the pleased surprise at the use of the given name (up to then I had felt that all the cast was being Southern and using "Miss" before my name because Charles Hamilton called Scarlett "Miss O'Hara" when he proposed), I moved over nearer the twosome and Clark and I had a long talk on the respective merits of the five-gaited and the three-gaited horse.

Thank goodness, I've listened to W. T. Anderson and Wade Stepp talk horses long enough to know my technical terms! I'm not sure I didn't give Mr. Gable the impression that I was practically born in the saddle and owned a string of fine horses. You know how it is—the further from home you go the bigger are the columns on the colonial mansion that was your grandfather's house!

Clark is an ardent lover of horses and owns a number of registered mounts. But he thinks we are pretty lazy because we prefer a single-foot to a trot. He reminds me of Roland Ellis, Jr., who always made fun of the riders who counted it a hard day's work to get on their horses at the edge of town, ride a mile to Wesleyan Pharmacy at Rivoli in a rack, dismount and drink a chocolate milk shake. Roland wants to ride fifteen miles and then when you get back home he says he thinks you've probably been two or three miles.

And speaking of homefolks reminds me of George Cukor's reference to Macon people. He told me the other day he counted his visit there two years ago as a priceless experience. He found the city so distinctly Southern in flavor, with its leisurely way of living, that he felt rested for being there. And he recalled with pleasure the morning he went with me to call on Mrs. W. T. Anderson, who was so kind about showing him the heirlooms which she had inherited from grandmothers and great-grandmothers. (Of course he didn't know that Mrs. Anderson is always kind to folks and she was showing those lovely old things to him because she wanted to be polite to an important visitor in town—so, I didn't disillusion him.)

My only regret about George's visit to Macon is he didn't stay long enough to eat a meal with the W. T.'s or the P. T.'s and find out what a real Southern meal can be like to prove that no cooking in the world can equal that of the Southerner.

Man! Would I like to get some spoon bread right now, made by that hundred-year-old recipe Mrs. Annie Virgin Hall brought from Virginia!

But it begins to look as if I'll be here at least for the duration of de wah and there is no spoon bread in California. They don't even know what waterground meal is, out here.

Tallulah Bankhead, once considered for the role of Scarlett O'Hara and who made great success in the London theater, today wired Mr. Cukor: "Tell Vivien Leigh that if a Southern girl could play *The Green Hat* in England it seems a fair exchange that an English girl should play a Southern girl here and I hope and believe America will show her the same good sportsmanship and hospitality that England did me under like circumstances."

Straight From HOLLYWOOD

Prissy Has Trouble with Her Lines but Finally Makes Grade

HOLLYWOOD, Calif.,—Do you remember how you laughed at Prissy when you read *Gone With the Wind*? Well, we've been laughing at her this week—in the flesh.

Butterfly McQueen, who plays the role in the movie version, has a high voice—higher than soprano—(I should say it is about as high as the top note on Kreisler's violin) and every time she opens her mouth we all laugh.

George Cukor (this was written before his resignation), gets so tickled at her sometimes he can scarcely direct, and when Butterfly sees George is amused she breaks down and laughs.

Cukor has gone Southern with a vengeance and quotes from the book constantly, threatening to sell Butterfly down the river if she doesn't get the action just right or calling to a prop man to get the Simon Legree whip. It is all in fun, of course, and Prissy enjoys the joke as much as any of us.

In a scene today, the men were shooting a close-up of Prissy and Scarlett, in the scene where Prissy acknowledges she knows nothing about birthin' and does not know "how come she tole sech a lie."

Cukor told Vivien Leigh where to begin to make the scene match with the long shot taken the day before. The usual calls of "Quiet" and

"Camera" followed, and Prissy muffed her lines completely, spoiling a take.

"What's the matter, Butterfly?" asked George.

"Mr. Cukor, I can't begin there. Miss Leigh'll have to start on the line back of that," piped Prissy in her most respectful tone.

Amid general laughter George said: "All right, Butterfly, if you must get temperamental! I guess we can begin back a line, can't we, Vivien? Prissy, you better be careful how you try my patience. We had one Prissy here before you came, and I really did sell her South."[9]

Finally, however, in spite of Butterfly's temperament, we finished the shot and then began on the scene where Rhett arrives with the decrepit horse and dreary wagon to take Scarlett, Melanie, the newly-born Beauregard and Prissy back to Tara as Atlanta is burning.

"Sue," called Cukor, "where would Prissy sit in the wagon? Would she be on the seat beside Rhett?"

I shook my head, and we assigned Prissy a seat in the bottom of the wagon.

The horse moved forward a few steps, Rhett called "Whoa," and the animal halted with alacrity. Rhett jumped out and Prissy started scrambling over the wheels.

"Sue," called Cukor once more. "Come here a minute. Would Rhett help Prissy out of the wagon?"

And then almost before I had time to shake my head, he said, "No, I knew he wouldn't."

The scene went on. But don't think it happened as fast as you can read this. Lights must be just right, not too strong and not too faint, and in just the right position; and the glare of the fire where the Confederates [are] blowing up the warehouse to keep the Yankees from taking the ammunition must be of proper brilliance.

Then the camera must be adjusted, and there are more rehearsals. So, it takes time.

But finally the scene progressed to the point where Rhett brings Melanie downstairs and puts her into the wagon, with Prissy toting the newly-born Beauregard Wilkes and Scarlett carrying the light, Charles Hamilton's sword and [Ashley's] picture.

The first time Clark Gable brought Melanie downstairs half the men on the lot sighed wistfully.

"Oh, boy! What wouldn't I give to be in his shoes, carrying Olivia de Havilland!" You could see them thinking.

But after Gable rehearsed the scene a dozen times I rather think most of the men were glad they were not playing the role of Rhett, for the steps at Aunt Pitty's are not so easy to make with even so slender a lady as Olivia in one's arms.

While rehearsals progressed I could scarcely keep my mind on the scene for watching Ina Claire, who was visiting on the set.

Dressed in a dark, warm, brown wool frock, brown, low-heeled pumps, and wearing a brown fur hat saucily on one side of her blonde curls, Miss Claire watched proceedings and made comments that were as amusingly vital as she is.

She fairly whooped with laughter when she took a good look at the weary nag drawing the wagon in which the refugees were to escape.

Not that she thought the poor animal was funny. She proved her humane instincts later by buying some sugar to feed him, and she begged for a carrot and an apple to give him.

But her laughter arose from the thought she voiced:

"Here is a fine anachronism. Here you are shooting a scene in mid-summer—look at the make-up girl squirting perspiration on Scarlett—and the horse has a winter coat on. Look at him! You can see the long hair sticking up all over him. He hasn't molted!"

And all our protests that the horse was supposed to look like he had never been curried availed us nothing. She continued to kid all of us about it the rest of the afternoon.

But when she was serious, Miss Claire said she was greatly interested in the production of *Gone With the Wind*, for she had found the book so fascinating, and she praised the dramatic efforts and the masterful sweep of the story in warmest terms.

"They really didn't need to write a script for this show," she vowed. "They could have just given the actors copies of the novel and let them read their parts from the book. I have never seen anything so perfectly suited for production."[10]

Miss Claire was not the only visitor on the set this week. Mrs. William Stufflebeem of Los Angeles, whose husband is manager of the Southern California Department of the Atlanta Retail Credit Company, talked to me about mutual friends in Atlanta and told delightful stories of Guy and Cater Woolford, whom she admires greatly.

When she was a bride, Cater Woolford came to dinner with her one evening and she laughs now at the panic it struck in her heart to have her husband's boss coming to dinner. She vows the only easy chair in their new little home was held together with strings and every time Mr. Woolford moved in the chair (of course, he sat in it, in spite of all their efforts to prevent him), she was in mortal terror. For she didn't know, then, what a human sort of person Cater Woolford is.

Merian Cooper, formerly of Macon and Athens, now a Hollywood producer, visited us too. He had served on the border in 1916-1917 with the Macon Volunteers, and we had a fine time chatting about mutual friends. Mr. Cooper, who is married to Dorothy Jordan, is related to Macon's Miss Caroline Patterson, and he asked about her first thing. Being kin to Miss Caroline, he is also related to Mary Bennett Dunwody and to the Lamars and the Cobbs. And he made me homesick talking about Macon people he knows.

In 1916, he declares, he was broke, and he enlisted with the Macon Volunteers and went to the border. He talked of Cooper Winn, Boyce Miller, Will Murphy, Bill Fenton, and Eugene Harris, among others. He asked particularly about Bill Fenton, who was a classmate at school.

And, of course, I was very happy when George Cukor said:

"Look out, Cooper, she'll write about you in the hometown paper."

And Mr. Cooper smiled at me and said:

"Oh, I have always loved the *Macon Telegraph.*"

Editor's Notes—THREE

[1]On 17 January Myrick wrote in her diary:

"Today I met Clark Gable.

"He would not have been worth a whole paragraph by himself before today because I have never liked him. But I did like him when I met him. He is dynamic, quiet, polite, human and fairly bursting open with IT. I mean what Elinor Glyn and I call IT, as exemplified by Lady Daisy Somebody who was Elinor's friend and always came into the room with a piping bullfinch.

"How'm I doin'? Falling for the movie idol of a billion femmes. George's secretary, a darling gal named Dorothy Dawson, called me and said would I come in please. Mr. Gable was in Mr. Cukor's office. I powdered my face, fixed my lipstick and went in. There sat the God on the sofa beside Cukor and before him stood Lambert, of wardrobe, Plunkett of costume design and two other men with note books.

"Clark had a dozen sketches before him. He rose as I came into the room—so did George—and G. said 'Miss Myrick this is Mr. Gable.'

"I murmured how do you do but he stepped forward, offered his hand, turning on the full force of smile and dimple and said 'I am so glad to meet you, Miss Myrick.' His palm was moist and he had a look of a man with so much red blood—so hot as it were—he couldn't help a little perspiration. His hair is too long and his eyes are very blue and his lashes beautiful. He wore a tan coat over a canary-yellow silk sports shirt, a tie of raspberry and yellow stripes (very yellow) and gray trousers and looked fresh-washed. His shoes were tan and had very thick soles.

"Geo said 'Sit down here and let's see the pix you have of neck wear.' I sat between Clark and George and showed a pic of a man in a collar with wing ends and with a tie soft and rather large and with a frill on his shirt and Clark was enthusiastic.

" 'That's the tie I meant, George,' he said, taking the photo from me and he demonstrated on his neck how that was a becoming line.

"George laughed. 'Yes, Jack Barrymore discovered that long ago.'

"Clark laughed. And then Geo asked how it is tied and both Gable and I said in concert 'wrapped around from the front then brought around again and tied in a bow.' And he gave me a look of 'Aren't you wonderful?' He is not upstage and he is friendly.

"They showed him materials for suits and many sketches and he liked this one and not that one and they made changes and in all we talked about half an hour."

[2]"Another object of constant concern to Selznick was the Southern accent—or its absence. One of Susan Myrick's responsibilities was to see that the actors laced the dialogue with enough inflections and cadences of Southern speech to capture the flavor of the South. After each take Fleming would turn to her and ask: 'Okay for Dixie?' If she said it was not the take was usually reshot. The worst offenders were Clark Gable and Leslie Howard. Gable had no ear for accents; Susan Myrick tried without success to get rid of his Midwestern 'r'. . . . She would go over each scene with him before shooting, but then in the effort of concentrating on the scene, the accent was usually forgotten. Leslie Howard ruined several takes. . . . 'Mr. Howard, please don't say 'bean' remember it's 'bin,' Susan Myrick reminded him after one ruined take. 'Oh, my word, of course, I forgot,' Howard replied. Vivien Leigh picked up the accent quickly and rarely fluffed a line." Roland Flamini, *Scarlett, Rhett, and a Cast of Thousands* (New York: Macmillan, 1975), pp. 267, 270.

[3]"Olivia told me that she had trouble with certain sounds in her 'Georgia' talk and that Miss Sue Myrick, acting as one of the technical advisors, made her practise saying 'I can't afford a four-door Ford,' and 'I can't dance in fancy pants.' Short-cuts, said Livvy, to acquiring a ree-fined So'thern accent, suh!" Gladys Hall, "Gone With the Wind: On the Set with Gladys Hall," *Screen Romances* 18:128 (January 1940): 70.

[4]McQueen was born in Florida and received her early education at Saint Benedict's Convent in Augusta, Georgia. She made her Broadway debut in 1937 in *Brown Sugar*, a musical by George Abbott. Malcolm Vance says: "She had earlier applied for the role of Prissy in *Gone With the Wind*, but was told she was too old (in the book Prissy is twelve when brought to Tara to live at the opening of the novel), too fat, and too dignified. After her hit in *What A Life!*, however, her agent secured the role for her and the part was adapted accordingly. The role brought her instant fame, although in later years she has spoken disparagingly about the novel and the character in various interviews. . . . Although Butterfly has said 'I didn't like being a slave,' felt she was taking a step backward, and objected to the fact that Rhett Butler was called upon to refer to her as 'a simple-minded darkie' (although Miss Mitchell's words are 'a simple-minded wench'), nevertheless she considers the role her best work (which indeed it was), and has stated, 'But it paid well. I went through a full semester at U.C.L.A. on one day's pay.'" Vance, *Tara Revisited*, pp. 121-22.

Myrick wrote Mitchell on 12 February: "Progress on the movie goes forward with dull moments followed by great fun as when George threatens to use a Simon Legree whip on Prissy or tells her we had a Prissy before her and he killed the last one. She is really good in the role though not so young nor pine-stem-legged as I could wish."

In an interview with Myrick many years later Ron Taylor reported for the *Atlanta Journal* (25 March 1976): "The most paradoxical dialect problem was presented by Butterfly McQueen who found the Uncle Remus-style dialect required by the film all but impossible."

[5]A long letter from Joseph I. Breen of the Motion Picture Producers and Distributors of America ("the Hays Office") to Selznick on 14 October 1937 was a response to a reading of an early draft of Sidney Howard's screenplay for *Gone With the Wind*. It made numerous comments on the "birthing scene." Some of them are: "With a view to cutting down much of the broad detail of the dialogue and action suggesting the birth of Melanie's child, we recommend that you endeavor to delete, wherever you can, such action and dialogue which *throws emphasis upon the pain and suffering of childbirth.* This . . . is of *very great importance*. To this end we recommend that, in scene 190, you rephrase Melanie's line, 'It began at daybreak' to 'I have known since daybreak,' and that you also delete from Melanie's line at the end of the scene, the phrase, 'She'd know when to send for him.' . . .

"Please do not over-emphasize the anguish in Melanie's voice. There should be no *moaning* or *loud-crying* and you will, of course, eliminate the line of Scarlett, 'And a ball of twine and scissors.'

"Note: Beginning with scene 210 down to the end of scene 227; we urge and recommend that these scenes of childbirth be cut to *an absolute minimum*, in order merely to suggest Melanie's suffering. We think, for instance, that you might very well delete showing her teeth 'biting her lower lip till it bleeds;' her holding on to Scarlett's hands in desperation; all of the business of tying the towel to the foot of the bed, and the dialogue accompanying such scenes.

"Scarlett's line in scene 218, 'She can't stand many more hours of this;' Melanie's line, 'I can't stand it when you're not here,' Prissy's line, in scene 219, 'Miss Meade's Cookie say effen de pain get too bad, jes' you put a knife under Miss Melly's bed an' it cut de pain in two,' and Scarlett's line at the bottom of the page, 'I think it's coming now,'—these scenes, together with all the business set forth on page 107, are enormously dangerous from the standpoint of both the Production Code and of political [i.e., local] censorship.

"It seems to us that you may carefully *suggest* these scenes of childbirth without *over-emphasizing the distress and pain attended thereto*. It may be possible to do this effectively by playing the camera on Scarlett's face, or, possibly, on the faces of some of the other characters. As now written, however, the scenes are hardly acceptable and should be *materially toned down*." Typed copy in the Sidney Coe Howard Papers, Bancroft Library, University of California, Berkeley.

[6]There was a doctor in the house. In her record for 18 February Gladys Hall wrote: "Later, Olivia told me that an expert obstetrician, Dr. Reuben D. Chier, had been retained to supervise the birth scene. I had noticed him, off-set, a stop-watch in his hand, giving signals at certain stated intervals, timing her spasms. She also told me that, before the scene was shot, she had gone to a medical lecture at the General Hospital and had even witnessed two

births, garbed in a mask and a nurse's uniform." Hall, "Gone With the Wind: On the Set with Gladys Hall," p. 68.

Gladys Hall's facts are to be taken with considerable caution: basically they ring true, but parts of her record sound like press-agentry, and her dates are not always to be relied upon. Here, for example, she writes under the date of 18 February about events described in Myrick's article in the *Macon Telegraph* of 14 February and about which Myrick wrote Mitchell in a letter of 12 February. Cukor had left the production by 18 February.

[7]On 12 February Myrick wrote the novelist: "We all nearly died laughing when we were re-shooting the birthin scene. While the camera men were fixing the million things they have to fix, Olivia lay in bed and read GWTW, once more. George saw her and ordered the 'still man' [Fred Parrish] to make a picture of it for you. He is sending it along, herewith. He asked me to write you since he is, he says, a poor letter writer. He talks of you often and admires you greatly."

Margaret Mitchell replied to this in a letter of 15 February: "The picture of Melanie in labor, with 'Gone With the Wind' clutched to her and Scarlett anxiously cooling her brow, was wonderful. John says that the expression on Miss de Havilland's face is precisely the expression I wore during the time I was writing the book."

[8]Myrick refers here to Mrs. Frances Boyd Calhoun's *Miss Minerva and William Green Hill* (Chicago, 1909). It is currently in print in a facsimile edition published by the University of Tennessee Press with an excellent introduction by Robert Y. Drake.

[9]Gladys Hall recorded this as of 18 February: "Vivien said, smiling, that the only reason they'd had to make more than one 'take' of the scene was because they had trouble trying to make Prissy play the part of a dumb little negress. 'Because she isn't really dumb at all,' said Vivien. 'When she rests between scenes, she's usually reading a magazine with quite a literary tone! The other day I asked her why she particularly enjoys the magazine, and she said, "I p'tik'ly enjoy Mr. George Jean Nathan's articles on the Theatre!"" Hall, "Gone With the Wind: On the Set with Gladys Hall," p. 70.

In his *Atlanta Journal* interview with Myrick (25 March 1976), Ron Taylor told the story a bit differently: "Miss Myrick recalls walking by Miss McQueen one day as the actress was reading Esquire magazine—a regular habit with her during filming—and asking why she was so taken by the magazine. Whereupon, the film's Prissy declared, with heavy rolling Harlem R's, 'I like to look at the dirr-ty pit-cherrs.' "

A note about McQueen in Myrick's diary explains how there would be two versions of the anecdote: "Butterfly McQueen, christened Thelma, acquired her name because she danced so well in Fed Art Project Midsummer Night's Dream. She reads Esquire—says she likes the pix and George Jean Nathan."

[10]"I got a great kick out of meeting Ina Claire who visited on the set the other day. I wish you could have heard her talk about the movie industry. It

was marvelous the way she made fun of the whole caboodle. She says GWTW is the finest book since Tolstoi wrote and that when she had finished the part where Beauregard is born and the group escapes to Tara she thought there could NOT be anything else to read—but found plenty more just as thrilling. Says it is the most marvelous book for sustained interest she ever read." Myrick to Mitchell, 12 February 1939.

ILLUSTRATIONS—1

THE COMPANY WILL APPRECIATE SUGGESTIONS FROM ITS PATRONS CONCERNING ITS SERVICE

1220-8

CLASS OF SERVICE

This is a full-rate Telegram or Cable-gram unless its de-ferred character is in-dicated by a suitable sign above or preced-ing the address.

WESTERN UNION

R. B. WHITE
PRESIDENT

NEWCOMB CARLTON
CHAIRMAN OF THE BOARD

J. C. WILLEVER
FIRST VICE-PRESIDENT

SIGNS

DL = Day Letter
NM = Night Message
NL = Night Letter
LC = Deferred Cable
NLT = Cable Night Letter
Ship Radiogram

The filing time as shown in the date line on full-rate telegrams and day letters, and the time of receipt at destination as shown on all messages, is STANDARD TIME.

Received at

DEC 10 AM 7 18

QA15 120 NL 1 EXTRA=LOSANGELES CALIF 9

SUSAN MYRICK=

    MACON GA=

ARE YOU IMMEDIATELY AVAILABLE COME HERE TO PERFORM THOSE
FUNCTIONS CONNECTION WITH OUR PRODUCTION "GONE WITH THE
WIND" WHICH I BELIEVE HAVE ALREADY BEEN SUBJECT OF
DISCUSSION BETWEEN YOU AND OUR REPRESENTATIVE NAMELY TO BE
ARBITER OF MANNERS AND CUSTOMS OF TIMES AS WELL AS TUTOR
MEMBERS OF CAST. BOTH WHITE AND NEGRO IN ACCENT
CHARACTERISTICS OF EACH CLASS AND TIME AND PERFORM SUCH
OTHER SERVICES CONNECTION THAT PHOTOPLAY AS BEFITS YOUR
CAPABILITY YOUR EMPLOYMENT WOULD BE ON WEEK TO WEEK BASIS.
WE WILL PAY NOT MORE THAN HUNDRED DOLLARS WEEK ROUND TRIP
TRANSPORTATION. IT WOULD BE NECESSARY FOR YOU LEAVE
IMMEDIATELY. PLEASE WIRE ANSWER COLLECT AS WE ARE
PRACTICALLY AT DEADLINE DATE FOR HIRING PERSONS PERFORM
THESE FUNCTIONS=

        ELZNICHS NT INTERNATIONAL PICTURES
        BY   D T OSHEA.

NT..

THE QUICKEST, SUREST AND SAFEST WAY TO SEND MONEY IS BY TELEGRAPH OR CABLE

Telegrams concerning Susan Myrick's Hollywood employment. The GWTW techni-cal adviser's job became hers on 14 December 1938. Susan Myrick Papers, Robert W. Woodruff Library, Emory University, and collection of Susan Lindsley.

1201-S

WESTERN UNION

The filing time shown in the date line on telegrams and day letters is STANDARD TIME at point of origin. Time of receipt is STANDARD TIME at point of destination.

Received at Western Union Building, 455 Cherry St., Macon, Ga.   1938 DEC 13 AM 7 19

QA9 66 NL=LOSANGELES CALIF 12

MISS SUSAN MYRICE=

    MACON TELEGRAPH MACON GA=

RE YOUR WIRE SITUATION CHANGED CONSIDERABLY SINCE MISS BROWN
HAD HER DISCUSSION WITH YOU LAST MAY BUT BECAUSE OF THAT
DISCUSSION WOULD BE WILLING GO UP TO 125 A WEEK WITH ROUND
TRIP TRANSPORTATION WHILE JOB WILL UNDOUBTEDLY LAST BETWEEN
8 AND 12 WEEKS WE CANNOT GIVE ANY SUCH MINIMUM WOULD BE
WILLING GIVE YOU 5 WEEK MINIMUM JUST BY WAY OF ASSURANCE
ADVISE BY WIRE=

    DANIEL T OSHEA.

1201-S

WESTERN UNION

The filing time shown in the date line on telegrams and day letters is STANDARD TIME at point of origin. Time of receipt is STANDARD TIME at point of destination.

Received at Western Union Building, 455 Cherry St., Macon, Ga.

QA485 24 NL=WUX TDS CULVERCITY CALIF 13   1938 DEC 14 AM 12 41

MISS SUSAN MYRICK=

    MACON TELEGRAPH MACON GA=

ITS A DEAL. HOPE TO WIRE YOU NEXT WEEK DATE FOR YOUR ARRIVAL
HERE. BARELY POSSIBLE YOU WILL NOT BE CALLED UNTIL AFTER
HOLIDAYS=

    DANIEL T OSHEA..

Susan Myrick as she looked when she left Macon to go to Hollywood. Photo by Coke's, Macon. Collection of Richard Harwell.

The Selznick International Pictures studios in Culver City. Wilbur G. Kurtz Collection, Atlanta Historical Society.

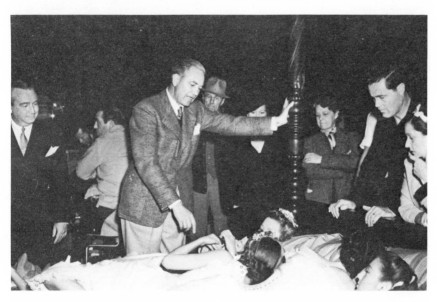

Susan Myrick (to the right of the bedpost) watches Victor Fleming arrange the scene of the afternoon nap at Twelve Oaks. Courtesy of MGM/UA Entertainment Co. Collection of Susan Lindsley.

William Cameron Menzies, designer of the production of GWTW and director of some of its scenes, with his drawings for the film. Courtesy of MGM/UA Entertainment Co. Collection of Richard Harwell.

Chief Electrician James Potevin, Producer David O. Selznick, Director Victor Fleming, and Head Cameraman Ernest Haller examine one of Menzies's drawings. Courtesy of MGM/UA Entertainment Co. Collection of Susan Lindsley.

Susan Myrick with Fred Crane (on her right) and George Reeves, GWTW's Tarleton Twins. Courtesy of MGM/UA Entertainment Co. Myrick Papers, Emory University Library.

Snapshot of Clark Gable and Susan Myrick taken in April 1939. Collection of Richard Harwell.

Susan Myrick poses in front of one of SIP's cameras on a GWTW set. Collection of Susan Lindsley.

Marian Dabney, GWTW's ladies' wardrobe mistress, and Edward P. Lambert, head of SIP's wardrobe department, examine a dress designed for Scarlett's honeymoon. Kurtz Collection, Atlanta Historical Society.

Susan Myrick rests during a break in one of the long days involved in bringing Margaret Mitchell's novel to the screen. Collection of Susan Lindsley.

FOUR
21 February—7 March 1939

Macon Telegraph, 21 February 1939

Straight From HOLLYWOOD

Olivia Pulls Trick on Gable but He Laughs at Himself

HOLLYWOOD, Calif.—We had a fine laugh on the set this week— one of the best gags of the season. We were shooting the scene where Rhett takes Melanie downstairs at Aunt Pitty's house to put her into the wagon for the flight to Tara. Prissy had repeated the words of Scarlett:

"De Yankees is comin'!"

And Clark was rehearsing the picking up of Melanie to take her away from the Yankees. Easily, he swung the lightweight Olivia de Havilland to his arms and walked off with her. Somebody began kidding him about being tired of picking up Olivia, and he vowed he found it a pleasant task.

Then, while cameramen moved the cameras, electricians adjusted lights, and Technicolor experts consulted, Clark went to his dressing room.

But not Olivia. Along with her stand-in, Ann Robinson [Miller], and several prop men, Olivia framed Clark.

When everything was ready for the take, Clark tried to lift the feather-weight Melanie and could scarcely move her. He groaned:

"What on earth's the matter here? Have you got her nailed down?"

"Am I heavy?" asked Olivia in her sweetest voice, looking very innocent and wide-eyed.

And after Clark looked completely flabbergasted and the crew began giggling, Olivia stood up and let fall the thirty-pound weight she had concealed in the folds of the quilt wrapped about her.

Everybody shouted, and Clark laughed as heartily as the rest of us.

Clark and I had a little chat the other day, and I was surprised (as I expect you to be) when he told me he used to work on a newspaper in Portland, Oregon. And you'd never guess what he did! He was on the police beat. He liked the work, too, and says he likes newspaper men and women because all he ever met were swell.

More interesting visitors have been on the set lately, too. Laurence Olivier, who doesn't like to have it said of him that he looks like a young Ronald Colman, dropped in for a while the other day. He did not look like Ronald to me! He is making *Wuthering Heights.*[1]

A young man from Louisiana, who designs costumes, visited us, too. He is a good friend of Edna Mae Oliver, and, since she is a friend of Cukor's, Rufus Lindsey of Minden (which he says is such a small place nobody knows about it except when he says it is near Shreveport) came over to visit. Lindsey's father is president of the senate, and Rufus is a wise son of a politician. For he refuses to discuss politics, preferring to talk about the dresses he designed for *Artists and Models Abroad* and for the recently-released *Cafe Society.*

A newcomer to the cast this week was Jesse Clark, who plays the role of Uncle Peter. He is thin, and his face is benign, and he looks much as I had thought Uncle Peter would look when I read *Gone With the Wind.*

He told me proudly that his mother belonged to the Adairs of Atlanta and was pleased when I told him I knew the name as one well-established in Atlanta. It was easy to see he is proud that his ancestors belonged to quality—not to po-white trash.

And he told me, too, that his father, Aleck Clark, was head waiter at the old Kimball House for many years. Jesse is sixty-three, he says, and though he has been long out of Georgia he still speaks fondly of his life there.[2]

I picked up a bit of interesting news today, talking with Hazel Rogers who designs the hair arrangements for the production. Hazel's husband does a lot of historical research as a sort of hobby and collects all sorts of newspapers and out-of-print books. And he found for her recently the name of a prominent hairdresser of Atlanta in the sixties.

She was Dale Waters, and the reference to her said she "excelled in the coiffure de Française" and that she went by appointment to the finest homes in Atlanta to arrange the tresses of the belles of that era.

Hazel has evolved some intriguing hair-dos for the feminine members of the cast. They are period in character in every case, but designed each time to best set off the charm of the particular character. For Melanie, the hairdress is simple and has dignity, while the arrangements designed for Scarlett are more zippy—if I may use such a term to designate a hair style of 1860.[3]

I have been reading in the *Telegraph* recently about the camellia shows and wishing I might be home to see them, so I have talked about the flowers in glowing terms. That started Will Price, dialogue assistant, who is from Mississippi, talking about his mother's camellias.

She is a rival of Dr. W. G. Lee, it appears, and he'll probably turn green with envy to hear that she has growing in her garden at McComb, Miss., forty-two varieties of the fifty-four possible in her locality. Of course, I wasn't going to let Mississippi get ahead of Georgia, nor was I thinking of handing any palms to Mrs. Kenneth Price over our own Dr. Lee. So I said Dr. Lee had forty-seven varieties. I hope he has!

All of us are looking forward to meeting Victor Fleming, the new director who starts work soon. We regret the resignation of George Cukor for everybody liked him, and we'll miss him.[4] But we have heard fine things about the new director, too.

And now for a story that sounds incredible. Not about the production of *Gone With the Wind*, nor about Hollywood—just about a queer thing that happened to me.

Somebody told me about a place where I could get the best grades of shoes at the cheapest prices; a store that bought out old stocks or broken lots, etc., and resold at low prices. The store stays open until nine in the evenings, so one night I strolled down.

The clerk, in a courteous fashion, showed me several pairs of shoes; and, while he went for a different size of a certain sort, I sat and gazed idly at the rows of boxes on the shelves. Suddenly I jumped, rubbed my eyes, and said to myself:

"My dear, you are working too hard. You should get to bed earlier and take more exercise. You are getting hallucinations."

Then I looked again, and it was true. There was a box bearing a name in script just like I'd seen a thousand times:

"Jos. N. Neel Co., Macon, Ga."

I nearly had a fit. I felt almost as if I'd seen "Uncle Joe Neel" and Roland and Blanche!

It would make a better story, of course, if I'd bought the shoes that had once been for sale at Neel's, but I didn't. They weren't the right size. But I did say to the man, who brought my shoes to try on, that I had been buying from Neel's in Macon for many years. And he said:

"It's a nice store, I guess. Those are high-class shoes that came from there."

Macon Telegraph, 24 February 1939

Straight From HOLLYWOOD

Change in Directors Gives Miss Myrick Time to Get About More

HOLLYWOOD, Calif.—There are those who insist that the high winds that blew over Southern California last week were in some way connected with publicity for *Gone With the Wind*. Believing firmly in the power of the press, I dislike to doubt it, but it does seem going a bit far.

Nevertheless the cessation of the wind that blew is welcome as will be the resuming of the other *Wind*. While it is pleasant to have a brief interlude of shorter hours now that we are not in production, all of us on the lot of Selznick International Pictures are expecting to begin any day—just as soon as Victor Fleming, the new director, has studied the script and becomes fully acquainted with the status of production. Everyone is enthusiastic about Mr. Fleming. He has directed some of the best pictures made here, including *Test Pilot* and *Captains Courageous*.

Meanwhile, property men, assistant directors, wardrobe people and others in the production department go forward with preparations. I, meanwhile, am continuing to work with the four principals of the picture on accent.

Saturday's lesson was especially pleasant for me because Leslie Howard invited me to have lunch with him while we worked. Vivien

Leigh, John Balderston, Leslie, his secretary and I sat in the walled garden with a warm sun pouring down on us and had a lunch that began with cream soup, followed by baked ham, a green salad, French rolls, Charlotte russe, and coffee and cheese.[5]

The cheese was a marvelous concoction of Roquefort and sherry and the salad dressing was a simple lime juice and olive oil. Believe it or not, there was no tea anywhere to be seen and the coffee tasted like American-made coffee. I learned that Vivien Leigh never drinks tea.

We talked of the delayed production of *Gone With the Wind*, naturally, but there was much chatter of Shakespearean folios: for Mr. Balderston (author of *Berkeley Square*) is a collector who possesses a first, second, third, and fourth folio purchased at some exorbitant price and highly valued. Naturally, the Britishers were particularly interested in those and they seemed a little envious.

During a considerable part of the conversation, I kept quiet and just listened fearing lest I show my ignorance as they talked of the apocryphal group of Shakespeare's plays.

But I understood the talk of polo which followed. Leslie Howard is an enthusiast and he was making plans to see a game between the British team and a California team. He said he hoped to see the international matches in New York later, but he thought he certainly ought to see this game as it was the only one he thought England would win in America.

His daughter, who is back in England, plays polo well, I learned, and Mr. Howard has a string of ponies.

I don't know whether my accent lesson did any good, that day!

I left the luncheon with pleasant memories of a garden where daffodils bloomed, green turf pushed through flagstones, bright sunshine filtered through pepper trees and pleasant people talked of interesting things.

It was especially nice to have a sunny, calm day once more, for the wind which had blown for three successive days was decidedly unpleasant. In Hollywood, and on the Selznick lot at Culver City, the wind did little damage compared to that done in Pasadena and parts of Los Angeles, where hundreds of trees were uprooted and windows were smashed by the force of the Santa Ana. (They call all high winds Santa Ana, here, because they are supposed to originate in the Santa Ana district about forty miles from Los Angeles.)

At the Lamar Trottis, where I had dinner the other evening, Louise and Lamar were fidgety all evening lest the wind blow down some of their newly-planted and greatly cherished trees.[6]

They have recently built a new home and Louise says trees are so scarce out here you have to buy them. She says the trees they planted cost almost as much as their house!

Lamar's picture, *Alexander Graham Bell*, has just been finished and he has another story ready for production. He has written the story of Abraham Lincoln, the young man, and John Ford will direct it with Henry Fonda playing Lincoln.

Somehow, in spite of the glamour of movies and stars and writers for the films, there is nobody so much fun, to my mind, as somebody connected with the newspaper business. So; it was a particular joy for me to have dinner the other evening with Bill Kirkpatrick. Bill works for the *Los Angeles Evening Herald and Express*, and he lives in Laurel Canyon with his lovely young wife, Virginia, and two-year-old son.

We talked of the legislature, of the press institutes, of whether there will be a sales tax in Georgia, of mutual friends in the newspaper business and mostly just about Georgia. For both of us have a vast fondness for the Empire State of the South and particularly for the people who live there. Both of us wished we might be transported in some fairy fashion to Athens for the Press Institute so we could see again some of the most delightful and lovable people of the state, the newspaper folks.

The interlude between directors which has given me shorter hours of work has enabled me to have some time for social life. The other evening I went to a party at the home of Mrs. Fairfax Proudfit Walkup, whom I have mentioned before as a relative of the Macon Proudfits. Mrs. Walkup had invited a group of graduates of the Pasadena Playhouse, where she teaches, and it was a merry party with the girls and boys telling stories of their work, their trials and their joys. One girl, who looked about twenty-two, grinned sheepishly when I asked her what sort of radio work she was doing, and admitted she gave advice to young mothers every morning at eleven. A handsome, dark-eyed boy who seemed about twenty-two also looked a little hacked and said he wrote the script for her.

I took to Mrs. Walkup the pictures from the *Telegraph* that showed the old Proudfit home, recently restored by Connie Proudfit

Hirsch and Mrs. Mark O. Daniel, and Fairfax showed it proudly to all the guests, bragging shamelessly on her kinfolks in Georgia.

The only thing that interfered with a perfect evening was the way I kept wishing for Mrs. Piercy Chestney. She'd have loved the talk of Little Theaters and she and Fairfax would have been good friends within five minutes. I reckon Mrs. Chestney's ears burned; for I told proudly of what Macon's Little Theater has done and I needed no urging to bring out of my bag the clipping I carried of Frank Hawkins' review of the last performance at the Little Theater.

How I wish I might have seen it!

Macon Telegraph, 27 February 1939

Straight From HOLLYWOOD

Gone With the Wind Shooting Will Be Resumed by Selznick Today

HOLLYWOOD, Calif.—Called in for a conference with David O. Selznick and Victor Fleming, new director for *Gone With the Wind*, yesterday, Wilbur Kurtz and I contributed what we could to the discussion of plans for shooting, which is scheduled to be resumed Monday.

Mr. Fleming, who is a handsome, blondish man with keen eyes and a tendency to fire questions at you so fast you can't even answer them, indicated a familiarity with details of Miss Mitchell's novel that bodes good for the production of the movie.[7]

And what he didn't know about Clayton county to begin with, he soon learned from Wilbur Kurtz. So well did Wilbur talk of historical background that Fleming leaned back in his chair and said:

"Kurtz, I'd like to get on a boat bound for Australia with you and spend the whole voyage listening to you while you told me all about the history of the South."

Wilbur grinned and said, "It's a date."

Well, I've no date for Australia, but I did have a fine date with Olivia de Havilland at her home the other afternoon. Olivia, who is having practically no difficulty with Southern accent is greatly interested in the locale of *Gone With the Wind* and asked many questions so that our accent lesson consisted largely of my talking about Georgia while she listened, with an occasional interruption such as:

"How do you pronounce 'there'?"

Olivia's living room is light and airy. The draperies are cream-colored of background, with soft rose and pale green flowers; and the taupe rug is brightened by the colors of upholstery on chairs and sofa. The room was further colored by the presence of two vases of American Beauty roses that perfumed the whole place.

Olivia's costume was perhaps designed to match the roses for her dull blue woolen frock was enlivened by American Beauty scarf and belt, and she looked very lovely as she poured tea from a Spode pot and served little hot rolled sandwiches to go with the tea.

Alicia Rhett arrived from Charleston, S.C., recently and she is what the office boy calls easy on the eyes, herself. Her red-gold hair frames a slender face, and many of us are remarking that she looks somewhat like Leslie Howard. Which is of course, as it should be, for Alicia plays the role of India Wilkes, sister of Ashley.[8]

Alicia was having a fine time, when I met her the other day, looking at pictures of hair styles of the sixties in a book that belongs to Hazel Rogers, head of the hairdressing department. But it was difficult for her to decide with Hazel on a hair-do because she was so pleased at other pictures and wanted to look at bonnets, hoop-skirts, and other costumes as they appeared in the old copies of *Harper's Bazaar*.[9]

Wednesday being the birthday of George Washington, the boss gave me the day off and I did so many things my head whirled from excitement.

Over at Pasadena, I had lunch with a friend at the Athenaeum club, which is at the California Technological School. (The Tech is known here as Caltech, which I find an intriguing word that somehow reminds me of Aztec Indians.) Only graduate students at Caltech, members of the faculty, and such scientists as may wish to come in from the observatories nearby are acceptable in the dining room, so I felt very important eating there. My friend has the good luck to be a daughter of a man who was a close friend of Blackmer, who gave the Athenaeum to the university; hence our entree.

After lunch we went to the visitors' gallery where we looked down into the cork-lined, insulated room that houses the two hundred-inch lens which is being ground for the giant telescope that is to be built at Palomar.

Of course, you have read how it took two years to make the glass and cool it at Corning, N.Y., and you saw pictures in your newspaper which showed the freight train that hauled the precious piece of glass out to California. Now, the process of polishing continues, where one piece of glass is ground upon another to smooth the two hundred-inch lens to the state of perfection required for proper refraction of light.

The campus and buildings at Caltech are lovely. Built in Mediterranean style, the dormitories, administration halls, library, and the other structures, are suggestive of monasteries with cloistered walks and arches everywhere. The liveoak trees are gnarled and picturesque, and they reminded me of Brunswick and Savannah—except there was no Spanish moss to beard the trees.

And I got a big kick from plucking ripe olives from the trees that border one of the long walks. All my life I had thought ripe olives grew in bottles or cans in grocery stores!

After we had toured the campus, we departed for a ride over Pasadena to view the handsome homes along Millionaires' Row and to moan a little over the desolation the high winds caused last week. Everywhere men were cutting trees that lay across sidewalks or lawns, blown down by the Santa Ana of last week. Thousands of beautiful firs and cedars and liveoaks and black acacia trees were uprooted or broken in the storm, and somehow a broken tree is a distressing sight.

I was cheered, however, by a visit to the famous Huntington Hotel, built many years ago by Henry Huntington, who founded the famous library at Pasadena [San Marino].

The gardens are lovely beyond words, with terraces leading down to a blue swimming pool set in an emerald of grass. Stock, calendula, phlox and myriads of daffodils, made brilliant spots along the terraces on one side; while the other sported every color of the rainbow, with blossoms nobody could tell me the name of. I recognized iris and thought the tall orange lilies were kin to our day-lilies.

Across the arroyo (creek bed to you) runs a bridge about an eighth-mile long, made of hand-hewn wood, picturesque with its steep roof and supporting timbers.

At intervals along the bridge roof where small gables come down enough for the visitor to see easily, are painted scenes of famous California spots.

Done by George Moore, they attract much interest, showing

desert, mountain, flowers, trees, old missions, and numerous sea-scapes, boldly done in warm colors.

Though we did not go to the races, we rode past the Santa Anita track, which houses 50,000 and was well filled for the derby. At least it must have been filled, for there seemed to me to be 50,000 automobiles parked in the area. The warm sun glinted down on them so that a million sparkles met our eyes as we drove along the road overlooking the parking spaces. And in the background the purple-blue mountains looked down calmly, unexcited over the spectacle of thousands going wild over the running of horses.

In spite of my efforts, I find it impossible to take on the calm air of the surrounding mountains out here. I was agog, for instance, at meeting John van Druten the other day. And when someone intro-duced me to Ben Hecht, I could barely remember my manners for the thrill it gave me.[10]

Mr. Hecht looks just exactly like you would expect the man who wrote *Front Page* to look.

Those two writers are just some more of the great and the near-great who wander on and off the movie lot at Selznick International Pictures. I met Nancy Carroll[11] the other day; and the day before that, I met Frank Morgan.

I'll get so I shall not be excited over it if the King of Siam arrives, I suppose, but up to now I am still tongue-tied at seeing celebrities.

Macon Telegraph, 2 March 1939

Straight From HOLLYWOOD

Myrick Gets Still More Inside Facts on How Big Studios Work

HOLLYWOOD, Calif.—Production meetings, consultations, conferences and such are going on all the time out here these days, and things are rapidly shaping for the new director, Victor Fleming, to begin shooting.

Walking down to the stage where the art department workers are building the sets for Twelve Oaks today, I chatted with Eric Stacey, assistant director; Lyle Wheeler, of the art department; and Reggie Callow,[12] assistant to Eric. I still think it's funny for an assistant to have an assistant, but I have found out how necessary he is. Eric has something slightly less than a million details to supervise, and Reggie can take care of a large number of these.

People may write plays and books that poke fun at assistant directors as yes-men, but the truth is those boys have plenty of work to do. There's the question of "breakdown" for instance.

I never knew what the word meant before. I had a vague idea it was something business men do to get figures to show the income tax man or prove the bonds they want to sell are O.K. But when Eric and Reggie get ready to break down a scene, that's something.

Shall we take the bazaar scene in *Gone With the Wind* as an example? The script writer puts down the dialogue and an indication of the situation with a few directions. But it is up to Stacey and Callow to figure out just how many persons will be on the set; how many wigs and costumes they'll need; how many men will have beards; how many will wear mustaches or sideburns; how long it will take how many hairdressers to do the hair properly; how many wardrobe girls will be needed to help get the extras into their hoops and low-necked gowns; how many men will be required to look after fitting of Confederate uniforms for the men; and so on. They must call for the right number of girls and men for the dances; see that music is ready for the dancing; notify the dance director to be on hand; telephone the principals about their hours; and, do goodness knows what else.

Stacey is of English birth, but he has been in the United States so long he is very much American in every way, particularly in pep. He came to New York City from England when he was about seventeen and started to work at (imagine it!) washing automobiles. He said he read an ad that advised boys to learn a trade, so he learned the way to wash cars, paying five dollars for three days' instruction. Then when he had been graduated, the teacher hired Eric to teach. From student to professor of car washing in three days is quite a record, I'd say.

Later, Eric got a job as captain of ushers at a movie house, and from there he moved on to California and to the job of assistant director in easy steps. (Call it easy if you want to!)

Anyway, the school of hard knocks may be accountable for Eric's unfailing good nature.

But maybe Monty Westmore's wisecracks and smiling countenance are accountable for the pleasant folks on this set. I don't know. I do know that Monty is always ready for a joke or a gag.[13]

It was he who was responsible for the sign on my office door the other day. Pasted on a sheet of paper labeled Interoffice Communication, was a clipping from a newspaper:

"Are you really from the South?"

The other day Eric and I were eating lunch together at the café on the lot when Monty walked in, sat down at our table and stared into space. Both Eric and I pretended Monty wasn't even there, and he kept still for just a moment. Then he grabbed Eric's check, added to it: "2 cups coffee, 10 cents," and told the waitress to bring him the coffee.

Eric paid the bill without a murmur.

Even the publicity department here finds time for occasional foolishness. One of the girls, whose folks migrated from Canada five years ago and who works in that department, was taking her final examination for naturalization papers the other day. While she was out, the boys framed a trick.

When she came back to work, a cameraman awaited to catch with lens and flashlight the surprised look on her face. He got it all right. She found lying on her desk an enormous roll of white paper, tied with the remains of a Christmas package ribbon, and marked Diploma. Back of the desk was a large flag, and perched on the window ledge was an eagle.

True, he was moth-eaten and looked as if he were molting, but he was definitely the American insigne of bravery and freedom.

Just above the eagle's head was a sign, hand-done with red and blue colored crayons that said: "Welcome to the United States."

The group sang "The Star-Spangled Banner" as the new citizen entered the room—that is, all except me. I insisted on singing "The Bonnie Blue Flag."

And that reminds me of something I wanted to tell some time ago and had forgotten. One morning when we were very busy on Stage 11, shooting a scene, someone called me to the phone:

Lou Forbes, music director, wanted to know if I knew the tune of "The Bonnie Blue Flag." I did. Could I come over and sing it to him, he wanted to know. But I couldn't leave the set right then, so Lou asked that I sing it to him over the phone.

Now, my friends and family know that I can scarcely carry a tune, and certainly I am no Geraldine Farrar so far as voice is concerned; but I had to stand up for Dixie, so I sang the first verse and the chorus.

The people standing near almost had convulsions, and the poor music director struggled to keep from letting me hear his laughter. But I told him to go on and laugh; I knew it was funny.

Anyway, he knows how the song goes—more or less.

Friday evening I had dinner with Mrs. A. O. Bowden, who is John R. Marsh's sister and whose husband is professor of archaeology at the University of Southern California. Mrs. Bowden is much like John, whose quiet wit and genial manner have won him many friends at the Georgia Power Company, and in Atlanta.

We went to see *Pygmalion* after dinner, and I enthusiastically recommend it to any movie goer. Leslie Howard plays the role of Professor Higgins, who also teaches accent you remember, if you saw or read the Bernard Shaw play.

Somehow, it was impossible for me to disassociate Professor Higgins from the Leslie Howard who is to play Ashley Wilkes, and I had a good laugh at the situation.

For: It strikes me as decidedly droll that I should be teaching accent to Professor Higgins who is supposed to be the master of all accents.

This morning, when I spent an hour at Leslie Howard's home working on Southern accent, we enjoyed a laugh about it together. Mr. Howard has a quick ear and a fluent tongue, and he picks up pronunciation of words easily. We agreed once more that the voice of a Southerner is closely kin to that of a Britisher, and Mr. Howard insists that the Southerner of the sixties had a pronunciation that was closer kin to Elizabethan English than is that of the present era stage diction in England.

As you who read this column have found out ere this all that goes on out here is new to me, and I keep in a constant state of excitement and wonderment. When I saw my first "dolly shot" (which means the camera is on wheels and moves around, though nobody yet has been able to tell me why they call it a "dolly") I got a big kick from it. And now they tell me Victor Fleming is going to make many "boom shots."

Near as I can make out, that means the camera (that $75,000 Brownie) is to rest on a long boom or arm so that it can go up to the ceiling and move on down to the floor with ease, showing the audience high and low views of what is happening.

Up to now I haven't seen the boom; but I know Selznick International Pictures Company owns one, and we are going to use it when we start shooting again. I hope to write you about how it works, soon.

An airplane flying upside down is nothing, to my mind, compared with a camera standing on its head.

Macon Telegraph, 7 March 1939

Columnist Dines with Cukor, Works on Film, Buys New Car

HOLLYWOOD, Calif.—You've read that the favorite pastime of Hollywood is playing what they call The Game, of course. Well, I went to George Cukor's to dinner the other evening, and we played The Game and I decided it is about the most fun of any foolishness I know about. The evening reminded me of a party we had last year at Eddie and Art Nims's when we played charades or something close to The Game.

Vivien Leigh, who everybody knows by this time is playing the much sought-after role of Scarlett O'Hara is the quickest thing you ever saw playing The Game. She looked so pretty in her wine-red crepe gown, cut square in the neck, that it didn't seem fair she should have both beauty and brains. But she did.

You know, this Game is a sort of charades affair, with each person given some name or quotation or song or just a crazy saying to act out. The one acting may not say a word except "yes" or "no" and his side has just three minutes in which to guess what he is trying to do.

Well, Vivien was given this perfectly absurd sentence to do: "They say she went to America on a very small boat." When Vivien read her slip of paper, she broke into a laugh, then started in; and she did the job so well the group guessed it in two and a quarter minutes. I shan't tell how she acted it out. Try it on your crowd next time you play The Game.

You'd have died laughing if you'd seen George Cukor acting out "I know a bank whereon the wild thyme blows." He pointed to the wrist watch and we all asked "Watch?" He shook his head and somebody said "Time?" and he nodded. Then he indicated that "time" was the eighth word in the quotation. He had already shown us it was a quotation by putting up his hands to wiggle his fingers like quotation marks and he showed it was Shakespearean by indicating a beard.

Well, I thought of "I know a bank whereon, etc."; but I was scared to say it because I wasn't sure it was Shakespeare. (I am not ordinarily quite so dumb, but I was awed at the guests present.) I thought I'd wait and see if he indicated a "wild time."

He didn't. He indicated he would act out the fourth word of the saying and he lay on the floor, posing after the manner of Cleopatra, first; then he began to pick at imaginary bits of grass (or so it looked to me) on the floor beside him.

I yelped, "I know a place where the wild thyme grows," and he nodded vehemently, pointing his finger to indicate I was on the right line but not quite correct. And Merle Oberon, who was on our side, called out the correct quotation.

Merle was looking very lovely, herself, in a midnight blue frock, decorated with bright Roman striped yoke and belt.

Adrian, costume designer, whose name you've seen countless times on the screen credit lists, was next. He had to act out a name, "Voltaire." I thought we'd never get it! He kept putting his hand on the electric light and jumping as if he were shocked, and we yelled such words as "shock," "light," "electric chair," "kilowatt" and so on. We couldn't get that so he started to act out the second syllable and kept making a noise that sounded like the wind, so naturally we all chirped, "*Gone With the Wind.*" Finally, a chap named Tommie Douglas[14] got it, though I'll never know why!

Dr. Bruno Frank, the German author, acted out "The Importance of Being Earnest" and I was amazed that a foreigner should not only be able to speak English but understood how to act in it!

We had a jolly time of it, all right. Mrs. Frank showed the same familiarity with the English language that her husband showed. And her mother, Fritzi Massary, Hungarian actress and singer, was good at The Game, too.

With Tommie Douglas, who is a top-flight decorator in Los Angeles, was his assistant, Rex Evans, who is about six feet three and weighs two hundred pounds and has done many bit parts in the movies.

And I could not take my eyes off the exotic Mercedes, who had the blackest hair and the most devastating eyelashes I ever saw. She wore a pale gray silk frock on the monk style, with very high boned collar and opened from neck to hem, with a wide belt of silver links, elaborately carved in relief.

But this is enough about social doings. For I am hard at work again shooting on *Gone With the Wind*. Victor Fleming is making some additional scenes and the first day's shooting at Tara on Forty Acres started at eight and ended at four. But that didn't end the day's work.

We moved on to Stage 3 and shot a new scene inside Tara's Halls, with our new Jonas Wilkerson (played by Victor Jory) asking what work he was to do the following day.[15]

We knew. We knew full well that Jonas didn't have to work next day, but we did. We shot the scene that showed the wedding reception after Scarlett's marriage to Charles Hamilton. And Charles looked so handsome in his Confederate uniform that all of us hated to think he had to die of measles in camp within a few short weeks.

One very funny thing happened on the Forty Acres lot the first day we were shooting. At least it seemed funny to me; most of the crew and actors took it as a matter of course.

A branch of an oak that shadows the side of Tara was in the way of the camera as it "dollied" back and forth to show Scarlett sitting on the porch with the Tarleton twins; so Eric Stacey told one of the ground crew to tie it back. (They think too much of live trees to cut a branch and this one was a real tree—not made in the studio as some of them are.)

Somebody yelled for a ladder but one of the crew started to climb nimbly up the tree, waving back the man who was coming on the run with the ladder. (They do everything in a hurry when the sun is right for shooting.)

Like a native of the South Sea islands, the man climbed high enough to catch hold of the branch, then calmly settled himself on the limb below and held the branch while the camera shot was made.

"Nice view you have up there," called Eric.

Victor Fleming is so handsome that I am not able to decide whether he is an excellent director or I just think so. Anyway, we are getting things done rapidly, and Mr. Fleming and cast and crew are on the best of terms.

He manages to get in a little kidding, too, though he is very business-like. The other day when I sidled up to him and suggested timidly (you see I didn't know him very well at first) that Jeems should take off his hat when he addressed the white gentlemen, he just muttered okay, and went on with his talk. Then he called just before he started the camera:

"Jeems, take off your hat before you start that speech. I've got the South right here on my neck."

The Tarleton twins looked very fine in their alike-as-two-peas suits—blue coats with black velvet collars and cuffs and pocket flaps, pearl gray vests, gold watch chains and pale yellow "britches" and black boots.

And the boys' hair just matches the color of their handsome sorrel horses.

Those horses, by the way, behaved well while their pictures were taken, but the hound dogs that we used in the picture were difficult. Poor Tarleton twins and Scarlett had to do their acts over and over because the dogs refused to lie still as they should have done.

And we had airplane trouble, too, with our outdoor shots. It is uncanny how those things can fly over with roaring engines just as Fleming calls:

"Are you ready fellows?" and Eric calls:

"Ready, sir. Roll 'em, Frank."

Of course, you know we can't take a shot of a front porch scene in 1861 while an airplane engine registers its noise on the microphone!

And speaking of engines, maybe you'd like to know I have bought a car so that the eight-mile trek from Hollywood to Culver City each day will be easier.[16] Not interested? Well, you will be in hearing about how I took the examination for a driver's license.

A courteous man looked at my Georgia license, then asked me if I still weighed the same or had grown any taller; wrote something on a card and told me to sign my name, then take the card to the notary over at the other desk.

I did. The notary witnessed the signature I had made, then sent me to read a chart on the wall, first with one eye; then the other. After that, I was passed on to a man who gave me a long sheet of paper, on which were many questions. It was a selective test, with three answers written for each question and I was to put a check mark by the right answer.

I missed two: I said twenty miles an hour was the speed limit in the residential district and I should have said twenty-five. And I thought a yellow line painted on the curb meant no parking as in Georgia, when out here it really means parking only for loading or unloading.

So; the teacher made me do the whole thing over.

Then, I had to drive my car about six blocks with a traffic officer in the car beside me. He made me do left turns and right turns and we drove to a crossing where there was a stop sign and then we drove to a street that was almost a blind crossing, but had no stop sign.

I stopped, anyway, because I couldn't see whether a car was coming. It must have been the right thing to do because the officer passed me, and I was all finished except giving them a print of my right thumb.

Now I cannot commit any crime like swiping the carved-stick fan that Scarlett carries in the bazaar scene—the one that is so lovely. I might get caught by my thumb print.

[1]Olivier was supposed to be banned from the set so not to distract Leigh from her work. Myrick confided to her diary on 3 March: "Vivien is a bawdy little thing and hot as a fire cracker and lovely to look at. Can't understand WHY Larrie Olivier when she could have anybody."

[2]Mrs. Kurtz wrote in her second article for the *Atlanta Constitution*, on 26 February 1939: "Another incident of my first afternoon on a motion picture set: As we were about to leave the O'Hara's coachman came up to us and said, 'I hear yo'all is some of my folks!' and I knew him from the accent, to be a Southern darky. Upon questioning him, I found that he was born in Atlanta in 1876, in a house on the corner of Old Wheat and Butler Streets. . . . His father was for many years head waiter in the first Kimball house, and many of the older Atlantans will remember him. . . .

"Seated on the high box, reins in hand, head up looking straight ahead, Jesse looks the part of the proud, 'aristocratic' Southern coachman. Watch for Jesse in the picture! You'll like him."

When the scene of the O'Hara's drive to Twelve Oaks was reshot by Fleming, Clark was no longer on the set and the coach was driven by Pork (Oscar Polk).

[3]"Did I tell you Hazel Rogers, hair dresser, threatened to resign because David wanted Scarlett's hair to hang down like what Hazel called a Hollywood floozy? She would have gone, too, if I had not told George I thought the hair-do was terrible and not of the period and that Mammy and Ellen would have killed Scarlett before they'd have let her go out like that. So George made David change the hair dress and Hazel withdrew her resignation." Myrick to Mitchell, 14 February 1939.

[4]This is a prime example of Myrick's self-censorship in her columns. She wrote a detailed account, however, to Margaret Mitchell on 14 February: "When the morning *Hollywood Reporter* said Cukor would quit I refused to believe it. But on the set, I knew there must be truth in the report for all faces were wreathed in gloom and crew gathered in knots of threes or twos to talk in

"Morning wore on and everybody asked everybody else about it. Finally, I got up nerve enough to ask Eric Stacey and he gloomily said he thought there was no hope of patching it all up and his only reaction was that George had been damned patient not to have resigned before.

"It is really and actually true; George finally told me all about it. When there was a lull and I had a chance I said to him I was upset over what I'd heard and he said come and talk to him. So, we sat down and he talked—not for publication he said, but because he liked me, felt responsible for getting me into a mess and wanted me to know the truth. He hated it very much he said but he could not do otherwise. In effect he said he is an honest craftsman and he cannot do a job unless he knows it is a good job and he feels the present job is not right. For days, he told me, he has looked at the rushes and felt he was failing. He knew he was a good director and knew the actors were good ones; yet the thing did not click as it should.

"Gradually he became more and more convinced that the script was the trouble. My dear Peggy, I notice you said in your letter that Garrett is just cutting the script. . . . You are wrong, my duck. David, himself, thinks HE is writing the script and he tells poor Bobby Keon and Stinko Garrett what to write. And they do the best they can with it, in their limited way. Garrett is just a professional scenario writer while Howard knows dramatic values and—o hell, you know what Howard is.

"And George has continuously taken script from day to day, compared the Garrett-Selznick version with the Howard, groaned and tried to change some parts back to the Howard script. But he seldom could do much with the scene. . . .

"And Peggy, I swear on my word of honor that we often get a scene (say about 2 and a half pages script) at five in the afternoon that we are to shoot tomorrow morning. How in hell can I teach Vivien how to pronounce words or Leslie how to say 'store' and 'love' and such words when he gets the lines at quitting time in the afternoon and starts acting them at 8:45 next morning! And how can George study scenes and plan out action when he doesn't know what he is to shoot some days until he comes on the set at 8 o'clock!

"So George just told David he would not work any longer if the script was not better and he wanted the Howard script back. David told George he was a director—not an author and he (David) was the producer and the judge of what is a good script (or words to that effect) and George said he was a director and a damn good one and he would not let his name go out over a lousy picture [and] if they did not go back to the Howard script (he was willing to have them cut it down shorter) he, George, was through.

"And bull-headed David said 'O K get out!'

"All this is written for brevity and therefore is not exact wording but the sense is right."

In her letter of 23 February Margaret Mitchell told Myrick: "If you see George C. these days give him our best and tell him that we understand (as well as people can understand at so long a distance) the reasons why he walked out."

muted tones. George came in a moment later, cheery as usual with a Good morning for everybody and no hint of anything unusual on his face.

[5]"Howard was a tireless Ladies' man; his current companion was Violette Cunningham, an attractive English redhead he introduced as his 'secretary.' Though the description fooled nobody it did keep up appearances, and she was able to accompany him to the set every day without complaint from Selznick—who had barred [Laurence Olivier], arguing that his presence would be too distracting for Vivien Leigh." Flamini, *Scarlett, Rhett, and a Cast of Thousands*, p. 224.

[6]Margaret Mitchell wrote Kay Brown on 6 October 1936: "I forgot to say that not only do strangers assault me about not having Gable and Hepburn and Bankhead in the picture but they assault me with demands that Lamar Trotti do the scenario. . . . Lamar Trotti is an Atlantan, you see, knows this section and has made a deep study of this period." Trotti had a long career in Hollywood as screenwriter and, later, producer with Twentieth Century-Fox.

[7]Myrick was so much a partisan of Cukor that her liking for Fleming was at first grudging, but she came to like and to respect him too. She wrote Mitchell on 23 February: "Fleming seems a bright chap though he is a sour puss if I ever met one. He is as keen as a whip, though, and the ideas he has about proceeding with the film seem good to me." On 12 March she told her friend in Atlanta: "Vic Fleming laughs at the script situation and told me the other day to write him some ad lib lines, that God knows they'd had fifteen writers [and] I'd just as well try my hand at it and probably couldn't be any worse than the others!" And: "Vic is no fool. He grinned back of his ears the other day when he asked me if we ever had anything like this Twelve Oaks in the South. I shook my head, grinning wryly, and he said, 'Maybe the po white trash would like it because they could say it was just like Grandpa's that Sherman burned down.' "

[8]Alicia Rhett was the most prominent product of Selznick's great talent search in *Gone With the Wind*. Cukor saw her in Charleston in a rehearsal of *Lady Windermere's Fan* and, according to Kay Brown (19 April 1937) "thinks she has talent." Miss Brown wrote Margaret Mitchell: "We are probably going to bring her up [to New York] for a month's work with [Robert] Sinclair [a stage director under contract to SIP] and make a test of her as Melanie on the hundred to one shot that she will be able to play it. If she can't play Melanie, which from our point of view is the most exacting acting role, then there is a chance that she will play Carreen." The next month she added: "Alicia is such a sweet, gentle person that I don't believe they really realize her actual potentialities. I have a feeling that she has real talent, and given the proper care, will go far." Rhett returned to Charleston after the filming of *Gone With the Wind* and participated in no further films.

Mrs. Kurtz wrote of her in the *Constitution* for 5 June 1939: "Everybody likes her. Alicia can be seen days when she is not working, with sketchpad on her knee making pencil drawings of the cast and crew."

[9]Myrick must have meant the nineteenth-century *Harper's Weekly*.

[10]Myrick wrote Margaret Mitchell on 23 February: "For yours and John's private consumption—Ben Hecht and John Van Druten are writing on the new script. Publicity refuses to permit the info to be given forth to the waiting public but it is true, none the less. I met both Van D. and Hecht at lunch with David, Fleming and Wilbur [Kurtz] the other day. Van D. told me he had just finished GWTW in fourteen hours straight sitting and he was punch drunk but prepared to go to battle with the script. And the Fleming, David, Hecht and Van D. combination were preparing to go into conference right after lunch. I'd give my right ear to have heard the conference!"

Haver (*David O. Selznick's Hollywood*, p. 271) quotes Hecht concerning Van Druten: "He was going to work with us, so I asked him if he had read the book. [Hecht had not.] He said, 'Yesss'—he was an English boy—and I said, 'What did you think of it, is it a good book, Johnnie?' 'Oh yess,' he said, 'it's a fine book—for bellhops'; well, David got furious and fired him on the spot." This statement is belied by Selznick's listing Van Druten as among the few of all writers who worked on *Gone With the Wind* who contributed to the final screenplay. (Flamini, *Scarlett, Rhett, and a Cast of Thousands*, p. 312.)

Hecht wrote an account in his *A Child of the Century* (New York, 1954; pp. 488-89) of how he rewrote the first nine reels of *Gone With the Wind* in seven days. His account is so fanciful that it is not to be taken seriously, nor is it supported by carefully maintained collateral sources.

[11]Kay Brown had noted in her letter to Margaret Mitchell on 24 January 1939 that "Nancy Carroll has the inside track" for the part of Belle Watling.

[12]Ridgeway Callow.

[13]In her letter of 23 February Myrick declared: "The gang around here is marvelous. I have got to know them well enough now to kid with them and they tell me all the cracks made and know I'll keep my mouth shut and it is fun to loaf in Eric Stacey's office and gossip at what we please to call production meetings.

"Monte Westmore who is head make up man is the funniest guy in the U S, including Canada. He was born in England but he talks like a rough house guy in a comedy, and as if he were born in Joisey. He swears with every breath and knows all the stars and tells their worst points. Like all the other folks out here, he hates the guts out of the actors and actresses and adores talking about their private lives and washing their very dirty linen for us while we roll on the floor with laughter. He told the other day about going to Mae West's apt to take measurements to make some wigs for her when he worked at Paramount. Mae's bed, he told us, is wide enough for six men to sleep in—then without a change of countenance he added 'no doubt six men had slept in it' and contd the tale. . . . I'll tell you more that he told if I ever get back to Georgia."

[14]Tom Douglas tested for the part of Frank Kennedy, as did Harvey Stephens, Conrad Nagel, and Alan Baxter. SIP call sheet for 20 January 1939.

[15]The scene at Tara between Jonas Wilkerson and Ellen O'Hara had been filmed on 28 January 1939, with Robert Gleckler in the overseer's part.

Gleckler died on 25 February and the scene was reshot with the new Wilker-son, Victor Jory. Pratt, *Scarlett Fever*, p. 150.

[16]"Bought 34 model Plymouth coupe for $348, including insurance et al. Seems pretty good." Myrick diary, 3 March 1939.

FIVE
12 March—1 April 1939

Straight From HOLLYWOOD

GWTW Staff Progresses with Colossal Task of Making Movie

HOLLYWOOD, Calif.—Victor Fleming is tall and broad shouldered and his graying hair has a tendency to get out of place. Down on Forty Acres the other day when there was a wind blowing from off the mountains, Vic's hair kept getting in his face and he'd push it back impatiently; but before he would make a take, he would call the hairdresser to rearrange Scarlett's tresses so they'd look just right.

You would think a star would get very high-hat and important-feeling, the way everybody does things for her, but Vivien Leigh is the most friendly person you ever saw with no tendency to be superior toward us—the hired help.

"Eddie," she calls in her lilting voice, "may I have a little powder?"

And when Eddie Allen, stand-by for make-up, runs over to re-powder her pretty face, she thanks him as sweetly as if it were not his business to make her look her best.

Eddie and Helene [Henley] and two or three others are always on hand and always busy. When a close shot is being made and the bottom of the billowing hoop skirt will not show, Helene rushes over to fasten the skirt up so that it will not trail in the dust. She is an ingenious girl, Helene. She has devised a trick to make it easy to hold up skirts. A wide tape to which six long narrow tapes are fastened, goes about the star's

waist. Attached to the six dangling tapes are clamps such as a stenographer uses to hold papers in place. The clamps are fastened quickly
to the edge of the skirt at intervals and thus there is no danger of a tear
in the delicate fabric, and there is some saving on cleaning bills.

Goodness knows what the cost of clothes will be, for they make two
of everything. You see, an actor might burn a hole in a costume with a
cigarette; somebody might trip over a full skirt and tear the gown; all
sorts of things might happen to spoil a costume. So: the wardrobe
department is prepared for any emergency. The director and the
camera crew and the rest of the outfit could not afford to wait a day or
two while a duplicate costume was being made.

The extras, of course, do not have duplicate costumes, but there is
expense for their clothes. You'd realize it if you'd seen the lovely gowns
worn by the girls at the wedding scene last week when we were shooting
the episode showing Scarlett's marriage to Charles Hamilton.

Handsome young men in Confederate uniforms made a soft background of gray with their gold and red sashes and girls were clad in
pastel shades and deep colors of expensive materials.

And Scarlett, dressed in her mother's wedding gown, wore ivory
satin that must be seen to be appreciated. When you see *Gone With the
Wind*, you will love that dress.

Ellen, wearing black taffeta, looked dignified and sweet; and
Suellen and Carreen, Scarlett's younger sisters, were very lovely.
Suellen's frock was dusty pink, trimmed with pleated frills of soft, dull
gray and it was very becoming to her blond beauty. Carreen wore blue,
and the hoop skirt was short enough to reveal the tops of the most
fascinating boots with squared toes and low heels suitable for a
thirteen-year-old in 1861.

We all felt like congratulating Barbara O'Neil (Ellen) on her beautiful daughters, Vivien Leigh, Evelyn Keyes and Ann Rutherford.

Alicia Rhett, who plays India Wilkes, wore a taupe taffeta frock
with coral ornaments and looked every inch the aristocrat with her pale
skin and auburn hair.

And one of the extras, an elderly lady with snow-white hair,
fascinated me in her gown of wine-red with a black lace cap, a black
lace shawl and a necklace of garnets.

She was Frances McCardell, who came to Hollywood from New
York State sixteen years ago and has lived here ever since. She
remembers when Hollywood was just a friendly little village, and she

lived at the old Hollywood Hotel where she knew Elinor Glyn and Rudolph Valentino and the De Mille brothers and even Will Hays.

Speaking of Rudolph Valentino—Monty Westmore, head of make-up, was telling me the other day about being on location with the famous Rudy when he made *Son of the Sheik*, and it was so hot he took five showers a day. There was a long pipe that had holes in it and water sprayed from the pipe all the time, so that the actors and helpers who were hot could just go stand under it.

Monty says he will never know how Rudy stood the heat, wrapped in the clothes that a sheik must wear. For three months, Monty said, they almost died with heat and dehydration.

Monty is one of five brothers, all of whom are tops in the make-up business with the movies.

The longer I stay here the more I am impressed with the efficiency of folks who work at the business of making moving pictures. There is William Cameron Menzies, production designer, at Selznick International Pictures. Bill knows everything in the world about artistic effects and does more work than any other ten men I ever saw. Yet, he has time for a joke or a good story, often, and keeps us in gales of laughter with his Cockney-accent imitations and his tales of Scotland. He says his Scotch mother merely shakes hands with him when he goes home after a year's absence! The Scotch are that effusive!

Bill was born in Connecticut of Scotch parentage, and he is an American citizen, but he has visited Scotland so often he can talk like a Robert Burns poem.

Bill has made sketches of every scene to be made in the picture *Gone With the Wind*, and when sets had to be designed, Bill made the sketches into elaborate water color designs. The set plans were so accurately scaled that an architect could trace his blue prints from them.

Menzies directed the H. G. Wells picture, *Things to Come*, and he was production designer for *Tom Sawyer*. He is famous in Hollywood—and rightly—for the sweep and beauty of his designs, and he is famous with the staff at Selznick International for his good humor and his grand stories.

While Menzies and Fleming and Garmes (head cameraman) were consulting the other day about shots, a group of us got started saying tongue-twisters. The one that bothered me most was "The United

States has six twin-screw steel cruisers." Try it and see what it does to your tongue.

We have made some recent takes on the scene where Gerald O'Hara rides his white horse.[1] Reports had been published that Hi-Yo Silver, the famous horse, had been replaced for the picture because the Technicolor camera didn't like the whiteness of Silver.[2] But David Selznick is anxious to be true to the book, *Gone With the Wind*, in every possible way and he insisted that Gerald must have a white horse. So the Technicolor man doctored up Silver's highlights with some ashy-blue powder and he is now back in the picture to stay.

I was surprised the Technicolor men didn't spray the horse. They're always spraying something on the set. And one man has devised an ingenious way of making the sprayed objects dry faster. He uses a hand-drier, such as the beauty shops used to have before the modern driers were perfected.

I watched one of the men spraying the posts of Scarlett's lovely mahogany bed the other day when we were making a take of Scarlett in her widow's weeds, just after Charles Hamilton's death. That room is such a pretty one! The most fascinating bit in it, to my eye, is a corner washstand with a pinky-gray bowl and pitcher on it. The edges of the bowl and the top of the pitcher are decorated with gold, and the soap dish matches, of course.

I discovered that day, when we were shooting Scarlett's bedroom, how one take fits into another. [It] has always been a mystery to me how the chief cutter made close-ups match with long shots—in other words, I couldn't see how he got a finished picture from the bits we shoot at a time.

But that day in Scarlett's room, there was a scene where Barbara O'Neil (Ellen O'Hara) sat down on the bed beside Vivien Leigh (Scarlett), and tried to comfort her weeping daughter. The camera was pulled back far enough to picture the side of the room and catch Mammy's frowning countenance at the edge of the picture.

When the take was finished, Victor Fleming said we would now take a close-up of Ellen and Scarlett, and the camera was moved forward about four feet. Then the scene began, and Fleming said:

"But Vivien, when we took the long shot, remember you had tears in your eyes. This must match. Start your weeping. And begin back a speech, so it will be easy to match."

Then I realized that a take always began just after the spot where the other one finished and the cutter, as he watches scenes in the projection room, can fasten one piece of film to another in just the right spot to make the action continuous.

We make at least two prints of each take so if there is any flaw, the cutter can choose the good one.

Oh! I promise you I'll never criticize any slips made in pictures again! You've no idea how hard everybody tries to get everything just right.

There is the matter of the Confederate flag, for instance, in *Gone With the Wind*. Wilbur Kurtz carefully studied every available work on the subject, and the flags for the scenes were made exactly according to specifications furnished by Mamie Chestney, authority for the UDC in Macon, and those from the booklet, published by the Richmond, Va., chapter, UDC.

But don't think we have not already heard from a number of persons that our flag is wrong!

And the funny part is, the flag is absolutely right!

As a last word in the controversy, Wilbur wrote to Miss Irene C. Harris, at Battle Abbey, the Confederate Memorial Institute at Richmond, and asked her to look at all the battle flags in the museum (the flags that had been in actual use in the battles of the War Between the States) to see if the flags had white borders around them. For, that was one of the criticisms made of the flag—that there should not be a white border around the battle flag. Miss Harris wrote Wilbur:

"We have at Battle Abbey, seventy-eight Confederate flags that were captured during the War Between the States, '61-'65. These flags were returned to Virginia, March 26, 1905. These flags with the exception of a few which have fringe (these are silk flags) have white borders, one and one-half inches wide—no fringe.

"The flag you are interested in (the battle flag) is number two in the flag book. Mr. Charles Hoffbauer, who painted the mural paintings at Battle Abbey, used this flag in the painting of Gen. Stonewall Jackson, viewing the arrival of his 'Foot Cavalry' and also in the painting of Gen Robert E. Lee and other Confederate generals."

So, we know the flags we are using are right, and we know a thousand and one more things are right, and we are making every effort to have everything exactly as it should be—all the way from the costumes of the Negro slaves to the accent of the leading lady!

Mrs. F. Marion Houser of Perry was a visitor on the set this week. She was excited over the experience, naturally, and I enjoyed seeing her thrill. It reminded me of myself!

Straight From HOLLYWOOD

Good Job Made of Difficult
Scenes Showing Action at 'Cue

HOLLYWOOD, Calif.—It is the first day of shooting scenes at Twelve Oaks, handsome colonial residence of the John Wilkses, a few miles from Tara.[3] Lovely girls in sprigged muslins, flowered challis, plaid cottons, and softly tinted gowns, all in hoop skirts and period hats, stroll around the porch and inside the large hall. Colored butlers wander about; colored grooms stand leaning against tall columns; two small Negro boys sit in the sun and watch, mouths agape; the O'Hara carriage, with its spanking bays, and another carriage stand waiting.

Hi-Yo Silver, Gerald's white horse turns a restive eye on the proceedings. Stand-ins for the O'Hara girls and for Gerald wait listlessly to be told where to go.

A score of men bustle about, busy at various tasks. The camera is down in a hole about four feet deep, fastened to a long arm of steel that stretches back for five feet to a sort of trestled support, thirty-five feet long, the whole mounted on a chassis bigger that most trucks and resting on oversized rubber tires.

The hour is 8:40 and I have just arrived on Stage 11 at Selznick International Pictures. It looks like bedlam to me.

And in a few minutes I feel as if I were in an insane asylum: for people begin firing questions at me so fast my head goes dizzy:

"Miss Myrick," calls Reggie Callow (assistant to Eric Stacey, who is assistant to Vic Fleming). And he bawls it out over the loudspeaker.

I go dashing madly toward Reggie who sends me on to Fleming, who wants a line for somebody to say to establish at once the identity of John Wilkes.

Before I can form an idea in my mind, someone says: "Miss Myrick, will you come into the hall a moment please?"

I discuss the line with Vic, get it to satisfy him and chase into the hall where the wardrobe man wants to know if the clothes for the servants are right. Before I can look at the mammys and butlers and maids, Reggie is calling for me again.

He wants to know if the ladies in the house should keep their hats on or take them off. I decide they'd be kept on; for the ladies are going out again in a few minutes to sit on the lawn and wait for barbecue time and no Southern lady would take a chance on getting a freckle. I quote Mammy's lines (the ones she says to Scarlett) about bleaching her with buttermilk to "get off dem freckles" she got down at Savannah that time, and turn to answer one of the wardrobe men who wants to know:

"Should the gentlemen have their hats in their hands or shall we take it for granted the Negro servants have taken their hats for them?"

Right after that somebody wants to know if the men can be moving up and downstairs as well as the ladies. Then I am asked why they are going upstairs when the juleps are downstairs!

Another wardrobe man comes to ask me if the little colored boys should be barefoot; then Vic wants to know if it is right for Gerald to come a-horse-back to the barbecue and not wear riding clothes, and I have to tell the groom where he should stand and explain to the little colored boys how they brush off the boots of the white gent'mun and tell the Negro who opens the carriage door that he must take off his hat, and explain to all the men-servants that when they address John Wilkes he is to be called "Marse John," and repeat to them that they always take off their hats to address white fo'kses and so on.

Meanwhile, Eric is the busiest man in the world, carrying out suggestions from Fleming, giving commands on his own, calling orders through a megaphone and getting some sort of order out of the milling group.

Meanwhile, I check with the extras who have bit lines to see that no "R" sound comes from a Southern voice and that all ad lib lines have a Southern flavor.

Then, when I come out of the hall again I find the camera has climbed out of the hole in which it first sat, is five feet in the air and moving up higher. This is the famous boom shooting I've been hearing about.

Astraddle the arm that holds the camera, feet in makeshift stirrups, sits Roy Clark, sighting through the lens, calling to the dozen assistants to lower or raise the boom a few inches. Then Vic motions for the camera to come forward and the men roll the truck along until the proper shot is reached. The place is marked with chalk, a man measures it with a tapeline and the camera slowly moves back and sinks into its pit.

Things are beginning to get orderly and Eric asks Vic if he is ready for a rehearsal. He is.

The carriage moves forward into place. Fleming calls "Ready," and things move with surprising accuracy for a first rehearsal.

Gerald rides up on his white horse just as the first carriage moves away, after the young lady and gentleman have stepped down and gone up to greet John Wilkes. Gerald dismounts and shakes hands with Mr. Wilkes; the O'Hara carriage, with Pork driving the horses, stops; the three O'Hara girls alight and the carriage drives away.

Up, up, rises the camera and forward it moves to catch a closer shot of Scarlett's greeting to India Wilkes who stands near the steps on the broad piazza. Then, farther and farther forward the camera moves to follow Scarlett right into the hall and catch her expression as she looks about for Ashley.

The way the camera poked its nose right through the front door somehow reminded me of a giant Peeping Tom.

Well, we had some more rehearsals and it took us until almost noon to finish two perfect takes, but we got it all beautifully—a shot that is considered difficult in any studio.

The camera never did stand on its head, but I am expecting that any day.

Between takes, I complimented Walter Plunkett on the beauty of costumes[4] and he told me an interesting thing, apropos of Gerald's riding a horse to the barbecue and not wearing riding costume.

When Walter was touring the Southern states, studying costuming and local color for *Gone With the Wind*, he talked to an eighty-four year old lady about clothes.

"One thing I've heard that I want to get straight," said Walter, "Maybe you can fix it for me. Did girls ever ride horseback in hoop skirts?"

"Young man," replied the old lady, "a horse was a means of getting somewhere in those days. If your wife has to run down to the corner grocery for a loaf of bread does she bother to put on a motoring costume? Certainly not. She wears the frock she is wearing around the house. In the sixties, if a girl wanted to go someplace and a horse was handy to ride, she rode in her hoop skirts. Then, when she arrived, she was properly dressed. If she'd taken off her hoops to ride, she couldn't have walked on the street without them."

So, that explanation ought to be sufficient for anyone who thinks it is strange Gerald rode horseback to the barbecue, dressed in his "Sunday clothes." At least Walter and I thought so.

Oh, yes! I almost forgot to tell you. That boom on which the camera rides weighs five and a half tons (including the truck), and it has an upward stretch of twenty-five feet and a forward stretch of twenty-six feet.

And, as if we didn't have enough excitement for one day, the first day's shooting at Twelve Oaks brought us visitors important enough to make us all sneak careful looks around. The Duke and Duchess of Sutherland were two guests on the set, and another was Marion Davies.

Speaking of guests, I was a guest Sunday at tea and a showing of the works of Isham Toor, sculptor, formerly of New York and Paris, and now of Altadena.

Mr. Toor has received high praise from critics and his fame is growing. At the San Francisco fair he has a dancer which is regarded as one of the best pieces of modern sculpturing.

At his home, the sculptor had the plaster model from which the dancer on exhibition was moulded. The lady in flowing gown holds high a tambourine, her graceful head leading toward the raised arm, her skirt flowing to the foot extended backward and upward. Fluid movement enwraps the whole. From every angle the dancer is graceful, beautiful, and stirring.

But there were dozens of pieces besides the dancer. The artist is versatile, working in various media and in many moods. Bronzes of a centaur, a boy bearing a bucket of water, a woman carrying a bundle of wood and others were strong and powerful. Some of the plaster models had the detailed work and the delicacy of Dresden pieces in their relief designs. Bronze models for fountains had the grace of flowing water in them.

And the wood carvings were the things that pleased me most. From maple and from birch wood, specially seasoned and readied, the artist has fashioned figures of such delicacy that one can scarcely believe they can possibly be carved of wood.

Mr. Toor's wife was a charming guide about the house and the garden, and told me the story of their coming to Altadena, with a little smile as she told it.

Mr. Toor, born in Armenia, came as a small boy to live in New York. He modeled many bits even as a child, studied art in New York and then in Paris. It was in Paris that he met the woman who was to be his wife.

"I didn't want to marry—nor did he," explained Mrs. Toor. "I liked my teaching and I wanted my career, and I knew he had no business burdening his artistic self with a wife.

"So we resisted each other for four years; then gave up and married. We went back to New York and pretty soon we decided there was no use being married if you weren't going to have a child so we wanted a child. But we knew a fourth-floor walk-up in New York was no place to have a baby, so we began looking for a place.

"That brought us to Altadena where we thought the climate would be right and there would be plenty of room out of doors for a baby."

She brought out the baby for us to see, later. He was a rosy little plump thing that looked healthy and fine and the Toors are happy at coming to California.

Of course I talked to Mr. Toor about Marshall Daugherty, Macon's sculptor, and when I spoke of Marshall's work with Carl Milles, Toor's face brightened and he said, "If the young man has worked with Milles he must have great promise."

He was much interested in Marshall and asked many questions about him. When he found that Marshall does not have models for his work he was greatly pleased and nodded his head over and over again in approval. And he expressed the wish that the young man would be able to keep the pot boiling without losing any of the genius that smoulders within him.

Macon Telegraph, 19 March 1939

Straight From HOLLYWOOD

Exterior Scenes for Twelve Oaks Barbecue Are Finished

HOLLYWOOD, Calif.—"Shooting on location" has an intriguing sound to me, and I have felt very envious of those script girls and sound men and others of the crew who have told exciting stories about being on location. So, I was all agog at the first day's location work on *GWTW*.

At seven o'clock in the morning I piled into a car at Selznick International Studios and, along with Wilbur and Annie Laurie Kurtz, two script girls, and an assistant to the camera crew, I started off for the spot near Pasadena where we were to shoot the exterior scenes for the barbecue at Twelve Oaks.

Mind you, we'd already had breakfast and driven eight or ten miles to Culver City before we started out for location. And the trucks with all sorts of equipment had left long before daylight. The hairdressing folks and the wardrobe people had been at work since 5:30 and we who left at seven were the loafers of the crowd!

It is still astounding to me that the folks who make movies go to work so early, work so late, and so hard. I always thought a star went to work at—say, eleven in the morning, took two hours off for lunch and quit at 5:30!

So, it is hard for me to realize that Vivien Leigh can be always prompt for make-up at six or seven, as the call sheet directs, be on the set right on time, and be cheerful about going to work at eight in the morning. And some evenings she works until after seven—always bright and chipper about it. You see, in this movie, Scarlett works all the time. Ashley Wilkes and Rhett Butler and Melanie and the others have days to work and days to loaf but Scarlett is always on hand.

Anyway, Scarlett and Ashley and Rhett and Melanie were all four on hand for the Twelve Oaks shooting the other morning and there was plenty to do to get ready for the scenes.

It is no small task to manage two hundred and fifty extra people who provide atmosphere and background, and Eric Stacey and a score of helpers dashed madly about getting things done.

Ladies in hoop skirts and basques, with gay bonnets and hats, and many of them with parasols, strolled about the lawn or sat at tables eating barbecue. Children, looking very quaint in their old-fashioned costumes, rolled hoops or skipped rope or played about the lawn, and mammys looked after them. Waiters toted huge silver trays of food to the white folks and colored maids helped with serving, so that the effect was as near as the movie could make it to that described in Margaret Mitchell's novel.[5]

It is easy enough for a script writer to say, "Children swarm over the place, Negro butlers pass tall frosted glasses, young people and elderly people sit at tables or wander about the grounds, etc." But it is something else for a director to get things just like the script wants them.

But finally all cues were ready, Eric Stacey called directions over the loud-speaker, and everybody knew what to do and when to do it.

Ashley, in a brown coat and fawn colored trousers and vest, stood on the balcony of the house at Twelve Oaks and talked to Melanie of the beauty of a civilization that could not last forever. Melanie in her gray frock with a rose-colored sash, looked very sweetly at him and promised to love him the same, even if war should come. And the camera recorded the lovely picture while the microphone picked up the sound of the voices.

Which reminds me that a fan letter asks me to tell how the movie folks put in the sounds of voices after they take the pictures. They don't. It's all done at the same time. While the camera records the actions the microphone picks up the voices. Camera and sound machine are synchronized and it is the sound man who calls out "Quiet, speed!" meaning to say that there must be no outside noises and that the camera and the sound machine are synchronized and moving at the proper speed.

Cameras are no longer cranked by hand. Electricity does the work. There is enough electric current used on the stages at Selznick International Pictures in one day to provide lights for a small city.

There are three members of the cast about whom I have said little so far because they have only recently started working. Howard Hickman, who plays John Wilkes, is an old hand in pictures and on the stage. He is a former Kentuckian whose great-grandfather gave the family name to the town of Hickman, Ky. He has been with the theater since 1903 and he is married to Bessie Barriscale, whose silent movie work old-timers will recall with pleasure.

Then we have Victor Jory for our Jonas Wilkerson, overseer of the Tara plantation. He replaces Robert Gleckler, who died several weeks ago.

And for Frank Kennedy, Selznick International has cast Carroll Nye, a former reporter on the *Los Angeles Times*. But before becoming a newspaperman Nye had played in stock and in silent movies.

Everybody on the lot talks about the races at Santa Anita track and that brought Eric Stacey to tell a racing story that brought down the house.

John Doe, we'll call him, went to the races, placed a $2 bet on the first race and won on a long shot, about $60. He bet the whole thing next race and won again. He continued betting, doubling his money several times, until the sixth race, when he had brought his two dollars up to $2,000. He put the wad on a horse and lost the works.

Sadly, John Doe leaned against the railing near the betting window. A man approached, drew six dollars from his wallet and said, "No. 6, across the board."

"I wouldn't do that if I were you," protested John Doe, in a hoarse whisper.

"What do you mean, it's none of your business," replied the stranger.

Still whispering hoarsely, John Doe said, "But I advise against it, Pardner. I just ran two dollars up to $2,000, bet it all on one horse and lost!"

"Whe'ew!" said the stranger in pitying tones, "Did you honestly? If I were you I'd cut my throat!"

John Doe pulled at his shirt collar and exposed his bloody neck: "Look!" he cried hoarsely. "Look!"

It was fun to have Clark Gable on the set again this week. He was not in the scenes we shot for several days and when he came back he was surrounded by men and women, all wanting to hear him talk.

He was looking very handsome in his dark blue coat and gray trousers with a ruffled shirt and the high collar and stock that befits his costume.

"How's your Southern dialect?" he wanted to know of me, and "I hope you all have had a pleasant time in the last few days."

And he hastily explained that he meant all the group when he said "you all," for the whole company has been thoroughly impressed with the truth that Southerners do not use the expression "you all" when they mean one person.

There were two extras working in the barbecue sequences who were sons of old silent stars. They are Bryant Washburn, Jr. and Carlyle Blackwell, Jr.

Blackwell is an amateur photographer and has won several prizes on his pictures. He belongs to a camera club and has invited me to come to a meeting next week. So I shall probably get bitten by the camera bug as about a hundred thousand others in California have been.

All the boys who work with the camera crew at Selznick International are camera fiends and they talk of stops and finders and telescopic lenses and depth of focus and the relative merits of various sorts of film.

Paul Hill, second assistant cameraman, has traveled all over the world in the movie business and he pooh-pooh's the movie camera work at which he is so good and adores talking about the still shots he made with a $12 camera or a dollar camera and so on.

But that Technicolor movie camera which films *GWTW*—that's sump'n!

Macon Telegraph, 24 March 1939

Straight From HOLLYWOOD

Sue Gets Thrill as Men Dash Away to Join Military Units

HOLLYWOOD, Calif.—It is nearly eleven o'clock in the morning at Pasadena where we are shooting exterior scenes for the Barbecue in *Gone With the Wind.* Since about nine we have stood about, watching anxiously for signs that the fog will lift. The weather man said it would be a clear day, and we trust he is right.

It is cold in the morning fog; and we shiver a little as we stand around, shifting the weight from one foot to another and talking.

Presently, there is a little sun peeping through. It looks like a possible shot in a few minutes.

Assistant Director Stacey, calls over the public address system for groups to get ready and mushrooms over the broad expanse of lawn become young ladies in hoop skirts, who rise and saunter to their places.

Dozens of horses, tethered to trees about the place, stamp nervously: young men gather in their assigned places; groomsmen practice managing the horses with one hand so they can pull off their hats with the other; Ashley Wilkes walks over to his chestnut mount; Melanie gets a final going over by the make-up girls and everything is ready.

"Action! Camera!" is the call, and in a few seconds I get the biggest thrill I have had since I first saw *Birth of a Nation.*

There is a thunder of hoofs and a rider dashes up waving his hat and calling. He pulls the horse to a dramatic stop, rearing the mount upward to full height and calls out:

"Mr. Lincoln has called for volunteers."

Rebel yells sound over the place and men and women call out: "War! It's come!"

Youths and men run toward their horses, which grooms unhitch and hold for their masters; horses dash madly away at full speed; carriages careen around the corner, filled with young bloods hurrying to join their troops; young ladies wave good-bye to men, embrace their sweethearts; wives and mothers weep a little at the news of war; housemaids and cooks stand gesticulating at the sight and wondering what it all means.

And Ashley, seated on his horse, bends down to kiss Melanie and say he must rush away but he will come back.

Well, when that take was finished, I found myself all choked up and my eyes were misty and my heart was pounding. Maybe it was the sound of rebel yells that were a cross between a Confederate veteran reunion and a bunch of gay young men at a football game. Anyway, it was the most exciting and thrilling shot I can imagine.

And when I got back to earth, I went over and congratulated Stacey and his two assistants for the task of managing the mob scenes of theirs, and they did a magnificent job.

Poor Eric Stacey had taken a lot of ribbing about the weather! We had been scheduled for outdoor shootings several days and Stacey had changed the call because of weather reports which said probable rain. And the days were the loveliest in the calendar, with no fog, no clouds, but smiling skies.

Vic Fleming had said to Eric, "I started to hire a fellow to get a wet raincoat and umbrella and come on the stage and talk to you this afternoon."

So Stacey had said we'd go to Pasadena for the shots if it poured rain. Luckily for Stacey, the weather report was right that time and the lifting fog gave us a beautiful five hours in which to work.

During the afternoon, while the cameramen were shooting the scene where Scarlett O'Hara sits under a tree, surrounded by beaux of Clayton county, eating barbecue and sending Charles Hamilton to get her dessert, there were several visitors on the set.

Somebody observed that in a group of four, all the visitors carried copies of *Gone With the Wind.* One of the publicity men introduced himself and discovered that the visitors were trying to find in the book the scene we were shooting. He obligingly showed them the place in the book, then borrowed my script for them to see.

One of the visitors was Irving Crick, weather man at California Tech.[6] Mr. Crick is a famous scientist to whom goes credit for first using high altitude readings as a basis of weather forecasting—a method that the United States Weather Bureau is studying for possible long range forecasting.

Two men from Georgia visited the set this week, both of them working for Frank Troutman in Atlanta, who married Miss Mary Frank Satterfield of Macon. The boys were Julius Lunsford of Reynolds and Glenn Johnson of Savannah. Glenn was a graduate of the University of Georgia and Lunsford, too, finished in law at Georgia, after preparatory work at Mercer.

Johnson declared as he left the set: "I'm going back to the hotel and write the longest letter to my mother I ever wrote. The folks at home will certainly eat up the news that I saw a part of the making of *Gone With the Wind.*"

And both boys declared they could hardly wait to see the picture now that they had seen the beautiful set and since they consider the casting so perfect.

Many of the boys and girls used as extras in this picture are Southerners and almost every day one comes up to talk to me and tell me he is from Alabama or Georgia or Virginia. One young man, Edward de Butts, Richmond, Va., is a brother of William Hunter de Butts of Macon, who married Mary Custis Lee, daughter of Gen. Robert E. Lee.

Magazine writers and reporters from several far-off newspapers have been in the set during the past week, one of the most interesting of whom was a young man who represents a Polish screen magazine. He spoke English with an accent which Hollywood would call "terrific" and I spent an amusing half-hour listening to him while the cameramen arranged a new setup. The poor man could not understand a word of what I said, but we both bragged about the homeland and had a good time. As he proudly referred to Pilsudski, Danilova, Madame Curie, Chopin and Paderewski, I just as boastingly spoke of Alexander

Stephens, L. Q. C. Lamar, Admiral Benson and Admiral Ellis. I had the advantage of the man; for he never heard of any of my famous ones.

You'll be interested to know, I am sure, that Margaret Mitchell's phrase "like a duck on a June bug" has created considerable stir in the studio of Selznick International. When she first accepted the role of Scarlett, Vivien Leigh told some reporter she never saw a June bug and the remark was widely quoted.

So, loyal Southerners proceeded to send June bugs to Miss Leigh. A box of them arrived and Miss Leigh's secretary opened the package, unsuspectingly. When the top was removed from the box all the June bugs flew out and whirled around the room, causing quite a commotion until they were recaptured. Vivien says she knows what June bugs look like now and they know what she looks like.

N. H. Giles of Atlanta was more careful and more scientific.[7] He sent the studio two specimens, dead, mounted in the proper fashion on pins and labeled with their Latin name, *Cotinus nitida*.

I discovered today, for the first time, that we have six cameramen in our crew and that four is usually considered the top number in a crew. The Technicolor camera needs more attention than a six-weeks-old baby!

Somebody is always oiling some part of it or polishing something about it and a man changes lenses every now and then and a good looking blond boy, whose hair is always in his eyes, squints through the finder and wipes off something and two men walk out on the set and squint at meters and hold up little round green discs and peer at them and then they change some more lights or adjust something about the camera.

Well, I think it's worth while. For the rushes we see after work, every evening, show the loveliest color I ever saw in movies. Wait until you see how the green velvet streamers of Vivien Leigh's hat impart a green color to her eyes and see the tints and shades of the gowns the girls wear!

Oh yes, I nearly forgot, the folks on the set are intrigued with what they call "Southern slang—" If you've got any choice phrases, like "a duck on a June bug" send them along.

Macon Telegraph, 26 March 1939

Straight From HOLLYWOOD

Imaginary War Is Chief Topic of Busy Culver City Colony

HOLLYWOOD, March 25.—Millions of people are talking about war; but out here in Culver City, we are still largely concerned with the war fought in the Sixties and we sing "When This Cruel War Is Over" thinking of the days of the Confederacy.

Funny, but somehow the movies get you. At least I suppose they get everybody. They seem to have got all of us on the Selznick International lot. I can't seem to worry much about whether Germany fights or even whether the United States fights. It is almost more than I can do to read the front pages of the papers.

My days are devoted exclusively to listening to accents to see if they sound properly Southern, deciding whether I think the clothes worn in various scenes are sufficiently dilapidated for the era, looking up some passage in Margaret Mitchell's book to check against some notion I have, sitting on a chair or a high stool or even on a step-ladder to watch the action as a scene is shot.

On the set we go around repeating the dialogue of the actors just as we used to do in the Macon Little Theater!

You see, we rehearse a scene—say five or six times—then the camera is ready and we make a take. Something may be wrong with the position of the camera as it pans and the take is no good; or maybe the director doesn't quite like some bit of action; maybe I don't like the sound of the Southern pronunciation of some word; perhaps the sound track doesn't pick up the words just right.

Anyway, something is not quite right so we make another take. Maybe we are lucky and get two perfect takes in succession. Even then we are just started with the scene. There must be Close Ups.

I suppose you were no more conscious of the number of Close Ups in a movie than I was. And I have found out that Close Ups are SO-O important to make a scene just right.

First we make a Close Up of Scarlett saying some important lines—maybe to Rhett—and the camera is turned so that Scarlett faces it. Then we make the Close Up of the same two, speaking the same dialogue, but this time Rhett faces the camera.

When the cutter gets through with the film it is so arranged that as Scarlett speaks the audience sees a Close Up of her lovely face; and when Rhett speaks, the audience looks at Clark Gable's smiling countenance.

So, you can see that by the time a scene is finished, we all know the dialogue quite as well as the actors themselves; and we go about telling each other: "The Yankees are coming," or saying: "You are no gentleman, sir," and so on.

Then, between times somebody like Jerry Wright, who has been script girl for the movies for about five years, tells me about experiences in the movie world. Like the time Jerry saw a plane hit the ground, jump an automobile, lose its undercarriage, bounce into the air, get up height and glide to a stop in the bay a few hundred yards away. And nothing happened except the pilot grumbled about getting wet.

And Eric Stacey tells about needing a wheel-puller. When he first began being an assistant director, Eric took a group on location for some scenes that required carriages and horses and wagons and mules.

Well, the location in that case happened to be a hundred miles from anywhere—in a desert. And the first time the horses tried to pull the carriage the wheels locked and the carriage wouldn't move a foot.

It seems that carriage wheels have a habit of "freezing" to the hub when the carriage is jostled in transit, and Eric had never heard of such a thing before.

Well, when somebody told him he should have brought a wheel-puller he thought he was being kidded—like sending a man for a left-handed monkey wrench; but he found out later that a wheel-puller is an essential. Now he never goes on location without seeing to it that wheel-pullers for carriages and wagons are available.

"Strange business, the movies," Eric told me. "Do you know the first thing I'd think to take if I started to go on location in—say Alaska—to shoot a picture? Snow!"

I thought he was kidding, but he wasn't. Seems snow doesn't photograph well; and when pictures are made with snow scenes, the director has to provide artificial snow.

One day, sitting around between times as the camera crew moved the camera to another location and electricians fixed lights, I talked to Ray Rennahan, who is a specialist on color photography and proper lighting for best color effects. Ray told me about some of the ways queer names come to be accepted terminology on movie sets.

"One director I worked with, many years ago," said Ray, "watched me as I took out a light meter and measured the amount of light on the subject we were photographing. A little later he asked me:

" 'Where is that Ju-ju, Ray? Get it out and measure up the light.' "

"So, for a long time we called a light meter a 'Ju-ju.' Then another fellow came along and called it a 'Jeep.' "

I also learned from Ray that when he calls to a helper to move "that gobo" a little, he is talking about a large, black piece of heavy cardboard that is used to deflect as much of a light as he wants.

" 'Gobo' is short for go-between," he explained. "The board goes between the light and the camera."

There are small, wooden stools that the property men and others use for lifting the height of tables or furniture to bring them to the proper height for best camera work and these are called "turtles."

So it goes. Every day I pick up some interesting conversation around the set at SIP.

Yesterday, I talked to Harry Davenport, who is playing Dr. Meade. (And what a perfect selection for the role he is!—talks so much like an old-fashioned Southern gentleman that I get homesick when I hear him, thinking he is the orator for Memorial Day.)

Mr. Davenport told me some of his experience on the stage—he's playing his sixty-seventh year now. For several seasons he and his wife played in Keith's vaudeville, and his story of his favorite act is delightful.

He played the part of a Scotsman and his wife was a young Scottish girl whom Harry was courting. The other man in the act was a sailor, who had brought home from a trip a small statue of Truth. The piece of statuary was endowed with supernatural powers and whoever told a lie in hearing of the statue would lose a part of his clothing.

The idea was planted in the mind of the audience as the play got under way with Harry and his girl sitting on a bench within a few feet of the statue. Harry begins to tell her how much he loves her, and suddenly his hat is whisked away. She replies that she loves him, and her hat disappears.

On it goes—with the audience shrieking with laughter, looking for the thing they know will happen and fairly falling into the aisles with pleasure when the expected occurs.

Harry tells the story with a gentle smile and says: "We lost first one garment, then another, until we got as far along as the audience of twenty-five years ago would stand for."

And his smile indicates that he realizes there is a great deal of difference between the standards of audiences of today and those of yesteryear.

Among the interesting visitors on the set this week the one who caused the most craning of necks was Noel Coward, who came on stage with Leslie Howard. With them was an actress, Isabel Jeans, who wore a ravishing black frock and draped over one shoulder was a dyed fur cape that left all the women on the set gasping with envy.

Many writers for newspapers and magazines appear on the Selznick International lot from time to time. One of them, this week, was Kirtley Baskette, a free lance writer who knows Betty Hay McCook very well. We had lots of fun talking about Macon people; for though Mr. Baskette didn't know many Maconites, he had heard Betty talk of many of them and spoke of them as if they were old friends.

Though this column sounds as if I had played a lot recently, that doesn't mean the making of *GWTW* is not moving forward. We have made many takes and every night when I see the daily rushes I feel a glow of pride and pleasure in them, though my own part in the making is so small a one.

Macon Telegraph, 30 March 1939

Straight From HOLLYWOOD

New Bazaar Shots Are Made and Gable Tells Sue of Ranch

HOLLYWOOD, Calif.—We are getting so Southern around the lot at Selznick International that it is rumored some of the crew threaten to refuse their checks if they are not paid off in Confederate money.

It is all because everybody is so thrilled and excited over some additional shots we made last week of the bazaar scene in Atlanta where pretty girls danced with dashing young officers and Rhett and Scarlett shocked everybody with their goings-on.[8]

The bazaar booths are decorated with smilax and it surprised me greatly to discover that June weddings in Los Angeles will be obliged to go smilax-less because Selznick Company bought the entire supply— more than a thousand dollars worth. The men hauled in three big truckloads to the set.

In Georgia, where smilax grows in the woods and all we have to do is go out and cut it for decorations, there is no such growing of smilax as there is out here in Ventura county where they make a business of supplying greenery for home decorations. This strange sort of smilax runs on twine strings and when the florist sells it he charges by the yard. He just cuts off string and all and the green stuff is ready to hang anywhere with ease.

On the set the other day we all giggled at Eric Stacey who called out over the microphone to the dancing girls: "Wipe that smilax off your faces and get to work." I almost picked up one of the two-pounders (cannon captured by Andrew Jackson at the battle of New Orleans) and hit Eric because I was mad he made the pun before I got to it.

It was fun to watch the dancers with their hoop skirts whirling and, after they had danced a while and a rest would be ordered, they'd sit down on the floor with skirts spread around so that they looked like those funny little china dolls that we used to make pin cushions of when I was little, or maybe like those dolls that are sometimes used to disguise the telephone.

There were several one-legged and a number of one-armed men on the set (no, they weren't dancing. Don't interrupt!), to represent soldiers home from the War Between the States. And one of the men had an especially interesting history. Wayne Castle, he was, a first sergeant in the U. S. Marines, First Regiment of the Fifth Division. He was one of the first of the American troops to land in France and fought all through the war unharmed until November 10, 1918, when he was shot five times in the leg.

Wayne was laughing heartily because he was wearing the uniform of a lieutenant general of the Confederate army and said he had never dreamed he'd be advanced so rapidly in rank.

Clark Gable looked his usual handsome self in his full dress clothes which even the uniforms of the officers could not overshadow. And Vivien Leigh in her widow's weeds was a pretty sight. I wish I could tell you all about the exciting scenes but it wouldn't be fair to spoil your fun when you see the picture.

They are doing the most amazing things that must cost a great deal of money to make the picture real. For instance, one of the men told me yesterday that they had ready nine tons of red dust to make the streets of Atlanta (which are to be shot on the Forty Acres) look dusty as they would have looked when the soldiers and wagons and buggies passed down them in 1863.

And speaking of shooting things, Ralph Slosser, one of the assistant directors, pulled a good one, too. Ralph was tired (we all were for we had worked late the night before) and sat humped in a chair with his feet on a stool while there was a lull in proceedings. Somebody called: "What are we shooting tonight, Ralph?"

"I think I'll just let them take me out and shoot me," said Ralph wearily.

But I didn't want to be shot (even if they do shoot horses). I sat on a high stool near Clark Gable (who has his own chair, painted white and marked with his name) and he told me about his ranch and his home which is almost finished.

"The finest thing about my place is it has trees on it," he said, smiling enthusiastically. "Down in Georgia you folks will probably not understand how rare trees can be out here in Southern California. We have so much desert and so much prairie type of country where trees just don't exist, though the trees are plentiful up in the hills."

"On my fourteen-acre ranch there are 987 trees—five hundred of them shade trees. There are pepper trees, eucalyptus, black walnut, oak, poplar, and so on. I have one huge old oak tree that men say is three hundred years old. It had started to decay somewhat and the surgeons have taken out all the dead wood and filled in the cavities just like a dentist fills a tooth."

Clark's face was as bright and his tone was as excited as a small boy's when he talked of his ranch and it was easy to see that he loved his trees.

"Some of the branches are tied up with steel cables," he went on. "I didn't want to take any chances on losing that lovely tree and the branches had been weakened by the dental work!"

He laughed.

"You see," he went on soberly, "high winds blow up off the mountains and I am afraid the branches might break."

Clark plans to play at farming; he was brought up on an Ohio farm. He has a fine crop of alfalfa already, he told me, and he hopes to raise some cattle, though his ranch is small.

"I have one of these big ice boxes, built-in," he said. "It looks like the kind you see in a butcher shop and you can walk right into it. I hope to raise some meat on my own farm."

Gable has brought a tractor for his San Fernando Valley ranch and likes nothing better than doing his own plowing. Maybe he will retire to the ranch and live the life of a farmer in ten more years, he grins.

The house, he insists, is "just a small house." It has two bedrooms, a living room, a gunroom, dining room and so on and is what he calls a farmhouse built on early American lines.

Some day, perhaps, I'll tell you more about the house. When it is all finished and things are moving right on the ranch he promised he will invite me down for dinner.

Everybody on the set is congratulating Harry Wolf, one of the assistant cameramen. He has a new daughter and every morning when he comes in somebody kids him about looking like he walked the floor with the baby all night.

Ned Lambert, head of wardrobe, is also a new father and we expect any day now to see a fight between the two papas who insist upon boasting about the finest girl ever born.

I went out the other evening with a young man named Paul de Witt whose brother, Cornelius de Witt, lives at 560 Hillyer Avenue, Macon. Cornelius is a graduate of William and Mary College and Paul thinks Cornelius knows my brother-in-law, Dr. L. C. Lindsley, of Westover Plantation, Milledgeville; for Doctor Lindsley taught at W and M just about the time de Witt was there. I told Paul to have his brother look up "Shorty" Jeffries; for I remember that he is also a W and M graduate.

Another Macon contact came for me the other day in a roundabout way. Catherine Causey, who works in wardrobe, here, is the daughter of a former Georgian. He is J. M. Causey and was born in Crawford county. His two brothers, Charles and Robert, still live at Knoxville and Catherine hopes to visit there before long. I spent a pleasant half-hour telling her all about how Knoxville and Roberta look.

Macon Telegraph, 1 April 1939

Straight From HOLLYWOOD

Railroad Station Shots for GWTW Fascinate Miss Myrick

HOLLYWOOD, Calif.—Every morning when I come on the set, these days, Victor Fleming begins grinning and humming "Marching Through Georgia." I have threatened to secede from the union if he doesn't stop it. So, we go on with our little game. GWTW has got all of us very Southern.

We have been doing such interesting shots. Down at the old railroad station that stood in Atlanta in 1860 (at least it is a duplicate of that old station though it is located on Forty Acres at Selznick International), we have been doing the scenes that show Ashley's arrival for his Christmas furlough in 1863; and the whole business fascinated me.

Wilbur Kurtz drew the plans for the station from old pictures and specifications he had received from various sources, and the set-dressing department did an excellent job of putting in benches and lights that looked as if they were half a century old.[9]

Soldiers in uniform were true to type, too, with faded and worn clothes; some of the boys dressed in butternut and some in sadly mixed combinations that the Confederate soldiers were forced to wear as the war went on and funds sank lower and lower.

Bandages for heads or arms looked blood-stained, and I asked the make-up man what they used to get the right color. He said that the stuff was put up under the name of "artificial blood stain" and that it was raspberry flavored.

That practically floored me! When I could get my breath again I asked why on earth they flavored it anyhow—was it maybe to give the boys the raspberry? But he explained it was made pleasant of flavor so that an actor who got some on his lip and tasted it by mistake wouldn't mind.[10]

I still think maybe I was being kidded.

But I was not ribbed about the bell on the funny, old engine that stood in the station. The engine was designed by Wilbur Kurtz (who is regarded by everybody on the Selznick lot as a wizard because he always knows everything and always gets things right) and built on the set, and it looks so much like the one in your old history book that you'll think the picture has come to life.

The bell on the engine is one the property department found at a museum. The bell came around the Horn to this country and was used on an engine on a train way back in the fifties.

We were very authentic about things on that railroad station set. One man was writing a note as he stood waiting in the station. He was dressed in a faded ragged uniform and leaned on a pile of old leather trunks as he wrote.

One of the crew laughed and called to the actor:

"Are you writing that note with a Southern accent?"

"Sure," replied the soldier, "look." And he brought his note over for us to see:

"Dear Sugar:" it began. "I haven't had time to write you since I left camp, but I want to drop you a line to let you know I am still lucky and I am not toting any Yankee bullets up to this time."

There were three bit players on the railroad station set who were interesting to me because of their work in the movies back in the old, silent days.

Josef Swickard played in the *Four Horsemen of the Apocalypse* many years ago. But long before that—fifty years ago, he says—he played in *The King's Fool* on the stage in Atlanta.

Mary Carr and Emmett King were two more players with small bits. King will be remembered by old-timers as the man who played General Jackson in *Barbara Frietchie*.

There is a game that people around the studio play when they have a few moments to spare. I am going to tell you about it but don't say I didn't warn you not to play. The thing will give you the running jitters if you don't watch out. Marcella Rabwin, Bobby Keon and Harriett Flagg are three girls who even play it at lunch, and they've got me doing it.

Get yourself a pencil and a piece of paper, and I'll play you a game.

First you make six lines crosswise, then six lengthwise so that you have five squares each way, making a total of twenty-five squares.

I'll take first go, and I'll give the letter "C" and I'll put it in the first space at the left. You may put it where you please. (I put it where I wanted to. There is no rule except that you must put the letter somewhere and you can't erase it or change it to another place.) Say you put the "C" in the lower left-hand corner.

Now it's your turn to give a letter and you had figured you'd use the "C" to begin the word "clamp;" so you give an "L" for your letter and put it next to the "C." I had thought of the word "clash," so I put mine next to my "C," also.

But I have also thought of the word "crimp;" so I give an "R" for my next letter and put it down below the "C" giving myself two starts toward five-letter words.

Meanwhile, you (smartypants) had thought of the word "colon" to use your "C" so you decide to put that "R" in the center of the bottom line so you could end a word with it eventually. And you give me an "O" for your next letter. Well, it suits you to use the "O" for "colon" but I have no thought about what to do with it so I just put it down in the space below the one where the "P" will be when I end the word "clamp" (in case I ever get the right letters for it) and hope to make a word of it, sooner or later.

And on we go until all spaces have been filled. Sometimes, you find yourself ending with words like "aobgr" or "prynr," as I did in a game today.

The winner is the one who scores highest; scoring ten points for each five-letter word you've made, four points for each four-letter word, and three points for each three-letter word. And plurals don't count. And you can't use proper names, either.

We had another visitor from Georgia this week. W. K. Meadows was here on business and came over to watch while we made some additional shots on Ashley's Christmas visit to Melanie in Atlanta. It was fun talking to Mr. Meadows, who knows John Sibley and Pope Brock very well because he works with the same firm.

And Mr. Meadows and I had a good laugh together over Vic Fleming's kidding remarks. In the scene that we were shooting, Uncle Peter carries the candelabrum upstairs to light the way for Melanie and Ashley; and Vic wanted the candles held in a certain fashion. So he took the candle stick from Uncle Peter and held it first one way then another in order that the camera might get the right slant on it.

As he stood with the candlestick in his hand, Vic said:

"This thing is heavy. If you don't hurry up and get the camera fixed right, I've got to get a salary raise."

Then he turned to me and said, "How do I say that Southern-style, Susan? Should I say 'I got to get paid mo' money'?"

But I had my turn laughing at Vic when he didn't know what the Negroes at the station were saying. I had told them to say, "Chris'mus gif'" or "Chris'mus give" as the colored (and many of the whites) do at home, and Vic never heard of such a thing!

Mr. Meadows roomed with Gus Sparks at the University of Georgia. He told me he and Gus named their room "The Benjamin Franklin Apartments," and to this day they never meet without giving each other the high sign and asking about the Benjamin Franklin Apartments.

Mr. Meadows married Nan Ivey of Boston, Ga., and he is a brother-in-law of Leonora Ivey, who is director of physical education at Valdosta in the woman's college. Both the girls went to GSCW in Milledgeville. So I felt as if I had had a visit home after I talked to Mr. Meadows.

Next week looks like a most interesting week on the set of *Gone With the Wind*. Hundreds of extras are being fitted for costumes.

[1]"Thomas Mitchell was virtually the only serious contender for Gerald O'Hara . . . and Selznick had to agree to a special clause in his contract that he wouldn't have to ride, because he was terrified of horses." Flamini, *Scarlett, Rhett, and a Cast of Thousands*, p. 181. Mitchell, therefore, had to have a riding double. The double was Carey Harrison. SIP call sheet for 29 June 1939.

[2]Wilbur Kurtz wrote on 8 January 1939: "We went to Art Hudkins' place near the Warner lot. Art and his brother have a lot of fancy stock. The prime item to my way of thinking is that splendid white horse 'Silver' used in the filming of 'Hi-yo Silver' [i.e., "The Lone Ranger"]. I never saw such an animal." Kurtz, "Technical Adviser," p. 121.

In her *Constitution* piece for 26 February, Mrs. Kurtz said: "We then went to the back lot of this stage, where the horses and dogs were assembled. Here I got the biggest thrill yet; I saw that gorgeous horse 'Silver' (of Hi Yo Silver fame); he is to be Gerald's horse."

[3]Myrick commented on Twelve Oaks to her diary on 12 March: "Shot scenes in hall of Twelve Oaks Thursday for first time and almost died at magnificence of the place. Looks like Grand Central Station or the Palace at Potsdam. I almost expect train callers to come bawling out the schedule. Hall is big enough to put Westover [The L. C. Lindsley family home in Milledgeville] in. Stairway comes from TWO directions and landing is about the size of ordinary hallway. Looks about fifty feet from floor of hall to next floor! Lordy! What movies do think about the intelligence of the public. I tried to tell David it was too grand but couldn't. Vic knows it is too grand. He laughs at it. Also Gable laughs at it."

[4]Myrick wrote Margaret Mitchell on 14 February: "Walter Plunkett told me today he hoped I would some day tell you he tried his damndest to have costumes as you wished them when you so kindly talked to him about them and he had read the book a score of times and that even if you did not believe it when you saw the picture he had TRIED. I saw his book of layouts and he had two hundred pages and quotes from the book every time to prove his costume

design. But Selznick wants the pix to be a sex affair between Rhett and Scarlett and by god he is going to have her look pretty no matter what!"

[5]This is the private account that Myrick wrote for Miss Mitchell on 12 March: "May God have mercy on the soul of Jock Whitney and his money for I swear these fools are spending enough to make ten movies. The castle they have built for Twelve Oaks! And the extras they are paying to decorate the lawn and the hall and the piazza for the set! There were 250 extras at the out door shots we made in Busch Gardens in Pasadena (incidentally the barbecue setting looked like the palace at Versailles) not including the twenty colored waiters and cooks the ten maid servants and five Mammys and ten little nigger chillun and fifteen white chillun! And that ten acre field of the Anheuser Busch gardens was stinkin with people and horses and tables and benches. And I bet Queen Mary hasn't as much royal silver [as] the Wilkeses had at that barbecue. You'd have died laughing if you could have seen my face when I went to inspect a plate they brought to show in a close up for Scarlett. I must have looked some of my disgust. On the plate was a bone about the size you'd feed a mastiff or a St. Bernard with a bit of meat clinging, a serving of potatoes that would have been enough for the Knights of the Round Table and a huge slice of cake—about what you'd serve five guests. I persuaded the prop man to remove the bone, put on a slice of meat take off half the other stuff and then walked off the set and frowed up. I can't decide whether to bust into a sort of wild insane laugh about it all or to walk off the lot and tell them where they can put the picture.

"But of course I'm sticking. In the first place, I know that I AM stopping lots of mistakes and gross errors so the few score I can't stop I'll just try not to think about. And naturally I am having some fun and I am curious to know just how many strange things they will do before it is all over."

Gladys Hall said in her record for 10 March: "I remarked to Vivien that Clark was certainly a triumph of the sartorial art. His coat was of midnight-blue cloth, trousers of fawn pearl, boot-straps and square-toed shoes of black patent leather. I must say that girls are going to be hard put to it to understand Scarlett's indifference to Rhett when they see him in *this* regalia!" Hall, "Gone With the Wind: On the Set with Gladys Hall," p. 69.

[6]Among other accomplishments, Crick developed methods for seeding clouds with silver oxide.

[7]This was Norman H. Giles, now a distinguished professor holding an endowed chair at the University of Georgia.

[8]One of the things Margaret Mitchell learned about the filming of *Gone With the Wind* that upset her most was that Scarlett was shown wearing a hat at the charity bazaar. In a long letter to Myrick on 10 February 1939 she commented: "Annie Laurie [Kurtz] . . . included casually a bit of information that turned my few remaining hairs white. She spoke of the bazaar scene with Scarlett and Rhett dancing together, and mentioned that Scarlett had on a bonnet and veil. In the name of God, what was she doing with a hat on at an evening party where everybody else was wearing low-cut gowns? My tempera-

ture jumped seven points at the news. I cannot imagine even Scarlett showing such poor taste. I foresee that I will get at least one good belly laugh out of this picture, and it will be during this scene."

She continued to be concerned on this point. "The more I look at the picture of the bonnet and the veil that Scarlett was wearing at the bazaar the worse it gets," she wrote on 15 February. "I suppose this must be one of the things that comes under the head of 'pictorial.' " And on 1 March she told Myrick: "If they do re-shoot the bazaar, I hope you get the bonnet off Miss Leigh."

Myrick answered in her letter of 12 March: "Yep, we are re-shooting the bazaar and Walter Plunkett and I are plotting to get the bonnet off but we are doubtful. You see, the fools paid John Frederics of N Y a hundred bucks for that bonnet and they are bound she'll wear it. If we get it off the fair Scarlett I'll buy you a dope when I come home! I am getting cynical now and sort of getting like Mr. _____ and Mr. _____ that time they drank the 'don't keer likker'. When the pix is shown can I go to Pango Pango with you to keep away from it all!"

Selznick wrote in one of his famous memos on 13 March: "The costumes of the picture, and the sets also, should have dramatized much more than we have done to date, and much less than I hope they will do in the future, the changing fortunes of the people with whom we are dealing

"I am hopeful that this will be corrected· in such things as the bazaar retake. I am aware that the former scene at the bazaar looked like a cheap picture postcard in its color values—but this was because we were foolish enough to overdress the set so that it looked cheap and garish, instead of neutralizing it as to color values, so that it was obviously an armory, and playing against this the beauty of the costumes, which gave us a marvelous opportunity for beautiful colors against the set, which obviously gave us no opportunities. The shots that Mr. Fleming has in mind on the waltz will fulfill their complete promise of beauty only if the costumes are lovely and colorful—so that Scarlett's black is a complete contrast." David O Selznick, *Memo from David O. Selznick* (New York: Viking Press, 1972), pp. 197-98.

[9]Wilbur Kurtz pointed out to Selznick and his associates on his first trip to Hollywood that one of the distinctive features of Civil War Atlanta was the depot that Margaret Mitchell referred to as the car-shed. It was, he said, "a huge barrel-vaulted train shed, three hundred feet long by one hundred feet wide, covering an area of 30,000 square feet. 'So that was the car-shed of the novel, was it?' It seemed that no one out there had the faintest conception of what Margaret Mitchell's reference to the car-shed meant—they thought it was a mere plank depot. However I had the transcripts of the original plans of this huge structure, having found the original [Edward A.] Vincent plans some years previously in an old trunk on Washington Street."

"Then we'll build it," exclaimed Mr. Selznick. Kurtz, "Technical Adviser," p. 21.

Mrs. Kurtz's article for the *Constitution* on 20 February begins: "The best known of Atlanta's war-time landmarks is the edifice known as the 'car-shed,' a replica of which has been constructed on the 'forty-acres' for certain sequences in 'Gone With the Wind.' It was built in 1854 and was burned by order of General Sherman in November 1864."

For the January 1940 issue of *Railroad Magazine* (27:2 [December 1939]: 58-61), Mr. Kurtz wrote an article, "Gone With the Wind," about the car-shed and other aspects of Civil War railroading as reflected in the film.

[10]In writing of the scene in which Scarlett shoots the Yankee deserter, Gladys Hall noted: "The take was repeated . . . several times, because it is a scene full of close-ups and the eye of the Technicolor camera is mercilessly keen. Paul Hurst played the role, his face painted with artificial blood, which has the flavor of raspberries, and poor Mr. H. said that he doesn't know as he'll ever enjoy raspberry shortcake again!" Hall, "Gone With the Wind: On the Set with Gladys Hall," p. 71.

SIX
6 April—16 April 1939

Macon Telegraph, 6 April 1939

Straight From HOLLYWOOD

Fun and Work Mix Well in Producing Gone With the Wind

HOLLYWOOD, Calif.—The *Atlanta Examiner* office in 1863, where Atlantans received news of the casualties that came from the Battle of Gettysburg, probably turned its ghostly body in its grave of ashes this week; for the office built on Forty Acres at Selznick International in Culver City is such a perfect replica of the original building that it must cause some heartache to the long-passed-away *Examiner*.[1]

Drab and sad were the people who waited for news of the war, dressed in their genteel best which showed the desperate condition that was beginning to obtain in Georgia when the war had yet another year to go.

Wardrobe and make-up had worked valiantly to costume properly three hundred and fifty people, and goodness knows what hour they began, for when I arrived at the set about quarter to eight the folks were all ready and waiting.

Carriages and horses, wagons, Negro men and women and little boys and girls, both white and Negro, added to the atmosphere, and as I stood on the high platform and looked down at the extras I felt a renewed surge of pity for those who wait and hope after a battle.

But there was so much to do and so many things to watch I had no time for sorrow. Were there enough widows in the crowd? Was there some girl in the foreground whose red fingernail polish might show? Did all the Negro men have their hats off as they stood near the white folks?

All these and many other things I had to think about, and meanwhile find time to laugh at wisecracks coming from here and there, stretch my body in gratitude to the warm sunshine (after working indoors for days on a stretch) and gape at prominent visitors who were on the set.

Mr. and Mrs. Walter Lippman and Mr. and Mrs. John Balderston were four visitors whom I met, and somebody pointed out to me the minister from the Netherlands and his wife, who were on the set.

But none of the visitors matched in attention the welcome given Clark Gable, who was grinning broadly at the congratulations offered him, for that was his first day at work since his marriage.[2]

Even the sad scenes shot that day could not dim the smile that Gable wore.

For that matter, in spite of the long list of casualties and the pathos of women weeping over the loss of loved ones, there were plenty of wisecracks. There was a scene where Melanie and Scarlett sat together in a carriage and Vic Fleming wanted Scarlett to have a purse in her hand.

"Has somebody got a purse for Scarlett?" he asked the Wardrobe.

Eric Stacey shouted "Wardrobe" through the loudspeaker, and as a girl came to the camera, Fleming said:

"I want a silk purse for Scarlett. Anybody got a sow's ear we can make one from?"

Then there was the crack somebody aimed at me as three men walked past, carrying buckets of red-brick dust to make Georgia's soil the proper color:

"There goes the Georgia bucket brigade," said Lyle Wheeler. "I declare, Susan, it would have been so much easier on us if Miss Mitchell had just located this story in Natchez, or New Orleans or some other place where the dirt isn't red."

"Well, you'd have had to go looking for Spanish moss," I answered, "if the scene had been laid in Natchez."

"You're all wrong," replied Wheeler. "We can manufacture Spanish moss in our shops that looks more real than the real Spanish moss."

Working out on Forty Acres is something like a picnic. (All except the work part.) Everybody seems to absorb some of the warmth of the sunshine, and there is much gay banter. And picnic lunch is served to all of us—crew and extras.

We stream down toward the other side of the lot when Eric calls "Lunch! Back at work in an hour;" for lunch is served in the old *Garden of Allah* set which gives protection from wind that sometimes blows cold off the nearby mountains. A box that contains sandwiches, a hard boiled egg, a carton of salad, an orange and a slice of cake is given to everyone and there is steaming hot soup for all who wish it and milk and coffee, too.

"Are you eating barbecue with me?" members of the group ask each other, for the barbecue at Twelve Oaks lingers in our memory. And at lunch somebody is always shouting "The Yankees is comin" and somebody answers back: "Aw Chris'mus gif'."

All this fun is good for the tired feet and the worried mind, for you needn't doubt we have both on the set—particularly the feet. There is so much standing up to be done. Sometimes I wish I were the cameraman who sits on a little stool that is attached to the carriage for the camera and rides back and forth when the camera moves forward and back.

That is, the man who rides is the head assistant cameraman. Ernest Haller, who is head cameraman, never sits down. He is always squinting through a little finder to see just what the picture looks like, and measuring the amount of light, and walking over to see what lamp is not casting the proper light, and waving a hand to see where the unwanted shadow is coming from.

Ernie Haller is regarded as one of the top cameramen in the world, and is particularly good at Technicolor.[3] He has been crazy about cameras ever since he was a small boy, he told me, and when he went to high school he never studied anything except physics and chemistry and art. At first, when he started to work, he thought he would be an artist or an architect and began a career in those fields; but his interest in cameras kept pulling at him, and, living in Los Angeles where the motion picture industry was growing so fast, he began transferring his interest to the movie camera.

He has invented more gadgets for movie cameras than you can count, and is one of the pioneers in color photography.

Ernie is a quiet, gentle sort of man, with reddish-blond hair and the sort of skin girls wish they had. And he is good company in spite of his enormous efficiency.

We had a new member of the *Gone With the Wind* cast on the set this week. Jackie Moran, who played Huck Finn, is taking the role of Phil Meade. Jackie is the pet of the lot because he is so modest and is just a little shy and is so good-natured. He is crazy about baseball, and I had a fine time talking to him about the Chicago Cubs. He was the mascot for the Cubs for several years before he left Chicago to begin his movie career, and he loves to talk about Gabby Hartnett, who is one of his best pals. He thinks Dizzy Dean is great and feels sure Dizzy's sore arm is going to be all right and that Dizzy will win many games for the Cubs this year.

Jackie was vastly amused when I told him about Little Willie, Macon's mascot, and he hopes some day he will get to Macon to see the Peaches and Little Willie.

The youngster has got the whole crew tossing balls around in their spare moments. Ann Robinson Miller, who is the pretty stand-in for Olivia de Havilland, hurt her thumb playing ball the other day and there are some sore arms on the lot, too.

We had a fine laugh on the lot last Saturday morning. The day looked a little dark at quarter to eight, and Eric Stacey was muttering in his beard that the weather man was crazy and he expected rain almost any minute. That would have been pretty bad, for the crew had started to work about five to get all the equipment hauled out to Forty Acres and set in place.

Ray Klune, production manager, was walking about, looking worried over the probable loss of several hours of work, and everybody was casting anxious glances at the clouds that darkened over the mountains. Eric picked up the loudspeaker and called:

"Attention, everybody! We're moving in. Boys, get your trucks ready so we can go in to work on Stage 14!"

There was a moment of dead silence. Some fifty men of the crew, who had been working briskly and chattering as they worked, dropped what they held and stood in absolute silence, gazing toward the sky where a bit of blue was appearing.

Ray Klune started toward Eric on the dead run, and all the extras on the set moved toward the wardrobe tents. Then Eric, with a high-school-boy grin on his handsome face, shouted into the microphone:

"April Fool!"

But even that wholesale announcement of All Fools' Day didn't warn us sufficiently. At lunch hour, when people were just fooling around and the lot was crowded with extras who sat about indolently, somebody planted a pocketbook in the street.

A few minutes later, along came the expected sucker. He picked up the purse, looked around and said: "Somebody drop this?"

Nobody paid any attention to him and he opened the purse to look for a name.

"Bl-oom-er-loom!" came a loud report, and the sucker jumped ten feet and threw the purse as far as he could.

So, with fun and foolishness at intervals, the work goes forward, and excellent work it is, too. I hope when you see *Gone With the Wind* you'll agree with me that it is beautiful. I believe you will.

Macon Telegraph, 10 April 1939

Straight From HOLLYWOOD

Sue Keeps Busy but Familiar Scenes Are Making Her Homesick

HOLLYWOOD, Calif.—This month, Harry Davenport, who is playing Dr. Meade in *Gone With the Wind*, will celebrate his sixty-eighth anniversary of work on the stage. And the sixty-eight years have been continuous, too.

He has played many roles on the legitimate stage and in the movies, and counts it a great thing that he played with Joseph Jefferson in *Rip Van Winkle*.

Mr. Davenport was telling me about his stage experience on the set the other day when we were shooting down at Forty Acres on the Atlanta street scene. Plastered on the walls of the wooden fence near the office of the *Atlanta Examiner* were hand bills announcing the coming of various events. Among them was a bill that told of the showing of Mrs. Riddle's company that would present *The School for Scandal*. Among the characters listed was Sol Smith, who would sing a comic song.

Mr. Davenport looked at the bill and caught his breath.

"Well, I'll declare!" he said. "I knew Sol Smith very well."

Another sign told of Bryant's Minstrels, which would show in Atlanta, and Davenport told me Bryant was his god-father. Then he smiled so that fine wrinkles tightened at the corners of his twinkling

eyes and told me he supposed I wouldn't like him any more if I knew his
wife sang "Marching Through Georgia" the first time it was sung, back
in 1888, in Atlanta.

I just laughed back at him, and told him he was much too nice a
man to be a Damn Yankee and I found it difficult to believe what he
was telling. So he grinned broadly and said he supposed those who
rebelled in the sixties would never outgrow it.

"Them's fightin' words, suh!" I told him. "All you have to do to
start trouble with me is to speak of the War of the Rebellion."

Anyway, we had a good laugh at the crowd last Saturday afternoon when a little rain squall came up while we were working on Forty
Acres. We told Eric Stacey and Vic Fleming that the reason for the rain
was apparent to anybody but a Yankee. Down South, we said, nobody
ever worked Sat'dy evenin' and the rain came just to prove there was no
sense in working on a Southern picture on Saturday afternoon.

While we sat around and waited for the rain to stop (it did stop in
about ten minutes and the sun shone brightly) I was talking to Olivia de
Havilland. She sat on a nail keg that was displayed along with churns
and coffee mills and other old-fashioned articles in front of one of the
Atlanta stores, and I sat on an upturned cedar bucket.[4]

Along came a lady who stopped and listened to our conversation
for a moment, then said:

"Aren't you from the South?"

Smiling, Olivia said, "Yes, indeed, we are." The lady returned:
"I just knew it. I'm from Mississippi. Where are you from?"

"Georgia," said Olivia, turning on all her charm (and she has
plenty) for the Mississippi lady.

"Well, I just knew your accent was Southern," the lady told her, "I
couldn't tell whether you came from Alabama or Georgia, but I knew it
was one of them."

Then Olivia confessed. But she was greatly pleased that the Southern lady thought her accent was so perfect for Olivia has been practicing hard to get her voice to sound properly Southern for her role as
Melanie.

I have been kidded a lot since I've been here about Southern
accent, and some of the people vow they don't understand a word I say,
but I got a fine compliment Sunday from an Englishwoman who was a
guest at George Cukor's house. I had gone there, too, for lunch and
George explained to his friend as he introduced me that I was a

technical adviser on *Gone With the Wind*, that I was from Georgia and said the lady would probably not understand anything I said.

"Oh! you are wrong, George," she replied. "I have been listening to Miss Myrick and I find her voice pleasing. I can understand her much more easily than I can the Californians. Miss Myrick's accent sounds very much like the accent in London."

I was pleased, of course, not only because the lady liked the way I talked but because she proved my contention that the speech of the educated Georgian is close akin to that of the Britisher.

It was beautiful at George Cukor's Sunday. The sun was warm and the weather was just what the chamber of commerce would have you believe it always is in California. We sat in the garden and talked and I watched the reflection of the azaleas in the blue water of the swimming pool and marveled at the enormous size of the daffodils.

Later, we walked through the garden, which is on three levels, for the house is built on the side of a small mountain and the garden rambles up and down stairs just as the house does.

Down in the basement garden are the fruit trees, oranges and lemons mostly. The orange trees were fragrant with the pearly white blossoms and gay with the color of the ripened fruit that clung; and the lemons are so large I thought they were young grapefruit.

On the edges of the garden are the grape arbor and the trellis on which the [boysenberries] grow, and the grass about is green with springtime and scattered over it are orange and yellow poppies. Shrubs of every sort you can name grow in lushness along the border and the white blossoms on the firethorn are lovely. Most of all, I think I liked the tea olive and the yellow jessamine, because they remind me of home.

A small formal garden has bordered walks and roses of yellow, red and pink and white blossom in profusion.

The second-tier garden has a border along the side of the hill that is about four feet wide and is filled with flowering plants—daffodils, stock, poppies, iris, candy tuft, daisies, coreopsis and goodness knows what. I don't recognize many of California's flowers and George calls everything some ridiculous Latin name like *Gladiolus hepatica*.

The flower bed lies right next to the hillside and flat against the hill wall are trained lemon trees and over all trails wisteria, just beginning to bud.

A flagged walk leads up the incline and at intervals stone steps have easy lifts, and where the stairs rise are statues brought from France and Italy to adorn the already lovely place.

At the top of the second-garden steps is the third garden, a sort of terrace with an arbor over which vines trail. Here are seats so that one may look out over the world, and on a clear day see all the way to Catalina Island.

At least they say one can see that far. I observe that in Los Angeles everybody tells you every view shows all the way to Catalina. It's just as in the Southern mountains where the guide always swears you can stand on the peak and look into seven states.

Anyway, you don't care where the view goes at Cukor's, for the garden is so lovely there is no sense in looking afar off.

The past week has been so crowded with excitement I can scarcely sleep nights for thinking about it. The street scenes that show refugees leaving Atlanta as the Yankees approach the city were (if you'll pardon my Hollywood expression) terrific!

Horses and carriages and wagons and mules crowded the streets, and five hundred extras worked in the lovely sunshine. Explosions from distant shells sent smoke over the scene and bursts of noise made everybody jump. Everybody—that is—except the horses. They are so well trained they behave no matter what happens.

Oh! of course, some of the horses reared on their hind legs and one or two of them tried to run away, but the men who handled them pulled the animals right back where they belonged and the scene went like clock work.[5]

Red dust was all over the place!

It made me fair homesick, I can tell you, to see the street that looked so like a small Georgia town with its thick red dust and its little boarding houses and "offices upstairs" and Negroes and mules.

During the lunch hour I walked down the Peachtree Street, and lying flat on the board sidewalks were stretched several of the colored men, fast asleep. That about finished me for homesickness. I had to get very busy and work fast to keep back the tears.

I know people in Georgia will get the biggest kick of all out of seeing the red dirt and the picture of a small Georgia town when *Gone With the Wind* finally comes to the screen. For, you know, the picture is in Technicolor, and to Georgians who love the wonderful shades of red clay, even Clark Gable and Vivien Leigh will fade for a moment into insignificance when the street scenes come on and Georgia soil shows brick-colored.

The days we worked in the street scenes, though, nobody on Selznick International lot liked the dust, except me. It got in our eyes and teeth and hair and clothes and shoes and I took a lot of ribbing about the dusty little Southern town where nobody could possibly keep clean.

I refused to admit how often I had driven over unpaved roads in Georgia in summer weather and arrived at my destination with clothes, face and hair red with the dust which I didn't think was so lovely then. But the red dust in *Gone With the Wind* makes me homesick.

Macon Telegraph, 13 April 1939

Straight From HOLLYWOOD

Officer's Understanding Makes California More Appealing

HOLLYWOOD, Calif.—The dust of Atlanta streets of 1864 is still in my eyes and ears and nose and is buried in the pores of my skin as I write this, for we have been shooting scenes for *Gone With the Wind* on Forty Acres for some days, and red dust (Selznick International Pictures bought nine tons of it, you know) has been kicked up by horses and the feet of many extras.

Caissons drawn by six horses can raise a lot of dust, and five hundred persons can kick up plenty of it. Even our hero, Rhett Butler, was coated with it before the day was over, for he drove his spanking pair of sorrel horses through the dust and the crowds to pick up Scarlett and take her back to Aunt Pitty's.

"Were you ever this dirty before in your life, Sue?" he asked.

"Never!" I lied cheerfully, refusing to recall the times I've tried to pass a car on a dirt road in Georgia when the driver ahead kept just half a block before me and would not respond to my honking.

Vivien Leigh, like the grand trouper she is, swallowed chunks of dust and never murmured a protest. The stuff rose in clouds that a visitor on the set vowed could be seen in Hollywood eight miles away.

I wouldn't know, though I live in Hollywood, for I go to work before the dust starts flying and don't get home until darkness has fallen.

Never an accident marred the work of the five hundred extras, though we did get excited when a wheel ran off a cannon-carriage and rolled down the street, missing a score of persons by inches.

Excellent drivers managed the horses; and when the wheel ran off the cannon-carriage, the men just drove the horses through with the carriage on one wheel, dragging a hub on the other side.

The extras who do special stunt work for the movie studios are known as the studio shock troops and they are men who are members of the Hollywood American Legion post. Their manager talked to me about their work one day on the set and told how they first began working as extras when a man without an arm or a leg was needed. Then the Legion organized the group of veterans and now they are on constant call at one studio or another for jobs that require men with plenty of nerve and the ability to do whatever is required.

And speaking of extras, it is fun to talk to various ones in the group. They love to tell of their past glories and to recall the days when they were working in silent movies either with stars or as stars in their own right. For many of the stars of silent days are now working as extras in the talkies.

One man who looked about fifty told me he had played in movies for thirty years. His name is Fred Behrle and he played in *The Birth of a Nation*, *Custer's Last Stand*, *The Veiled Mystery*, *The Clutching Hand* and many, many others. He loves to talk of Theda Bara and Ruth Roland and others whose names are almost unknown to the younger moviegoers of today.

As he talked to me, he rolled a cigarette with the mastery of long practice and there was a hint of sorrow in his voice as he talked of the time when coal-oil lamps had to be kept near the camera to provide heat "so that static would not interfere with the fillum."

"The static would make the fillum flicker," he explained, and I nodded, though I didn't quite understand.

"Thirty years and now nothing but an extra at $8.50 a day!"

Another extra, who used to live in Tennessee, talked to me about Georgia, where she had visited, and of Copper Hill, where the "bad lands" are so awesomely beautiful in their denuded, eroded hills, where red and orange and magenta earth is gashed with gullies, and small peaks lift up their wounds toward the blue skies.

But it was not an extra with whom I had the most fun on the Atlanta sets. Laura Hope Crews, who is Aunt Pittypat, invited me to come to her dressing room for a while during a camera change, and it was a delight to listen to the charming woman whose experiences on the stage began nearly fifty years ago.

She talked of *The Silver Cord*, which Sidney Howard wrote and dedicated to her many years ago and of the new plays she has been reading. While she is exiled here, far from the New York stage that she adores, Miss Crews whiles away many hours by reading all the current plays she can find in book form. She praised Lillian Hellman and Philip Barry and expressed enchantment over the Oscar Wilde play she had just read—the one produced the past season in New York.

As we talked, I heard someone call over the P.A. system: "Miss Myrick! Come to the camera." And I jumped to my feet and hurried away.

But it was only Victor Fleming wanting to kid me a little. He had a "shin-plaster" and wanted to know how much I'd give him for it. I offered a dime and he said it wasn't worth that much so he'd just give it to me. I thanked him prettily and vowed that any Confederate money was worth a lot to a Southerner.

"You know," he grinned, "you Southerners are a sentimental lot. If you hadn't been so sentimental, we'd never have had to make this picture and I wouldn't be swallowing all this dust."

Vic likes to kid about the South because he loves it. He often refers to trips he has made to the deep South and speaks lovingly of the people he has met there and the fun he has had and the hospitality shown to him by Southerners.

"I guess Atlanta has outgrown this dusty state by now," he teased, "but Macon now, it's just a little town isn't it? I guess this town we've built looks just about like Macon, doesn't it?"

"Sure!" I grinned back. "Only we have one or two streets paved now."

Then I told him how Macon was quite a town when Atlanta was just Marthasville and, since he was interested, I told him how the people of Clinton thought the newly-born town of Macon would never grow because "it was too close to Clinton." He was greatly interested in Georgia's lost towns.

But he still kidded me as he walked away to resume his duties as director, for he hummed "Marching Through Georgia."

Each week I discover something unusual about the business of making movies. I was agog, for instance, the other day when I found the sound man tying a leafy branch to the end of the mike. I asked how come and he told me the sun was in such a position that it was impossible to prevent a shadow of the microphone from falling in the picture; so he tied the branch on and the shadow looked like a tree shadow. Isn't that something?

And now, if I may be personal, I'll tell you about how I got arrested!

I was going home from the studio about ten the other evening and as I approached a crossing, I slowed up. There was a blinking light, which I took to mean "slow down and look out" so I looked both ways and went on across without stopping.

"Pull over to the curb," said a stern voice about a minute later and you know how your heart skips a beat when you hear such a summons, no matter how innocent you may be.

The cop proceeded to get out a little book of tickets and a fountain pen and I proceeded to be scared to death. But I turned on my most polite manner and said I'd take the ticket if he said so but I had no idea what I'd done wrong. He said that was a stop boulevard and I said I didn't know it, that I thought a blinking light meant slow down and look.

"Where's your driver's license?" he demanded.

I fumbled in my pocket book and brought out the license issued by the state of California, but I also managed to hand him the Georgia license left over from last year and I talked fast, telling him I'd only been here a short time and so on.

"Well, I thought you talked like you'd come from somewhere in the South," grinned the cop, looking over the Georgia license. "I'll let you go this time, but remember, next time you come to a red light, stop! No matter whether it is blinking or standing still. Amber lights, blinking, means slow down but a red light means stop in any language, Deep South or whatnot."

So, what with the marvelous sunshine we're having, the singing birds, the spring warmth, the kindness of cops and the progress of *Gone With the Wind*, I am beginning to be sold on California.

Easter Sunday was a fine day for me. I had lunch at George Cukor's and what a fine lunch, with fried chicken and baked ham and string beans and fresh green asparagus and a salad of grapes and avocado with curly endive, followed by a dessert too beautiful to eat. It was ice cream, frozen with little yellow bunny shapes in the middle and with it were served strawberries and fresh pineapples that were piled in a hollowed-out pineapple shell.

And such fun to listen to the gay conversation! First of all there was Fannie Brice and you know it was fun to hear "Baby Snooks." She looked very young and very charming in a yellow light-weight woolen frock that had a brown and cream plaid coat and it is difficult to believe she has a son who is six feet four, as she vows he is.

Of course it was nice just to sit across the table from Errol Flynn and look at his handsome face. Then there was Vivien Leigh and there was Olivia de Havilland, whom I have grown accustomed to seeing, but they are both good company. On my right was Lord Warwick, a handsome fellow who wore white trousers and a double-breasted, navy coat with brass buttons that had the insignia of the Royal Yachting club on them.

Most pleasant was Mrs. Charles Brackett, who was so cordial and friendly as soon as she learned I was from Macon and knew Fliss Guttenberger. Everybody laughed heartily at us for talking about "The Matthews Girls" but they couldn't stop us, for she is an ardent admirer of the Matthews as are all of us in Macon. Mr. Brackett was there, too, but he went away and talked to someone else after George Cukor told him he thought Brackett had married a woman far superior to him.

"See here, Charles!" said Cukor, "your wife is kin to the Matthews girls of Pee Wee Valley and Macon, Ga. You can't be worthy of that!"

There were many more guests but I couldn't quite get them straight in my mind. Only I did know that a lady who came in later was Constance Collier.

But the big excitement of the day came for me at 5:30 when I arrived at the home of Carl Lindquist in West Los Angeles and talked over the shortwave radio to friends back in Macon.

Saturday night I planned to go to sunrise services but Sunday morning I was just too tired and sleepy to get up. But thirty-five thousand persons did get up before daybreak to go to Forest Lawn where the Philharmonic orchestra under the baton of Dr. Otto Klemperer played the overture to Oberon and Ann Jamison sang Franck's Panis Angelicus.

Thirty thousand more went to Hollywood bowl for sunrise services and another fifteen thousand to Mount Rubidoux.

But today we are back on the stage and Clark Gable is a prisoner in a Yankee jail on the *Gone With the Wind* set.

Macon Telegraph and News, 16 April 1939

Straight From HOLLYWOOD

Southern Atmosphere Pervades Ante-Bellum Scenes of GWTW

HOLLYWOOD, Calif.—Southern atmosphere has certainly pervaded the whole staff at Selznick International Pictures. It is amazing the way one person after another tells me his grandmother or his great-aunt Sally was a Virginian or a Georgian or a South Carolinian. And during the past week while we were shooting the scenes with Rhett Butler in jail in Atlanta, it was too funny the way everybody looked down their noses at the actors who were playing the roles of Yankee officers.

First thing, I threatened to trip one of the Yankees—you see I have to keep up the spirit of the South; and I just had to do something about one of the officers who looked something like General Grant and wore a Union suit.

When I spoke to Bill Menzies, of the art department,[6] Bill grinned and said:

"Don't hurt the poor boys. One of them is sure to be from Alabama or Georgia; and if he isn't, his grandfather was."

Then Bill admitted that he felt a sinister something in the air when the Yankee officers came on the set for the first day's work.

"I've got so accustomed to thinking and feeling Southern and all my sympathies are with the South and the Confederacy so that those

Union army uniforms sort of make me mad, and I feel like I must hate those poor fellows," he said.

The Yankee boys did splendid jobs, just the same; and though I hate to admit it, they do add to the picture. You won't notice them after Scarlett appears, though. She is so ravishingly lovely in that frock you read about in *GWTW*—the one she made from the curtains.

And the trouble that frock has caused! It's so heavy (it is actually made from the material that was used for the curtains at Tara. You'll see them in the parlor when you see the picture) poor little Vivien Leigh can hardly tote it. But the main trouble was in getting the color to suit both Miss Leigh's eyes and the Technicolor experts as well as the other important persons connected with the show.

You see the Technicolor experts know all sorts of strange and fascinating things about colors that ordinary mortals like me don't understand at all. Anyway, when Dick Mueller says something is not quite right in color there seems to be always a good reason for what he says and changes are always made accordingly.[7]

But the curtain-frock is beautiful, so I forgave Mr. Mueller.

He does the strangest things, anyway. While we were shooting the scene in the jail, Dick stood talking to me; and all at once he darted off like a Yankee was after him. He sidled up to one of the cameramen and then talked to Eddie Boyle, the set-dresser, and to Ray Rennahan, the other Technicolor man, and he fussed and fidgeted all the while Vic Fleming was having a rehearsal.

After a while I found out what was giving him such fits. There was a bottle, wrapped in white paper in the foreground of the picture, and Dick knew that would make other colors look a smidgeon wrong. At least that is what I got from his conversation. Anyway, the bottle wrapping was changed to a sort of cream-white and half the wrapping was removed so the green of the bottle showed.

Dick spent the next half-hour muttering to me:

"Look at that beautiful green. See how that bottle looks now and what a difference it makes in the whole picture."

Dick doesn't even see the action when he goes to a movie. All he looks at is color. The other day Miss Leigh asked Dick if he had seen the daily rushes and he said he had. So she asked how a certain scene she played looked. Dick said it was beautiful and she said:

"Were there tears in my eyes, Dick?"

Poor Man! He was so embarrassed because he didn't know. He didn't even remember what the scene was about. All he knew was Vivien Leigh's eyes looked green and lovely and the color of her skin was just the right creamy shade and showed the smooth texture just as it should be shown.

He goes to rushes to see colors. I go to listen to accent and to watch for anything that might look un-Southern. Eric Stacey goes to see what the background action is like. (You see, that is largely Eric's responsibility). The sound technicians go to hear the rushes. They sometimes sit through the picture with their eyes shut.

I guess only Victor Fleming and David O. Selznick actually look at the rushes as a whole picture.

Something brand new to me pops up every week on the moving picture set. This week, I spied a beautiful spider web over a window in the jail, and I said to Stacey:

"How did you ever manage to get that spider to spin a web in the right place for you?"

Eric Stacey grinned. (He looks like Mark Ethridge when he grins.)

"I put it on the call sheet," he said. "I ordered a spider to begin work this morning at six so the web would be ready for the cameras."

But some kind-hearted soul explained to me later that the spider webs are manufactured as easily and quickly by the property department as they could be by a spider. And the prop men always get the webs in just the right place. They're more durable than real webs, too.

The prop man promised to show me the next free time we have. The trick is done with some sort of air gun that blows a spray of gum.

After I found out about spider webs I wasn't the least surprised to hear Stacey call out as the director prepared to shoot a scene that showed dead and wounded soldiers:

"All the dead men come to the camera, please."

In spite of my admiration for California climate and people and especially for the efficiency of the men who work on the business of making *Gone With the Wind*, I still get a thrill when I meet Georgians visiting Southern California. The other day, Mrs. Howard Hanna, who owns Melrose Plantation at Thomasville and who has spent her winters in Georgia for thirty years, was a visitor and I felt I had found a long-lost friend.

For Mrs. Hanna adores Thomasville and the whole state of Georgia; and though she is only a part-time resident of the state, she knows and understands Georgia and its people and problems. She got as much pleasure out of the red dirt as I did. And when she found I knew Mrs. Arthur (Caroline) Little and Dr. Little, she hugged me.

Like everybody else who knows the Littles, she thinks they are the finest folks in the world. So, of course, we had fine fun talking of them and of other Georgians.

Mrs. Hanna, whose uncle, Mark Hanna, was one of the first out-of-state men to recognize the beauties of Georgia's winter climate, has traveled over the whole world and still thinks there is no winter climate to equal that of Thomasville.

And now if I may digress from my moving pictures, I should like to boast a little. I am so proud I am scarcely able to speak to my friends because I won a second place at the salon the other evening at the Hollywood Camera Clique, of which I am now a full-fledged member.

The picture was one I took when we were shooting at Pasadena. It showed in the foreground Ashley leaning from his horse to kiss Melanie good-bye, while the background showed activity of men and women and horses and dogs following the announcement of the rider that Lincoln had called for volunteers.

Of course, my picture of part of *GWTW* is a minor affair compared with the picture, itself, but to me it was very exciting to win a place in the first photograph competition I ever entered.

Editor's Notes—Six

[1]*Examiner* was a completely fictional name for an Atlanta newspaper.

[2]Gable was returning after six days away from the set. During that time he had married Carole Lombard in Kingman, Arizona. Gladys Hall wrote for 31 March: "When Gable showed up at ten o'clock for his scenes this morning, Vic Fleming started singing 'Happy Bridegroom to you!' One thousand extras took up the refrain, for Clark had been married the day before. No work was accomplished that day! The colored extras played a card game they call cooncan. Clark and Vivien settled down to a dignified (they hoped) game of Hop Ching. Intellectual extras had a go at backgammon. There was one table of bridge, one of hearts and one of draw poker. 'Nice festive honeymoon atmosphere,' said Clark, with his famous grin." Hall, "Gone With the Wind: On the Set with Gladys Hall," p. 70.

[3]Haller had replaced Lee Garmes. Ron Haver wrote in *David O. Selznick's Hollywood* (p. 272): "Selznick got rid of the last of his lingering dissatisfactions when he removed Lee Garmes as director of photography, replacing him with Ernest Haller . . . Garmes commented: 'It was very sad. I didn't want to leave the picture. I loved the story and I was very friendly with David, but he just didn't quite understand the softer shades and tones that we were able to get with the new faster stock, so we agreed to disagree.' "

[4]Several passages in Kurtz's journals tell of his trips with Harold Coles, Selznick's manager of properties, to find antiques of all sorts for the sets of *Gone With the Wind*. In his journal for 7 January 1939 ("Technical Adviser," p. 120), he noted a visit to Joe Weisberge's First Street Furniture Store in Los Angeles: "This genial personage began stocking hand props for G W T W some thirty-five years ago! The first thing I saw on entering was the slave bell at Tara. Before we got away we saw hanging lamps, Frank Kennedy's stove (at the store), complete equipment for a plantation blacksmith shop, tools for the negro labor battalion, iron clothes pots, big coffee pots for the barbecue, wooden tubs with proper stave handles, baskets (among them the one Scarlett carried when she went to look for vegetables), wheelbarrows, hospital beds, plows, and I don't know what else—unless 'twas the cast-iron teakettle Kennedy kept on his potbellied stove."

[5]Hall wrote of the work on 5 April: "Vivien passed her first 'stunt' test today. She took a post-graduate course in daredeviltry which made hardened stunt men gasp. The scene was one of the many incredible scenes of the evacuation of Atlanta. Horses and wagons were careening at full tilt down the street. And only the hoop-skirts which Vivien wore saved her. For, refusing to permit a double to run this danger, Vivien dashed sure-footedly between the galloping teams. A horse reared toward her. She stopped abruptly, and her heavy hoop-skirt flared up, making the horse shy off—and a star was saved!" "Gone With the Wind: On the Set with Gladys Hall," p. 71.

[6]The roster of personnel of Selznick International Pictures of 24 September 1938 listed William Cameron Menzies as Art Director, and Lyle B. Wheeler as Assistant Art Director. The credits for the film say "The production designed by William Cameron Menzies" and "Art direction by Lyle Wheeler."

[7]Selznick, as already noted, had very strong ideas about color and how it could make dramatic points. Haver quotes him (*David O. Selznick's Hollywood*, p. 273) concerning the Technicolor consultants: "The Technicolor experts are here for the purpose of guiding us technically . . . and not for the purpose of dominating the creative side of our picture as to sets, costumes, or anything else."

In 1939 Technicolor was still relatively new. In his memo concerning color, on 13 March, Selznick wrote: "I cannot conceive how we could have been talked into throwing away opportunities for magnificent color values in the face of our own rather full experience in Technicolor, and in the face particularly of such experiences as the beautiful color values we got out of Dietrich's costumes in *The Garden of Allah*, thanks to the insistence of Dietrich and [wardrobe designer Ernest] Dryden, and despite the squawks and prophecies of doom from the Technicolor experts. . . .

"Examine the history of color pictures: the one thing that is still talked about in *Becky Sharp* is the red capes of the soldiers as they went off to Waterloo. What made *La Cucaracha* a success and did so much for the Technicolor company were the colors as used by [stage and screen designer Robert Edmond] Jones for his costumes. . . .

"I know from talking to Walter Plunkett that no one feels as badly about the limitations that have been imposed upon him as he does. But if we are going to listen entirely to the Technicolor experts, we might as well do away entirely with the artists that are in our own Set and Costume Departments and let the Technicolor company design the picture for us. The result will be the unimpressive pictures that have been made in color by contrast with new and startling color combinations such as we achieved in *The Garden of Allah* and such as I hoped we were going to vastly improve upon in *Gone With the Wind.*" Selznick, *Memo*, pp. 198-99.

Selznick was justified with the fine reception the color work in *Gone With the Wind* received from critics and public. *The New Yorker*, which had reviewed *Gone With the Wind* unfavorably as a novel, gave the film as a whole an, at best, equivocal review. In that review, however, John Mosher declares: "Technicolor has never made a screen so opulent before. Its ruddy and atmospheric hues contribute, perhaps for the first time in movie history, to the action of the story. Here anyhow, Technicolor is a triumph." *The New Yorker* 15:46 (30 December 1939): 47.

SEVEN
18 April—30 April 1939

Macon Telegraph, 18 April 1939

Straight From HOLLYWOOD

Scenes Are Made of War Between the States

HOLLYWOOD, Calif.—A chilling wind blew over Culver City one day during the past week, and it was cold enough to light the heaters on Stage 14 where we were working. But in spite of the temperature, I felt warm; for we were shooting some *GWTW* scenes of the War Between the States and the sequence was dated summertime. So the Confederate soldiers in the hospital quarters provided by kindhearted Atlantans were provided with perspiration and fans and the effect of heat was created so effectually at Selznick International that I could scarcely refrain from borrowing a fan from one of the nurses.

They were a sorry-looking lot, those Confederate soldiers with their ragged uniforms, worn-out shoes and with beards of many days' growth on their faces. Just as the real Confederates were in the latter days of the war when clothing was almost unobtainable, so were the men enacting the roles of wounded Confederates in the scenes we shot.

In fact, I felt so sorry for the poor fellows that I almost offered to help Dr. Meade with his work.

Dr. Meade (Harry Davenport) looked exactly like he ought to look—as if he stepped out of the pages of Margaret Mitchell's novel—and he carried a thermometer and a stethoscope of the period of the sixties as he tended the wounded.

One of the wounded soldiers, whose leg was in a home-made splint and was suspended in a sling fastened to a piece of scantling, was wearing a pair of burgundy socks. Well, I almost had a spasm trying to find a moment when Victor Fleming could listen to me. When I did get a chance to speak, I said the man couldn't be wearing such whole or such modern-looking socks.

"Go away, Susan! Don't bother me. All you do is give me trouble," said Vic sternly.

I looked my amazement and he broke into a teasing grin:

"Don't worry, Susan," he said, "the man's feet don't show in this shot."

Then he turned back to the camera crew, gave some directions and presently called to the suffering Confederates:

"All right, boys! Groans and moans now. Let's have some more sweat and blood and make this shot before Susan finds something to complain about."

And this incident I tell to show you that we do have fun making the picture though the days are long and the grind goes on. Somebody always livens up the day with wise cracks. As Eric often does by calling out after a take is finished:

"All right! boys, it's a new deal," which is to say it is time for a new setup.

One day we had a sort of hash, picking up little bits that had been left over on other days. We shot part of the hospital scene on Stage 14, made a new setup on Stage 12 for some scenes with Prissy, looking for Rhett Butler, and then shot a scene of Rhett Butler at the barbecue.

Moving the camera so much necessitated rather long waits[1] so the make-up men and some of the property men and Clark Gable and some of the rest of us hired help had a lot of fun with tricks. Clark is a favorite with the men on the set and no wonder.[2] He is so good natured about things. One of the men started off by bringing a paper and pencil to Clark, asking for an autograph.

Clark, always obliging, took the pencil and paper and started to write his name. The pencil was the sort that you screw the end to let the point down and Clark twisted the pencil for more point.

"Pop!" came a noise like a cap pistol and Clark jumped a foot and joined the shouts of laughter that came from the crowd.

Before the day was over a dozen of us bit on the same gag, too. I was so proud to be asked for an autograph that I was a little shamefaced to discover it was just a joke.

But the crowd had fun with their tricks. One of the make-up men used to be a magician in vaudeville and he is full of tricks. He can put cards up his sleeve while you are looking right at him and you never see him do it. And he gave Clark two tiny sponges to hold, one in each hand.

"Now you choose the one you want to keep and I'll take the other," said Ed.

Clark chose the sponge in his left hand, closed his fist tightly and waited. Ed took the sponge from Clark's right hand, pretended to throw it away and it vanished. Then he made passes at Clark's fist and said:

"Open your hand."

Clark opened his hand and there on his palm were two sponges.

None of us ever found out how the trick was done but we made poor Ed repeat it over and over until Vic Fleming called out:

"Quiet!" and started rehearsal.

I must tell you of a remarkable coincidence that occurred when Annie Laurie (Mrs. Wilbur) Kurtz was out driving the other day with friends, who stopped to show her the campus of the University.

Mrs. Kurtz wanted to know something about a building and her friends couldn't tell her so Annie Laurie called to a group of girls who were passing and asked them.

One girl courteously came over to the car and started talking and Mrs. Kurtz said:

"Your voice sounds like a Southerner. Where are you from?"

"Atlanta," answered the girl.

Well, to make the story brief: it turned out the girl, Betty Barlow, was a friend of Annie Laurie Kurtz, Junior, who is now at Wesleyan in Macon, and the two girls had been at prep school together.

I, too, have discovered another Georgian. Dr. P. W. Griffith, who was born and reared at Eatonton, and is living in Los Angeles and practicing medicine here. He and I had a chat over the telephone and he is bringing his wife to meet me soon.

One evening last week I had dinner with some friends who are from England and of course there was talk of the possibility of war and of the Munich pact and Chamberlain.

The daughter of the house had brought over her gas mask with her and showed it to me. I had a creepy feeling when I took the mask from its box and thought of the frightened days the English people must have had when they were fitted with the masks and given their instructions about what to do if London were bombed.

The young Englishwoman showed me too, her copy of the book that was sent to every home in England—a pamphlet that listed the ways English men and women might be of service to their country when war broke out.

My hostess had been secretary to a prominent Britisher for her service bit when the war seemed to be imminent and she told me stories of the work accomplished that filled me with admiration for the preparations made by the English government. With wonderful efficiency the most minute plans were perfected and everything was in readiness in the event of war, declared or undeclared.

Oscar Polk, who is playing the part of Pork, the servant of Gerald O'Hara, in *GWTW*, brought me a copy of the *Chicago Defender*, Negro newspaper of Chicago, so I might read his admirable defense of the picture. There had been some criticism of the play by members of his race and Oscar Polk's defense is intelligent and worthwhile. I quote a part of it:

"I am from the South and am as familiar with Southern traditions as any member of my race. The characters that appear in the picture, Pork, Mammy, Prissy, Uncle Peter, Big Sam and Jeems, are all true to life—all of them could, in fact, have lived. As a race we should be proud that we have risen so far above the status of our enslaved ancestors and be glad to portray ourselves as we once were because in no other way can we so strikingly demonstrate how far we have come in so few years."[3]

And speaking of the colored persons in *GWTW*: I can hardly wait for the picture to be shown so you can laugh at the scenes where Prissy does her stuff. Butterfly McQueen is a good actress and the script writers have done a wonderful job of giving her lines from the book that everybody has enjoyed. Everytime Prissy works in a scene we have a grand time. I know you'll get laughs when you see her in *Gone With the Wind*.

Straight From HOLLYWOOD

Joys of "Going on Location" Experienced by Miss Myrick

CHICO, Calif.—Remember how I said once in this column that I was jealous of the people who talked about "going on location"? Well, here I am on location in northeast California, about a hundred miles from San Francisco and—say—four hundred miles from Los Angeles.

A group of us have come up here to shoot some exterior scenes and we expect to begin work early tomorrow morning.

Meanwhile, Ralph Slosser, one of the assistant directors, told me to "Go take a bath and relax." We arrived at one o'clock in the afternoon and I have nothing to do 'til tomorrow, which seems very strange for me, since I've been accustomed to working every day except Sunday from early morning until late evening.

Yesterday, before I left Culver City, we were shooting on the exciting scene where Scarlett and Melanie with India and others, wait in Melanie's parlor while the political riot is taking place. It is a difficult scene and it took a good deal of time for rehearsal, so I sat and watched the group as they studied the lines and Vic Fleming made plans for shooting.

At nine o'clock, promptly, Vivien Leigh was sitting in her chair on the stage, wearing pink slacks and beside her sat Clark Gable, in a tan flannel coat, tan whipcord jodhpurs, and wearing a burgundy scarf about his neck. Leslie Howard, dressed in light tan pants, a brown and dark-green plaid coat, leaned on a chair, while Olivia de Havilland rocked gently in an old-fashioned rocker. She wore a soft woolly pink suit with a white blouse.

Victor Fleming, in his gray trousers and tweed coat, sat on a corner of the sofa in Melanie's parlor and near him sat Harry Davenport (Dr. Meade) in a tweed suit and a navy beret that gave a Puckish look to his face and seemed to belie his silver hair.

It seemed strange to see the cast in other clothes than costumes for I have grown so accustomed to hoop skirts and Jim-swinger coats and Confederate uniforms that I can scarcely recognize our principals in street clothes.

It is hard to decide which color is most becoming to Vivien Leigh. When she wears green (as she does often in *Gone With the Wind*) I think it suits her best; then she appears in pink slacks and I am sure that is just her color. But the other evening when I had dinner at her house, she wore a soft blue trailing gown and I just knew that was the loveliest of all colors for her.

The dinner at her house was very exciting and thoroughly delightful, too. Will Price, dialogue assistant, who is from Mississippi, had sent Vivien a country-cured ham and we talked a lot about country hams and I told of how Mary, Mr. W. T. Anderson's cook, had gone to Atlanta to teach the Henry Grady [Hotel] chef just how a ham could be cooked to bring out the best in it. Of course we argued about the respective merits of hams from various parts of the country and the way I finally shut up Will Price (who was boasting about Mississippi) was to remind him of a line in *Gone With the Wind* where some one speaks of a "coarse Westerner from Mississippi."

Sidney Howard was a guest at Miss Leigh's party and he is lots of fun. For that matter, everybody was fun, and the gowns worn by the women were enchanting to my country-girl eyes.

There was Isabel Jeans, English actress, who wore a gown of black crepe with a burgundy cummerbund and whose dyed fox furs were so lovely I could scarcely keep from trying to take them home with me by mistake. Ann Mercedes wore a frock of silver cloth, made in monk-robe style, caught about her slender waist with a silver belt studded with semi-precious stones. There was another gown, too exciting for words, too. It was worn by a pretty dark-eyed girl, whose name I never learned and it was a fascinating shade of dull pink with the tiniest of fluted pipings of black and white checked taffeta.

But I must get back to Northern California. The bus picked us up at Selznick's at six yesterday evening and we had a gay time, singing like co-eds on a trip with the football team, on the way to Glendale where we took the train. We had dinner on the Southern Pacific and then crowded into the club car to listen to the returns on the Roper-Louis fight. (I had picked "sixth round, Louis," out of the hat!) Then to bed.

I woke at 8:30 this morning, thinking there must be some mistake or maybe it was Sunday. But, no! we were merely going on location.

Just as I finished dressing Ralph Slosser knocked on the compartment door and said we were coming into Sacramento and if I'd hurry he would take me to see the city. I hurried.

We had a half-hour's ride over the capital of California and it is a city quite different from anything I ever saw. Many of the homes in the older section of the city are of the gay nineties era, with gingerbread trimmings, but they are enchanting because of the riot of flowers everywhere. Purple iris, enormous pansies, gay tulips, bright poppies of every shade, scarlet sage and roses, roses, roses! The roses are everywhere, growing in beds, climbing on the sides of houses, sprawling over trellises and growing into trees.

Twice, as we rode along, I exclaimed with pleasure and surprise at seeing a house that looked like it might have been built in Macon or Savannah in the fifties—houses with pillars reaching to the second story and with iron-grill balconies. But most of the older houses were frame dwellings with outside stairways and many little cupolas and balconies that looked very strange and interesting.

The capitol is handsome and of white marble and looks about like the one in Atlanta, with its dome and greening lawns. There are magnolia trees and magnificent oaks and a few palmetto palms and in the park that occupies the adjoining block are hundreds of brilliant flowers.

Back to the station we drove, passing the baseball park and the almost completed Roaring Camp, which occupies two blocks and is to be the scene of the anniversary celebration for Sacramento next month when the city is a hundred years old.

Past Sutter's Fort, built a hundred years ago to protect the white seekers of gold from attack, we drove and presently we were again on the train, headed for Chico.

I saw my first almond trees and beautiful they are, in straight rows, like the Georgia peach orchards, but standing much taller than peach trees. Fig orchards, hop vines, grape vineyards and long stretches of grain fled past the windows and along the sides of the railroad track were thousands of yellow California poppies and myriads of lavender-blue lupine.

Far away, in the distance, we could see the snow-capped mountains and closer to us the blue-shadowed foothills. This is indeed a beautiful part of the United States.

And there was one touch that was so homey and fine I must tell you about it. As we passed a small town and the train slowed up a little, I looked out and saw, lying on the lush grass near the tiny depot, a man in overalls, arm thrown over his eyes and obviously enjoying the warm spring sun. His right leg was thrown over his left knee and sticking up in the air was a bare foot.

I envied him and I had a brief wave of homesickness at the sight of his pose of complete ease.

You see, we keep so busy shooting on *Gone With the Wind* that there is practically no time for ease out here.

I had Sunday dinner with John Marsh's sister, Sunday, and it was so pleasant to be once more in college atmosphere. Dr. Bowden (John Marsh's brother-in-law) is professor of anthropology at the University of Southern California and the other guests at dinner were Dr. Garland Grever and his wife. Dr. Grever visited Macon last fall, gathering material on Sidney Lanier, about whom he is writing a book. While in Macon, Dr. Grever met the R. L. Andersons, Mrs. Walter Lamar, Oliver Orr and others and he recalled names and places and talked about Macon like an old-timer.

He spoke in the kindest terms of Macon and said nowhere had he found people so helpful and accommodating. Naturally, I beamed and purred and felt very proud of my home town.

And then he began talking about Milledgeville and I purred all over again. He remembered the Sidney Lanier room at Dr. Allen's sanitorium and spoke of how lovely the old capitol is and how handsome are the buildings at GSCW.

All-in-all, it was a most delightful day for me; for the Bowdens are charming and Southern and I felt so much like a part of the family. And more proud than ever of Georgia and *Gone With the Wind*.

Macon Telegraph and News, 30 April 1939

Straight From HOLLYWOOD

Clouds Finally Come and Crew Gets Artistic Camera Shots

HOLLYWOOD, Calif.—The clouds which our unit has been looking for have materialized in soft, beautiful fleeciness and at least this section of Selznick International is feeling good over the progress we are making on *Gone With the Wind*. Chico's mayor or the secretary of the chamber of commerce or somebody has evidently been working on the weather. Anyhow, we needed clouds to make our scenes more artistic.[4]

Or, maybe the clouds have come because Chester Franklin, who is directing our unit, bought four red bandanna handkerchiefs for luck. (No, he doesn't use them all. He gave one to Wilfrid Cline, head cameraman and one to me to help out with the luck.)

To me, a novice in the movie business, it has been vastly funny to watch Cline and Franklin study the skies. They look upward through a little glass, something like a monocle, only dark-colored, and the talk goes something like this:

"Will, I think those clouds are moving to the left and upward, aren't they?"

And Will Cline says: "No Chet, I think they are moving slightly camera-right and downward."

To my untrained eye the clouds are standing stock still, but I keep quiet and Ralph Slosser, assistant to the director, murmurs in my ear:

"Look at the way those clouds are moving. Do they move that direction in Georgia?"

But the funniest of all the remarks was when Chester Franklin looked at the sky in which floated nary a cloud and he said:

"Well, it's too hot to shoot now."

I have found out by this time that something "hot" is something that has too bright a light on it so I realize the "hot sky" is one that is too sun-lit but I still think it's funny to say it's too hot to shoot. Sounds to me like going on a quail hunt and resting until after about four in the afternoon so the birds will not be sleeping in their beds because of the heat of the autumn afternoon.

Anyway, by the time the sun is sinking pretty well toward the horizon and clouds have formed in soft masses the director makes two or three takes and he and Cline survey the skies anxiously between shots.

Then they rush madly to get the camera set up in another location to point toward some more clouds. The property men and the fellows who handle all sorts of heavy boxes and things think nothing of grabbing up everything in sight, rushing madly up a hill and working like hornets to get set right for a cloud formation that looks promising.

For, you see, clouds are worse than time and tide about not waiting for man.

There's another thing that amuses me greatly! It's the way directors and cameramen talk to each other with their hands. I watched Cline and Franklin all week and they never discuss a set-up without illustrating the movements of the camera. I had observed the same thing about Ernest Haller and Vic Fleming back at Culver City.

"We take this angle," begins Will, spreading his hands, palms downward and separating them so they indicate an angle of about forty-five degrees. Then he moves the hands, slowly to left or right and goes on:

"We pan over this way."

And all the time he illustrates with his hands how to "dolly," how to "pan" and how to raise the camera angle.

When I kidded him about it the other day Cline looked at me very intently and murmured:

"Remind me to have you sent back to Macon tomorrow, will you?"

I get ragged considerably about being a technical adviser and I gather from some of the talk that next to the earthworm or maybe the doodle, a technical adviser is about the lowest form of animal life in the eyes of the movie makers. George McNulty, who is our script clerk and a sort of assistant to the director, tells a fine one on technical advising. He was the adviser on *The Informer* several years ago. (He is from Ireland and is as funny as Irishmen are supposed to be.)

George declares a friend of his from London was technical adviser on some picture that showed the cabinet in session at Ten Downing street and the adviser went with the director to look at the set, preparatory to shooting the scene. The adviser was horrified to find cuspidors had been placed beside the chairs for the honorable gentlemen who shared the responsibility of ruling the far-flung British Empire.

"Brass cuspidors!" groaned the adviser, "Oh, how terrible!"

"Terrible! This is awful," echoed the director, "Anybody ought to know better."

And turning to the set-dresser the director growled:

"Get some china cuspidors in here right away!"

One delightful thing about the picture-making business is that they love to tell jokes on themselves. They laugh about the way they treat technical advisers, but at the Selznick studio, I must say, they are very kind to us and they consult me about things in such a manner as to make me feel very important.[5]

As for Wilbur Kurtz, he is practically king of the place.

Max Steiner has been signed to arrange, compose and direct the musical score for *Gone With the Wind*, David O. Selznick has announced.[6] Mr. Steiner did the scores for *Bird of Paradise, Bill of Divorcement, Little Lord Fauntleroy* and others. He won the Academy Award for his score on *The Informer.*

Outside of the fun we have and the plans we make for working and the work we do, the outstanding thing about this location business is the efficiency of the crew. On the studio lot at Selznick International I was continually thinking how amazing it was that every man who worked on *Gone With the Wind* was always about two jumps ahead of anything that might possibly be required.

But up here, more than four hundred miles from the Selznick lot, the crew is even more amazing for its efficiency.

Suppose, for instance, you knew at nine in the morning you had to take thirty people on an overnight train journey at six that evening and you could not fail to do everything necessary because when you're taking a crew on location you have to take along everything you might possibly need. Wouldn't you have a conniption fit?

I remember how I sometimes planned for a supper out in the country, say thirty miles from town, and I would plan and make notes and fume and worry for fear I'd get out in the country and have no salt for the tomatoes or have no flour to fix the chicken for frying. If I had the responsibility that assistant directors and property men and camera crews have, I think I'd worry myself into an early grave.

As for me, I had only to bring some clothes and my typewriter. But since I've been here, there has been plenty to do.

In spare moments, however, I have seen some of the sights of Chico, chief of which is the magnificent tree which stands near here that the enterprising chamber of commerce has labeled the "largest oak in the world." Maybe it is. When I first heard about it I was inclined to scoff, remembering the huge old oak at Brunswick and the wonderful oak at Charleston. But when I saw this one at Chico I had to acknowledge it looked to me like the biggest one.

The oak stands 101 feet tall and its graceful limbs spread over an area that has been computed as large enough to shelter 7,780 persons, allowing two feet of standing room for each person.

The head cameraman with this unit is Wilfrid Cline and he has been everywhere and seen everything so I plague him to tell me about places and scenes and shots he has made. He made an early serial of Tarzan, in the days of silent movies, and he has spent eight months in New Zealand, shooting things for the movies, and he thinks Tahiti is the loveliest spot in the world.

Some people seem to have luck and he is one of the lucky ones. He was sent to Tahiti to make some test shots for a possible movie (which may be made some day) and spent gorgeous hours lying on beaches and admiring scenery as well as many interesting hours in a diving helmet walking on the floor of the ocean to hunt for the most beautiful scenes. I never have quite understood how they did it, but they water-proofed the camera and took it under water, too.

Of course, the stuff was Technicolor (I say "of course" because by now you must have realized we are shooting *Gone With the Wind* in Technicolor) and Cline, with the artist's eye for coloring, describes the underwater scenes in a way to make you wish you were a mermaid.

I have made up my mind to advise every youngster, who is trying to make up his mind about a vocation, to be a cameraman. It takes years of training and study but it certainly would prove a fascinating way to make a living and provide possible trips (at the expense of the producer) to all sorts of places in the world.

I had the shock of my life the other day at the Oaks Hotel in Chico when I walked into the lobby after a day's work and found Lee Hutchins sitting there. Dr. Hutchins, who was for many years at Fort Valley, investigating the diseases of peaches, is now working on some sort of disease that cherry trees have developed in California.

Another Georgia contact has given me considerable joy here in the north of California. Charles A. Clifford, who lived for seven years in Macon, back in the late eighties and early nineties, called me the other day (he had seen in the local paper that I was here) and asked if he could come by the hotel to see me.

Mr. Clifford, a native of Massachusetts, visited his cousin, Walter B. Hill, in Macon. Everybody in Georgia, of course, knows that Walter Hill was at one time chancellor of the University of Georgia and Mr. Clifford was pleased that I recognized the name at once.

He told me how he came to Macon to visit a few weeks and stayed seven years, which I think is a marvelous tribute to Macon's hospitality. He said he got his first surprise in Macon when he rode horseback downtown on the 26th of April and saw floating over the Confederate monument a strange flag.

He puzzled over it a while, then went to his cousin's office (the firm of Hill, Harris and Birch) and asked about it. That was the first time Charles Clifford ever saw the Confederate flag or knew that Memorial Day was celebrated on any day but May 30.

The young Massachusetts boy became charmed with Macon and when his cousin suggested Charles should stay there and learn a trade, the boy acquiesced readily. At the jewelry store of George Beeland, he began working and stayed there for seven years. Among the boys who also learned a trade at Beeland's, Mr. Clifford remembers was Guy Armstrong.

One day Charles Clifford, interested in Macon's history, went to the library and asked for permission to see the old files of the *Macon Telegraph and Messenger*. He explained he was from Massachusetts and wanted to look up some history of the war.

The librarian curtly refused to let the boy see the files. Charles reported this strange incident to his cousin Walter Hill at dinner time and Mr. Hill laughed heartily.

"Your approach was wrong," he said, "next time, don't tell the librarian you are from Massachusetts. Just say you are a cousin of Walter B. Hill, visiting here, and you'll get whatever you want."

Mr. Clifford is greatly interested in *Gone With the Wind* and says he knows it will be the most important picture ever made.

I think he's right; at that!

[1]Lydia Schiller, Selznick's principal assistant in charge of the script ("production continuity" is the phrase in the credits) recalls: "The camera rehearsals were what took so long. The lighting, steadying the camera, just moving that Technicolor camera was a massive operation, and Mr. Selznick did like his moving camera shots." Haver, *David O. Selznick's Hollywood*, p. 273.

[2]Ridgeway Callow recalled Gable's work on the set: "He worked well with everybody, but the crew didn't like him. I know at MGM they were supposed to be crazy about him, but they were not at Selznick. He was very aloof." Haver, *David O. Selznick's Hollywood*, p. 273.

Myrick remembered differently. She always had praise for Gable. In a 1974 article she wrote: "Clark was a 'sweet' man, generous with his time and kindliness; everybody on the GWTW sets adored him—hairdressers, makeup men and women, electricians, grips, cameramen—everybody. He could do no wrong." "Forty Years of 'Such Interesting People,' " *Atlanta Journal and Constitution Magazine*, 8 September 1974, pp. 44, 47.

[3]There had been considerable criticism of *Gone With the Wind* in the Negro and leftist press. David Platt wrote in *The Daily Worker* (New York), 29 October 1936: "Miss Mitchell's pretty story deals with the Reconstruction Period of the Civil War and among other things glorifies the Ku Klux Klan and slaveocracy, defends lynch law as a protective measure against the barbarous Blacks, hurls insults by the yard at Negro people and at the scandalous North for setting them free, and all in all gives as complete and deliberate a misreading of history as Thomas Dixon's 'The Klansman,' [sic] which David Wark Griffith embodied in 'The Birth of a Nation' back in 1915." Platt declared that Booker T. Washington called for protests against Griffith's film. "Today, 1936," said Platt, "the danger of a Klan film is infinitely greater. 'Gone With the Wind' was read by tens of thousands of people who were persuaded by the contemptible bourgeois literary hacks that the book is a masterpiece of literary genius. The film if it is made will be seen by tens of millions who may be even more misled by smooth direction and color into accepting for gospel truth this vicious libel on the Negro people.

"The film must be stopped. The Klan must not ride again."

Writing from Hollywood for the Associated Negro Press, Ruby Berkeley Goodwin filed a story that was published in the *Atlanta World* on 12 February 1939. "It is with decided relief," she wrote, "that I can report from no higher authority than George Cukor, director for the opus, that the objectionable term 'n——-' which was used a thousand times (to put it at a moderate figure) by Miss Mitchell, has been cut entirely from the script of 'Gone With the Wind.' Only in a very few instances will the term 'darkey' be allowed.

"Not only will all objectionable terms be omitted but the picture will present Negro characters in lovable, intelligent roles. They will speak dialect, of course. It must be remembered that prior to the Civil War very few Negroes spoke anything else. . . .

"Readers may be surprised to learn that many of the characters were given contracts upon the final O.K. of Susan Merrick [*sic*], technical adviser, who is Miss Mitchell's representative in Hollywood. Miss Merrick has insisted on the actors maintaining dignity.

"She explained this to the studio executives when she said one day in conference: 'In the finer southern homes, the servants are not expected to be clowns. They reflect the dignity of the people they work for. Many people without a southern background do not know that this distinction exists. Many times, the Negroes, though in the capacity of servants, actually ran the estates, attended to much of the business, and treated their bosses as though they were children.' "

Hall Johnson was a black musician from Georgia who worked in *Gone With the Wind*. In writing to Myrick on 17 April 1939, Margaret Mitchell thanked her for writing in her letter of 9 April that Johnson "thought G W T W was good and that it made him 'unhappy that some of his race failed so miserably to understand it and criticized the black and white angle' of it."

Mitchell continued: "I do not need to tell you how I and all my folks feel about Negroes. We've always fought for colored education and, even when John and I were at our worst financially, we were helping keep colored children in schools, furnishing clothes and carfare and, oh, the terrible hours when I had to help with home work which dealt in fractions. I have paid for medical care and done the nursing myself on many occasions; all of us have fought in the law courts and paid fines. Well, you know what I mean, you and your people have done the same thing. The colored people I know here in Atlanta had nothing but nice things to say, especially the older ones. Shortly after the book came out the Radical and Communistic publications, both black and white, began to hammer, but all they could say was that the book was 'an insult to the Race.' For two years they could not think up any reason why. I asked a number of Negroes and they replied that they did not know either but guessed it was some Yankee notion. The Radical press tried to use 'Gone With the Wind' as a whip to drive the Southern Negroes into the Communist Party somewhat in the same manner that 'Uncle Tom's Cabin' was used to recruit Abolitionists. Of course you know how happy it made me to have the Radical publications dislike 'Gone With the Wind.' I couldn't have held up my head if they had liked it, but the Negro angle bothered me, for Heaven knows I had and have no intention of 'insulting the Race.' Recently the Negro press has discovered the way in which they have been insulted. It is because I had various characters use the terms 'nigger' and 'darkey.' I am enclosing a couple of clippings on this subject for your interest, and I'd like to have them back when you have finished reading them. Regardless of the fact that they call each other 'nigger' today and regardless of the fact that nice people in ante bellum days called them 'darkies,' these papers are in a fine frenzy. I am wondering if they think I should have been inaccurate and had 1860 characters refer to them as 'The Race' or 'Race Members.' I have had enough twisted and erroneous and insulting things written about me and 'Gone With the Wind' to make me sore on the whole Negro race if I were sensitive or a fool. But I do not intend to let any number of trouble-making Professional Negroes change my feelings toward the race with whom my relations have always been those of affection and mutual respect. There are Professional Negroes just as there are Professional Southerners and, from what I can learn from Negroes I have talked to, they are no more loved by their race than Professional Southerners are by us. If you see Hall Johnson again please give him my very sincere thanks for his words."

Neither Myrick nor Mitchell realized that, though their attitudes towards blacks were genuinely kind and generous, they represented a kind of race relations that by the late 1930s Negro leaders regarded as degrading, patronizing, or—at best—paternalistic. The attitude of militant blacks was reflected in a long and damning review of *Gone With the Wind* that Carlton Moss, a black dramatist, wrote for the *Daily Worker* of 9 January 1940 as "An Open Letter to Mr. Selznick."

"Whereas 'The Birth of a Nation' was a frontal attack on American history and the Negro people," said Moss, " 'Gone With the Wind,' arriving twenty years later is a rear attack on the same. Sugar-smeared and blurred by a boresome Hollywood love story and under the guise of presenting the South as it is in the 'eyes of the Southerner,' the message of 'Gone With the Wind' emerges in its final entity as a nostalgic plea for sympathy for a still living cause of Southern reaction."

Moss wrote of the parts played by Blacks: "As to the principal Negro characters, they follow the time-worn stereotype pattern laid down by Hollywood. There is shiftless and dull-witted Pork, young Prissy, indolent and thoroughly irresponsible, 'Big' Sam with his radiant acceptance of slavery, and Mammy with her constant haranguing and doting on every wish of Scarlett. It is made to appear that she loves this degrading position in the service of a family that has helped to keep her people enchained for centuries. This false collection of two-dimensional characters is insulting to the Negro people."

⁴The principal mission of the trip was to film Gerald O'Hara's riding scenes. Myrick does not mention this as it was Carey Harrison, not Thomas Mitchell, who was to do the riding. She quoted Mitchell in her diary on 29

June as saying (not necessarily on that date): "I hate snakes, and I'm scared of rats too [and] if I had my way I'd never go near a damned horse."

[5]Myrick had felt relations with several of the SIP staff, particularly with Walter Plunkett, constrained during her first days on the studio's sets. As early as 13 January she noted in her diary: "Talked with Eddie Boyle who gave me a new slant on technical advisers! He said when Platt came to do sets he (Eddie) was scared to death and soon found to his delight Platt was human and fine. Then I said everybody is so fine and he said 'Christ! we like human beings. You just don't know. The technical experts who have come out here and told us how to run our business have been terrible.'

"Then I realized they expected me to be a butt and they are pleased that I am not. S'funny. I was scared of them and they were scared of me."

[6]Selznick noted in a memo of 8 March 1939 that his choice to do the score for *Gone With the Wind* was Max Steiner (Selznick, *Memo*, p. 193). Lou Forbes, SIP's Music Director, handled the questions and problems connected with music during the filming. Steiner's employment had been arranged before the completion of the film, but he did not begin his work till later.

On 14 August Selznick wrote his Vice President and General Manager, Henry Ginsberg: "In my opinion, Max Steiner should go on our payroll immediately and should start composing all his themes and selecting his basic music for 'Gone With the Wind.' Bear in mind that the scoring job on the picture is, if only because of its length, exactly twice as big an undertaking as any other picture, and also that no matter how much we speed up Max, obviously we can't overcome what will be his natural desire to do the greatest score ever written, and I don't even think that we should try to overcome this—so that this also means extra time." Haver, *David O. Selznick's Hollywood*, p. 298.

EIGHT
5 May—14 May 1939

Straight From HOLLYWOOD

Back from Location, Sue Finds Much Work Done on Picture

HOLLYWOOD, Calif.—Back in Hollywood seems sort of like homecoming after two weeks on location.

When I got into Glendale Monday morning I didn't even stop to eat breakfast but hurried on to the studio in Culver City to find out what was going on and what had happened since I left. Of course, I knew that Victor Fleming was on sick leave and that Sam Wood was directing in his stead, but I wanted to find out what else had happened.

Over on Stage 3 I found the company shooting scenes for *Gone With the Wind* as calmly as if neither Victor Fleming nor I had ever been away.

But how Tara had changed!

When last I saw the lovely old Southern home it was clean and beautiful but now the scenes were those after Sherman's march and broken windows, torn plastering, furniture that had been badly mistreated, and other signs indicated the depredations that came with De Wah.

Vivien Leigh, dressed in a frock that looked as if it had actually been worn for three years and worn for hard work at that, was telling Mammy about the difficulties of raising the tax money to save Tara.

The story of Scarlett's frock worn in the after-war sequences is astonishing to me, unaccustomed to movie doings. Since Technicolor shows with astounding accuracy actual conditions, it was necessary to get the aging of that dress just right. You see, Scarlett appears to wear out a dress right before the eye of the camera. So: it was necessary to make fifteen dresses, each one a little more worn than the one preceding; for we couldn't actually expect Vivien to wear out the dresses for us![1]

Under the direction of Edward Lambert and Marian Dabney, of the studio wardrobe, Mrs. Mary Madden did the aging of the dresses. She specializes in breaking down clothing and with knives, steel combs, sandpaper and all sorts of things she makes a dress look older than Methusaleh in no time at all.

At intervals during the day Monday, I gathered from various persons the story of what had been done in my absence. Of course I knew part of the story because the studio had telephoned me several times in Chico to ask questions about technical points but I was astounded to find out what a lot of work had been done while I was away. I sort of felt as if the production could not go forward in my absence and my ego got a deserved rebuke at the progress made without me!

Among other things I learned that Scarlett's frock, worn for the birthday reception Melanie gave for Ashley, was one of the handsomest gowns she has had for the picture. By that time, you see, Scarlett is married to Rhett Butler and she has plenty of money, so the dress is very rich-looking. Made of garnet velvet the dress is princess in fashion and has a bustle. With it, Vivien Leigh wore a necklace of garnets and all the folks on the set told me I missed it in a big way when I was gone during the shooting of the birthday party scene.

A new member has been added to the *Gone With the Wind* cast, too, since I went away. Little Mickey Kuhn is playing the role of Beauregard, the son of Melanie and Ashley Wilkes.

In fact, much water has flowed under the bridge since I have been absent two weeks. There are now four units shooting scenes for the picture. Sam Wood, substituting for Vic Fleming,[2] heads the first unit and he is my new boss. But with the second unit at Chico, there are still two more units making shots of exterior scenes and it begins to look as if *Gone With the Wind* is going to be greater even than I had thought.

But I must tell you a little more about our location trip and our search for clouds. While we waited one afternoon I amused myself (and, to a lesser degree, the company) by writting doggerel verses. Here they are, with MY apologies to Lewis Carroll:

> He thought he saw a tiny cloud
>> A-floating way up high
> He looked again and saw it was a
>> hot and shining sky
> "If I don't find some clouds," he said
>> "I think that I shall die."
>
> He thought he saw a wisp of cloud
>> A-lying on the bed
> He looked again and saw it was a
>> pillow there, instead.
> "I WISH that I could find a cloud,"
>> He moaned and shook his head.
>
> He thought he saw a little cloud
>> A-floating in the air
> He looked again and saw, indeed, a
>> cloud WAS floating there.
> "Oh, my!" he cried, "it cannot be!"
>> And pulled out all his hair!

But when the clouds did appear the way we worked was amazing. One morning we got a shot "in the can" before eight o'clock. ("In the can" is Hollywood for saying a lot of film is exposed and ready to go to the Technicolor plant for developing.)

A wild scramble followed the finish of the shot, for while clouds were banked we had to rush to another place where cameraman and director had planned another set-up. Men dismantled the camera, packing it away in its special truck; other men piled equipment into other trucks and wardrobe girls and hair dressers packed things hurriedly and everybody piled into cars or the bus to hasten to the next spot. We got a fine shot about ten o'clock.

During the afternoon we sat beside the third location, talking and playing games while Cameraman Cline and Director Franklin discussed the condition of sky and light. Presently the two men got into a car and drove away.

A group of men pitched horseshoes; others tossed an indoor baseball about; several of us played anagrams. An air of listlessness pervaded the place.

Suddenly Assistant Director Ralph Slosser rushed up in a car and began calling out orders. Franklin had found some clouds over a hill about a mile away and we must get there in a hurry.

A fireman, dressing for the fire call, never made better time than we did.

The way those boys get a camera taken apart, loaded on a truck, unloaded again and set up in the right spot in next-to-nothing-flat is a marvel.

Being on location was fun but it is pleasant, too, to get back and see the old friends at Culver City. Vivien Leigh and Leslie Howard and Olivia de Havilland were all three on the set today, and I was glad, also, to see Hattie McDaniel, who is Mammy, and Oscar Polk, who is playing Pork.

Late this afternoon, I also had a brief chat with Evelyn Keyes (Suellen O'Hara) who was looking very lovely in a pink frock and wearing a fuchsia and pink 'kerchief over her brown hair. She was offering to give away a kitten. Her prize cat had given birth to seven of the fluffy little black things.

Me, I don't want a cat. I'm too busy with *Gone With the Wind* to take on any pets.

Straight From HOLLYWOOD

Movie Work Gets Back to Flight from Atlanta to Old Tara

HOLLYWOOD, Calif.—I declare, we skip around so in shooting a picture that it is a wonder to me the finished product doesn't start at the wrong end and wind from here to there and back again. It seems weeks ago that we were shooting the scenes where Rhett, Scarlett, Melanie, Prissy and the newly-born Beauregard were leaving Atlanta for Tara. Since then we have shot some scenes where the group of women met at Melanie's house to wait for word from the rioting that brought about the death of Frank Kennedy.

And now shooting of *Gone With the Wind* is back once more to the flight of Rhett and Scarlett to Tara.[3]

A day or two ago we made the scene where Scarlett tries to get Ashley to go to Atlanta with her to help her start the sawmill business.

Of course Hal C. Kern, who is film-editor-in-chief, will get it all straight, but it's a mystery to me how he does it.

However, that is not one of my worries. Folks around Selznick International are always kidding each other about "staying in your own department" so I'll stay in mine.

Anyway, it is fun to watch the scenes being made and continuity never worries any of us on the *Gone With the Wind* set; for we know Margaret Mitchell's novel almost by heart by this time and you can scarcely mention a scene that somebody can't tell you the exact page in the book.

It was great fun the other day when we shot a scene that used little Beau Wilkes, about a year-and-a-half. The youngster, Gary Carlson, was making his first appearance before the camera and he was so cunning as he crawled over the top of a table, squirmed about to play with the paper balls the prop man offered him and generally acted like a little gentleman worthy of the name of General Beauregard, while the director got last-minute things ready.

"Quiet! Speed!" called the sound man and Director Sam Wood called "Camera!"

And little Beauregard acted like a veteran as Olivia de Havilland picked him up and went into her scene.

It was an interesting scene from the standpoint of clothing, too. Walter Plunkett did a wonderful job of making the old clothes for the after-the-war sequences look like they ought to look. He even went so far as to take a frock that Carreen wore to the barbecue and combine parts of it with an old piece of taffeta from Aunt Pitty's wardrobe to fashion a skirt for Melanie. Her blouse was an old piece of sacking, obviously homespun.

Suellen and Carreen wore dresses equally made-over and badly worn and both the girls (Evelyn Keyes and Ann Rutherford) laughed a great deal about their shoes made from old pieces of carpet. Over her shoulders Suellen wore a piece of carpet as a shawl, too, and her soft braids were tied with old pieces of string.

"Were people actually that poor?" somebody asks me almost every day on the set. I vehemently avow that they were quite poor and tell the questioners to go back and read the book again.

Each time the questioner shakes his head (or her head) and murmurs, "No wonder Southerners remember the Confederacy."

I am beginning to feel acquainted with Director Sam Wood and it is not hard for me to believe I have known him a long time because he resembles so closely Wallace Miller, attorney, and former mayor of Macon. He has the same sort of piercing brown eyes that are almost black and his hair is grayed through its black and he has something of the same kindly twinkle.

Director Wood is a great football fan and he talked to Vivien Leigh between takes today about the Rose Bowl games of many years and about various of his favorite players. He is greatly grieved because he missed the game last New Year's day, for he was in England making a picture.

But he plans to see the movies of all last year's games at the University of Southern California as soon as he can find time. And until Vic Fleming gets well enough to come back to his job, Mr. Wood will have no spare time, I am sure.

Sidney Howard, who has been here for several weeks, writing on script, has gone back to New York and I miss him a great deal. He loved to talk about the South and about the stage and he told many fascinating stories of plays and players.[4]

Former Governor Al Smith and Mrs. Smith were visitors on the set this week and I almost walked up to the once-candidate-for-president and said:

"How are you Old Potato? Remember, I voted for you that time the Republicans held an election and didn't let the Democrats know it."

Mr. Smith looked so like the pictures of him looked when he ran for president some ten years ago that I should have known him anywhere, even if I had not been told by a dozen persons that he was a visitor on the *Gone With the Wind* set.

Alicia Rhett was with us again this week, too. She worked while I was in Chico, but I hadn't seen her in some time and we had a nice chat. I discovered that Georgia has a new claim, now, on *Gone With the Wind*, for Alicia was born in Savannah, though she is now from Charleston and though she is descended from a distinguished Charleston family. Her grandfather, Col. Alfred Rhett, was commanding officer of Fort Sumter during the time it was held by the Confederacy and served with distinction during the War Between the States.

We have a new sound man on the picture now. He is a brother of Ramon Navarro. Every time I look at him I remember Ramon in *The Pagan*. Strangely enough, I recall very well, too, where I saw that movie. I was spending a weekend in Quitman where I had gone to make a talk to the Woman's Club at the request of Edna Cain Daniel and it was with Edna and Royal Daniel that I saw the picture in Quitman.

There is a lot of talk about the trouble in Europe—and how valuable our motion picture spotlights would be to our military forces. But I am too much fascinated by a thousand other things to bother about what we could do with what, in case of war. So far as I know there has not been, nor will there be, any war but the one we are making a movie of in *Gone With the Wind*.

I forgot to tell you, before; I found Douglas Hume at Chico. He left his card at the desk for me shortly after I arrived and a few days later came in one evening for a chat. He is in charge of dramatics at the State Teachers' College at Chico and he was so busy with rehearsals for *Hamlet* that he had no time evenings. And I had no time in the daylight hours so I only saw Douglas briefly.

Macon Telegraph, 11 May 1939

Straight From HOLLYWOOD

Real Danger Attends Filming of Exciting Scenes for Movie

HOLLYWOOD, Calif.—Many exciting scenes have been made for *Gone With the Wind* during these past weeks; but I think the biggest thrill I have had since I've been here came last week when we were working on Forty Acres on the sequence where Scarlett is searching for Dr. Meade in downtown Atlanta, wanting him to come to Aunt Pitty's to help about the birth of Melanie's son.

Of course, you remember from the book that there was plenty of trouble in Atlanta about that time, with the Federal troops hammering at the doors of the little city, and troops marching toward the front.

In the particular scenes we were shooting, Scarlett was meeting various sorts of troops, as she hurried through the streets to find the doctor. Several times, it appeared to me, the lovely little Vivien Leigh was in a hazardous spot close to the wheels of cannon or the feet of horses. But Eric Stacey and Reggie Callow, assistant directors, assured me everything was so carefully planned and timed that she was actually in no great danger.

As infantry lines marched past, dispirited, tired, dirty, bedraggled, and footsore, Scarlett started across the street. She was stopped by a group of men and women hurrying from the warehouses from which they were bringing free food. Again she darted through the edges of the crowd, finally rushing through just before the troop of cavalry dashed past, followed by caissons drawn by six horses.

Those men who played the roles of cavalrymen were "hand-picked" by the directors for daring and for keeping cool heads in emergencies. So far had the directors gone in their careful planning that the six leading horses of the cavalry were jumpers and the riders were the best to be found. Thus, if Vivien Leigh had by unlucky fortune tripped over her long skirts, the leading horses would have hurdled her prostrate form.

As it happened, Vivien crossed the street safely and there was no need to take any unusual steps for her protection. But one exciting thing did occur.

One of the men, wheeling a barrow of food, heard the horses behind him, saw they were close upon him and leaving his wheelbarrow in the street, ran to the sidewalk. The leading horses jumped the obstruction and thundered on past the cameras.

And the men who ride the caissons! Those men are such good riders that they can put the wheels of a vehicle, drawn by six horses, within two inches of the mark set by the director.

At full gallop, the horses dashed down Decatur Street, and at the intersection, made a right turn into Peachtree, still running as if Sherman was right behind them.

As the guns went around the corner, the wheels of the carriage hit a sandbag in the street and the men riding the carriage bounced high in the air.

I thought they never would come down!

But they did—and hit in the right place on the gun carriage when they landed.

Wilbur Kurtz had worked out for the directors the number of men for the unit. There were thirty men, a captain, a lieutenant, two sergeants, a guidon, and a bugler, who rode separate horses.

Then came four teams of six horses, with twelve men riding; and there were twelve men riding the caissons and guns. Besides these, there were twenty-four cavalrymen; and there were fifteen men on the ox-drawn siege gun.

Red dust flew over the place and when the day was ended everybody—crew, cast, and actors—had turned out to be red-headed.

And speaking of red-heads, I met Ona Munson, our Belle Watling, the other day. Walter Plunkett, costume designer, called me to come to his office to see some clothes for Belle. I found Miss Munson looking very lovely in a dark red velvet dress and a too-red hat trimmed with scarlet plumes.

Miss Munson is quite as charming as one would expect of a girl who has had a long and rigorous training in dramatic art. She is blue-eyed and blonde and is a college graduate with a major in English literature.

Maybe you saw Miss Munson in *Five Star Final.* Or, perhaps you had the good luck to see her on Broadway in *No, No, Nanette*, with Charles Winninger. She also played in *Petticoat Fever*, in New York, the role that Myrna Loy played in the film.

We have been working long hours this week, staying at the studio until ten one evening, and until midnight another evening. With four units at work on the picture, much progress is being made, and the good humor of all who keep long hours is one of the amazing things about this moving picture business.

On the set one day, for instance, a group of us, waiting for the change in camera setup, laughed ourselves sick at Hattie McDaniel, who plays Mammy in *Gone With the Wind.* Hattie was seated in a big chair (it takes a big chair for Hattie's two-hundred-odd pounds) with a pencil and paper in her hands and making the queerest motions, her lips moving the while and her feet, occasionally doing a sort of jig.

"What on earth are you up to, Mammy?" I demanded, my curiosity getting the better of my good manners.

Mammy laughed, her whole soft, big frame shaking the while.

"I'm just writing myself an act for the time I may do a personal appearance," she told me.

Then she eased herself out of the chair and began demonstrating an act she did in a vaudeville tour some months ago. It was fine entertainment, too, I can tell you. With that marvelous smoothness that fat persons often display, Mammy went into a tap dance, humming in her lush contralto voice "Way Down upon de Swanee River."

She turned and she kicked, and she did limping steps and she rolled her eyes, and she demonstrated the ways in which a male chorus does its stuff in a dance routine.

A little later, we were vastly entertained by Oscar Polk, too. Oscar who is (to my mind) the living embodiment of Pork, house servant of the O'Hara family, tried to throw a package of cigarettes to one of the men who roost on a very high catwalk to take care of arc lights for the company.

Oscar, perhaps envious of the attention we had bestowed upon Mammy, assumed poses like baseball players and threw the cigarettes over and over toward the man perched about fifty feet up. Finally, he got the package high enough and right into the hands of the fellow who was suffering for a smoke.

And that wasn't the end of our foolishness.

There is a young man who works in the unit who is about as fat as Fatty Hardy[5] used to be when he jerked soda years and years ago at one of Milledgeville's drug stores. Fact is, the man looks about like Dickens' Fat Boy. He has stringy, red-blond hair and he waddles when he walks and he is always laughing in a schoolgirl giggle.

Red was wearing a blue and white striped sweater the other day, the stripes going around, and a pair of tan britches that were pleated in the latest fashion at the waist line.

"You must have a date, Fat," one of the men kidded him.

"Oh, no," shrugged Fat. "These are just my campus togs."

Somehow the idea of Fats in campus togs was too much for us, and we laughed until we were weak.

Fat pulled another good one, too. Some visitor on the set was pointed out as a very rich man and Fat took a look at him.

"What has he got that I haven't got?" he shrugged. Then cocking an eyebrow, he added:

"Except my room rent?"

There is much activity around the lot at Selznick International Pictures these days; for in addition to our four units working on *Gone With the Wind*, plans are under way for starting another production right soon. David O. Selznick will produce next *Intermezzo*, starting late this month, with Leslie Howard as the leading man and acting, also, as associate producer.

Work is going on, too, toward the production of *Rebecca*, which will be directed by Alfred Hitchcock, winner of New York critics' award for the best direction of 1938. Mr. Hitchcock is a rotund gentleman with a keen sense of humor, and he waddles around the lot with a grin on his plump face much of the time.

And while we are on the subject of fun about the studio, I must tell you one of the wisecracks pulled by Reggie Callow, assistant director.

Reggie was reading the scene in the script where Scarlett shoots the Yankee officer. Directions indicated that the Yankee officer would bleed considerably and Reggie pointed it out to me:

"Here is a fine place for a little comic relief," he said in his best Shakespearean manner. "At this point, Prissy can come trucking in singing 'Gory, Gory, Hallelujah!'"

Well, it's a fine thing the way the folks can laugh about things. Otherwise, we would be too depressed to work these days while we are shooting such sad scenes as those when Scarlett comes back to Tara to find her mother is dead and the Yankees have wrought utter destruction.

I know Uncle Remus warned that it was a mistake to prognosticate and avowed you'd usually have to chew up your words and spit them out, nevertheless, I am bold enough to prophesy that Vivien Leigh, as Scarlett O'Hara, is going to receive the greatest acclaim ever given a film actress.

And in addition to that, I prophesy that critics and public are going to say Olivia de Havilland gives not only the finest, but the most colorful performance of her career when they see *Gone With the Wind.*

Macon Telegraph and News, 14 May 1939

Straight From HOLLYWOOD

Gloom, Tears and Fun Still Mingle in Making of GWTW Movie

HOLLYWOOD, Calif.—Gloom, tears, snifflings and long faces pervaded the *Gone With the Wind* set at Selznick International the first of the week because we were still shooting the sad scenes where Scarlett returns to Tara to find everything ruined, nothing to eat, her sisters sick and her mother dead.

But more gaiety came the next day when Scarlett shot the Yankee standing at the foot of the stairs.[6] While our unit worked on those scenes, another unit, headed by Bill Menzies, made some close-ups of Belle Watling and some of her girls.[7] Ona Munson, as Belle Watling, wearing a bright purple frock and a scarlet hat trimmed in red roses, charmed everybody with her laughter and friendliness.

But the thing that made the first part of the week a huge success was the visit we had from Vic Fleming, who is feeling better and came over to see how things were progressing.

Last Sunday was a day to make even Californians boastful of the weather. The sun shone bright and hot and the breeze was just cool enough to make a coat feel comfortable.

With some friends I drove to the beach and watched the people who swam. That is, they didn't swim much. It was still too cold to do much playing in the Pacific. Most of the bathers shivered themselves into the water for a few minutes then came out to run up and down the beach, turn handsprings, dig frog houses, build sand castles and eat lunches.

We had a sea-food lunch and I never knew before that fresh salmon, broiled and served with lots of lemon-butter could be such a marvelous dish. Up to now, I have known salmon only as it comes in cans.

Fresh salmon and canned salmon are as far apart in flavor as are the peaches one buys in New York from the fresh, deep-ripe ones we buy in Georgia.

And I must tell you about roads in Southern California. I never saw anything like them before. I mean from two standpoints.

First, they are all four-lane roads or six-lane roads or eight-lane roads. They have to be. Thousands of cars run over them all the time and if the roads were two-lane roads nobody would ever get where he was going.

It scared me to death when I first started driving out here to have cars passing me on both sides. But I got accustomed to it and drive as nonchalantly as if I were on Cherry Street.

And the way the streets and the roads twist themselves in strange direction is another thing unusual about them. You start out on a street that runs due east, thinking it is the way you want to go. First thing you know, the street has headed south by southeast and presently it is running due south. And just as likely as not, it changes and goes southwest in a few more blocks.

Street names in Los Angeles had me completely stymied for a while, too. How to pronounce La Cienega, for instance, puzzled me greatly and I asked a filling station man how to get to La Canada Street and he said he never heard of it.

I called it as it looked to me—Canada, like the dominion to the north of the United States.

After some discussion the filling station man exclaimed:

"Oh! You mean La Canada" and he pronounced it with the Spanish do-funny over the "n" as in "canyon."

"Oh! You mean La Canyada!"

A fine name I saw the other day on a station wagon downtown. I haven't the faintest idea whose wagon it is but I'd like to know who was clever enough to think up the name, which was:

"Rancho En Escrow."

Wilbur Kurtz was telling me the other day about the Confederate rifles we have used for *Gone With the Wind*. Five hundred of them were required, Wilbur said, and the need set in motion a search that ended in the exploration of almost every gun collection and antique armorer's stock in Southern California.

Some museum pieces and a few treasured old guns from the South were loaned, or leased to Harold Coles, Selznick International property man, after Wilbur had checked them and authorized their use.

A percussion cap muzzle-loader was the standard gun for the War Between the States, according to Kurtz, and the ammunition was a waxed paper cartridge, consisting of a fixed charge of black powder and a lead bullet tied together with a heavy thread.

Before the cartridge was rammed down in the gun the rifleman had to bite a piece off the breech end so the sparks from the percussion cap could ignite the powder charge.

Wilbur declared a recruiting officer would first look at a man's teeth to make sure he could bite off a cartridge. A soldier might lack an arm or a leg, but he had to have teeth, Wilbur said.

Katharine Brown called me on the set the first of the week. Of course Georgians remember Katharine with the blond hair and the charming manner, who came down to Atlanta and to Macon, more than two years ago, in a search for talent for *Gone With the Wind*. Katharine, who is with the New York office of Selznick International, is visiting the West Coast on business.

She talked gaily of the fun she had in Georgia and said she found the state a marvelous place for hospitality and kindness.

You should have seen the faces Vivien Leigh made when she first found she had to drink corn whiskey from a gourd. You know how gourds smell when they are not yet fully dried. Well, in the scene with Gerald O'Hara, after Scarlett comes home to find her mother dead, you remember Scarlett takes a drink. And she wrinkled her pretty nose and shrugged her shoulders when she raised the gourd to her lips in rehearsal.

But when I told her water tasted better from a gourd than anything else and Hattie McDaniel (Mammy) agreed with me, she drank a man-sized drink from the gourd and the scene went on smoothly.

Vivien Leigh is the most enthusiastic person I ever saw. She puts her whole self into everything she does. Even to playing games. You remember how I wrote of her ability at "The Game." Well, she plays anagrams or what-have-you with equal ability and enthusiasm.

The other day she asked me to come into her bungalow between scenes and play "Sinking Battleships."

I don't know who started it on the set but the battleship game is very popular right now with all of us. You probably played it when you were a child. You make ten squares each way on a sheet of paper, so you have a hundred squares in all, place one battleship, two cruisers, two destroyers and one submarine in whatever squares you choose and then your opponent tries to sink your fleet by guessing what squares you have marked.

Well, Vivien beat me every game and she would get so excited when we were each reduced to one ship and be as enthusiastic as any child over sinking my whole fleet before I could sink hers.

Eric Stacey would stick his head in the door and call "All right, Fiddle-dee-dee, need you on the set."

And Vivien would reply, "Can't you wait just a minute, Eric, until I have one more turn? I almost have Sue beaten!"

And Eric would answer, "Costing money to wait Vivien, must do!"

Vivien's portable bungalow is the cutest thing you ever imagined. It is a little room, built so it is easily moved to whatever stage she is working on. It has light-tan walls, a dressing table with a mirror, a chaise lounge, two chairs and all the furniture is done in gay rose, blue and tan chintz.

I could hardly keep my mind on Sinking Battleships because of the lovely vase of deep pink roses and delphinium on a tiny table in one corner of the bungalow. The roses in California grow to positively indecent stages of size and beauty, anyway.

I certainly do feel like a provincial lady out here. Everybody talks nonchalantly about the places they've been like Bali and Tahiti and the Philippines and Africa and I just have to listen because nobody out here is impressed when you tell them you've been to grand places like Quitman and Thomasville and Eatonton and that you lived within a stone's throw of the old capitol at Milledgeville.

Sam Wood's private secretary tells me about how she just spent six months in England where Mr. Wood made *Good-bye Mr. Chips* and how she bought an Austin and rode all over the island. Then the camera crew chat modestly about the time they made the picture in

Alaska and someone else tells about how he flew low over Manhattan Island to make the airplane shots in *Made for Each Other.*

Well—anyway, I do hope that when I get back to Georgia you all will listen to me as I talk about making the epic of the moving picture world, *Gone With the Wind.*

Editor's Notes—EIGHT

[1]Myrick said there were *fifteen* dresses. In *Scarlett, Rhett, and a Cast of Thousands* (p. 260), Flamini recorded: "Vivien Leigh is seen in a calico print dress she wears through a third of the picture, in Atlanta and at Tara. Twenty-seven copies of the dress were made in gradual stages of disintegration that seemed to mirror the collapse of the South. Two were in mint condition for the earlier sequences; a couple more were soiled for use during the birth of Melanie's baby; four were scorched and torn for Scarlett's dash through the burning city and her long homeward trek; the others were sandpapered, frayed, and faded for use during the long hard days at Tara. Selznick was obsessed with the importance of careful aging of the costumes to make them look worn and authentic, and the clothes and uniforms were subjected to numerous rinses in a washing machine in a solution of water, sand, bleach, with a dingy dye added when the clothes were supposed to look particularly dirty. The last of the series of Scarlett's calico print dresses, however, had to be made with the reverse of the material, because no more color could be squeezed out of the right side even by this strenuous method."

William Pratt (*Scarlett Fever*, pp. 124-25) described five versions of the calico. (At least two of these were used in more than one scene, so, assuming Myrick was correct in saying duplicate costumes were always made for the stars, and the dress appeared in eight scenes, as many as sixteen copies of it can be accounted for.) Mrs. Kurtz set the number of versions of this dress as eight or ten in her *Atlanta Constitution* piece of 26 February. Fifteen, twenty-seven, sixteen or ten versions of the same dress! Such is historical scholarship. Let the reader choose the number.

[2]Selznick had written on 14 April: "I have for some time been worried that Fleming would not be able to finish the picture because of his physical condition. He told me frankly yesterday that he thought he was going to have to ask to be relieved immediately, but after talking with his doctor was told that it would be all right for him to continue. However, he is so near the breaking point both mentally and physically from sheer exhaustion that it would be a miracle, in my opinion, if he is able to shoot for another seven or eight weeks." Selznick, *Memo*, p. 201.

On that same day Myrick told her diary that Monty Westmore prophesied that Fleming would not last. She wrote: "I think he is right. Vic told me today he was tired to death and he was getting the jitters and he thought he would just have to quit."

On May 2 Selznick wrote Howard Dietz in New York: "As you have no doubt heard and read, our troubles are by no means over. Vic Fleming collapsed on us, and we had to make another directorial switch. But Sam Wood seems to have taken over beautifully and I don't think there is going to be any letdown in quality. I have two other units shooting presently, and there is one stage of the picture at which five units will actually be shooting simultaneously!" Selznick, *Memo*, p. 205.

[3]Hall wrote of Rhett and Scarlett on the road from Atlanta: "I walked along a muddy road today, with Rhett and Scarlett who were fleeing Atlanta. She protests against his leaving and gets a rough kiss for her pains. He says, 'Here's a soldier of the South who loves you, Scarlett, and wants to take the memory of your kiss into battle with him!'

"The scene grew hotter, little red and yellow lights, supposedly from the flames of burning Atlanta, licked against the two flames which were Rhett and Scarlett. He said, then, his tone a mixture of arrogance, mockery and passion as red as the fire, 'You're a woman sending a soldier to his death, with a beautiful memory. Kiss me, Scarlett, kiss me!' Then Scarlett's voice, cold to hide its own fire, 'You low-down, cowardly thing!' The flames, not from burning Atlanta, seemed to consume them." Hall, "Gone With the Wind: On the Set with Gladys Hall," p. 70.

[4]Myrick wrote to Mitchell on 9 April: "To being with—SIDNEY HOWARD IS BACK ON THE SCRIPT! Came back last week. I haven't the faintest idea how many folks that makes in all who have done script. I lost count after the first ten and all I know is Howard is somewhere about the sixteenth, though he may be the twentieth."

Margaret Mitchell replied on 17 April: "I know you'll have a crown in Heaven for the great joy your letters have given us. Your last one, which announced that Sidney Howard was back on the script, kept us laughing all day. Every time we thought of the history of the script and the full circle which has been made we laughed again. It is all too incredible. I suppose Mr. Howard discovered that there was practically nothing left of his original script. I would not be at all surprised to learn that the script of the sixteen other writers had been junked and Mr. Howard's original script put into production."

Somewhat naively she added: "For months I have had to restrain myself from writing Mr. Howard and telling him about the goings-on over the script. Something told me he'd be the type who would appreciate the information. But, as usual, I kept quiet, for I never discuss anything about the picture with anyone. I have never met Mr. Howard but his letters have led to me believe that he is a grand person and one who has a sardonic appreciation of the strange ways of Hollywood." Mr. Howard knew a great deal more than she or Sue Myrick ever would about the "goings-on over the script."

Howard had been brought back for two weeks in April by much persuasion (backed by a high stipend) on the part of Selznick. He wrote his wife on 5 April, during his first day back on the set: "I came over here and reported for duty. I was shown the cut film up to the scene they were just shooting when I walked on the set. Namely, the scene in which Rhett leaves Scarlett at the cross roads. I thought the stuff was beautiful in color, dull and cold in action. Leigh quite extraordinarily fine as Scarlett though not really an actress of much accomplishment. Gable simply terrible as Rhett, awkward, hick, unconvincing. . . . They have done nothing much to my script except put in a lot of unnecessary movie construction in the matter of connecting scenes which has required them to cut down the good playing scenes of the book." Howard to Polly D. Howard, Culver City, Calif., 5 April 1939, Howard Papers, Bancroft Library, University of California, Berkeley.

A few days later Howard wrote: "I have been working very hard and very long hours. . . . My job was to lay out the end and put it back in shape for shooting. Selznick is the same. He is still obdurately refusing to cut the story or to condense and combine and I have already seen a full length picture up to the return to Tara. . . . I shall be finished early next week. The problem arises then: when will he read what I have written and clear me? I leave, of course, whether he clears me or not. Then he will put still another writer on my new script which he will not have read and the new man will spend another two weeks re-doing what has been done so often." Howard to Polly D. Howard, Beverly Hills, Calif., 8 April 1939.

As his contractual stay drew to a close he declared: "My difficulty in breaking away is not going to be leaving the script unfinished because I can finish it easily and may even get it OKed. The jam I see ahead is the hypersensitive state of everything connected with the picture. I have never been placed in quite this position of having everybody come to me to take their troubles to David because I am the only person around who doesn't upset him. And he feels that and calls me in to listen to all manner of problems with which, as writer, I have nothing whatever to do. And I want to get home."

Howard declared a "miasma of fatigue" surrounded him. "Fleming," he said, "takes four shots of something a day to keep going and another shot or so to fix him so he can sleep after the day's stimulants. Selznick is bent double with permanent, and I should think, chronic indigestion. Half the staff look, talk and behave as though they were on the verge of breakdowns. When I have anything to say I have to phrase it with exaggerated clarity." But he stayed a third week, reporting to his wife: "I can stay on here almost indefinitely at $500.00 a day. Nothing would please Selznick more in spite of the fact that I persuaded him to let me go this Wednesday." Howard to Mrs. Polly D. Howard, Culver City, Calif., 18 and 24 April 1939.

Myrick wrote Mitchell on 28 May: "Sidney Howard has long gone and I miss him. He was so delightful and so understanding of the true situation.

When he left, he came to say good bye to me and I asked if the script were finished. He said yes it was but no doubt David would rewrite it and it would not surprise Howard if D O S called him back from New York in a month or so to rewrite it once more. You know, I think, that the script is now about fifty pages more than when Howard first wrote it and is twenty pages more than Howard wrote it the second time after fifteen more writers had rewritten it." (Caution: this last sentence contains a heavy portion of hyperbole.)

[5]Oliver Hardy.

[6]This scene was reported by Gladys Hall in her entry for 11 May: "The scene, again, was in Tara. The scene where, after shooting the cavalryman, Scarlett and Melanie perform the ghoulish task of rifling his pockets and then start to drag him out. Most of today, Vivien and Olivia worked with this 'corpse.' Up and down stairs they went, over and over again." Hall, "Gone With the Wind: On the Set with Gladys Hall," p. 71.

[7]These shots were not used in the film.

ILLUSTRATIONS—2

Susan Myrick's identification card as a member of the staff of Selznick International Pictures. Myrick Papers, Emory University Library.

Form 73A—20M—#-38—K-J Co.

SELZNICK INTERNATIONAL PICTURES, INC.
CULVER CITY, CALIFORNIA

Inter-Office Communication

TO Miss Susan Myrick   DATE 3/10/39

FROM David O. Selznick   SUBJECT dialogue GONE WITH THE WIND

Dear Miss Myrick:

The actors are getting confused by so many amendments coming through to our dialogue, and I have therefore asked Miss Keon to be sure to check with you on each scene for such suggestions on dialogue as those which you sent me today, which are very useful and valuable and which I appreciate -- but which would be even more valuable if we received them in time to make the changes before the script goes into mimeograph.

DOS

k

A "memo from Selznick." Myrick Papers, Emory University Library.

A snapshot taken by Susan Myrick during the filming of GWTW's barbecue scene at Busch Gardens, Pasadena. Myrick Papers, Emory University Library.

Susan Myrick's snapshot of Leslie Howard and Vivien Leigh catches them at the Atlanta car-shed when Ashley arrives during his Christmas leave. Collection of Susan Lindsley.

In this snapshot by Susan Myrick, Victor Fleming gives directions to Leslie Howard, Laura Hope Crews, and Vivien Leigh for the Christmas dinner scene at Aunt Pittypat's house. Collection of Susan Lindsley.

Wardrobe assistants make last-minute adjustments on the costumes of Harry Daven-port (Dr. Meade) and Howard Hickman (John Wilkes) for the scene of the Confeder-ate wounded at the Atlanta car-shed. Vivien Leigh stands between the columns in this snapshot by Susan Myrick. Collection of Susan Lindsley.

Susan Myrick took this snapshot of extras costumed as refugees from Tennessee for a scene written into the GWTW screenplay but not included in the film. The posters were designed by Wilbur G. Kurtz and based on texts sent to him by Telamon Cuyler. Collection of Susan Lindsley.

Melanie Wilkes and her newborn son Beauregard in the wagon in which they fled Atlanta with Scarlett, Rhett, and Prissy. Collection of Susan Lindsley.

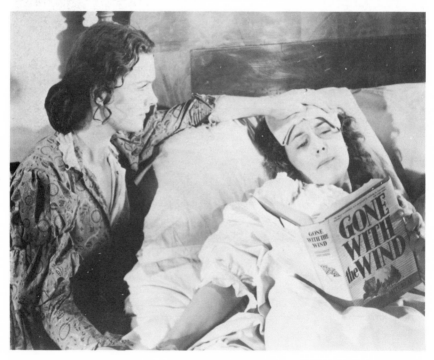

George Cukor, GWTW's first director, had this picture taken to send to Margaret Mitchell. Susan Myrick wrote about the filming of the Atlanta scene in her column of 14 February 1939. Courtesy of MGM/UA Entertainment Co. GWTW Museum, Atlanta.

Susan Myrick describes this GWTW *scene in her column of 28 May 1939. The note tells how Gable substituted Scotch whiskey for Hattie Mc Daniel's tea. From the MGM release* Gone With the Wind, © *1939 Selznick International Pictures, Inc. Copyright renewed 1967 by Metro-Goldwyn-Mayer, Inc. Margaret Mitchell Marsh Papers, University of Georgia Libraries.*

*Susan Myrick coaches Evelyn Keyes of Atlanta on the Old South accent and deport-
ment needed in her role as Suellen O'Hara, Scarlett's sister. Courtesy of MGM/UA
Entertainment Co. Myrick Papers, Emory University Library.*

Leslie Howard and Susan Myrick in a publicity photograph released by Selznick International Pictures during the filming of GWTW. *Courtesy of MGM/UA Entertainment Co. Collection of Richard Harwell.*

*Susan Myrick with Laura Hope Crews (Aunt Pittypat Hamilton).
Collection of Susan Lindsley.*

*Susan Myrick with Jane Darwell (Mrs. Merriwether). Collection of
Susan Lindsley.*

Susan Myrick found Georgians at almost every turn in California. She is pictured here with Ricky Holt, one of the children who played Beauregard, and his mother, Martha Massey Holt, whose parents lived in Macon. Collection of Susan Lindsley.

Susan Myrick's "Straight from Hollywood" columns in the Macon Telegraph *appeared as "On the Spot Stories of 'Gone With the Wind'," in the* Atlanta Georgian. *Myrick Papers, Emory University Library.*

AT TARA, THE O'HARA PLANTATION IN GEORGIA
BRENT TARLETON ....*FRED CRANE*
STUART TARLETON ....*GEORGE REEVES*
SCARLETT O'HARA ....*VIVIEN LEIGH*
MAMMY ....*HATTIE McDANIEL*
BIG SAM ....*EVERETT BROWN*
ELIJAH ....*ZACK WILLIAMS*
GERALD O'HARA ....*THOMAS MITCHELL*
PORK ....*OSCAR POLK*
ELLEN O'HARA ....*BARBARA O'NEIL*
JONAS WILKERSON ....*VICTOR JORY*
SUELLEN O'HARA ....*EVELYN KEYES*
CARREEN O'HARA ....*ANN RUTHERFORD*
PRISSY ....*BUTTERFLY McQUEEN*

**AT TWELVE OAKS, THE NEARBY WILKES
PLANTATION**
JOHN WILKES ....*HOWARD HICKMAN*
INDIA WILKES ....*ALICIA RHETT*
ASHLEY WILKES ....*LESLIE HOWARD*
MELANIE HAMILTON ....*OLIVIA DE HAVILLAND*
CHARLES HAMILTON ....*RAND BROOKS*
FRANK KENNEDY ....*CARROLL NYE*
CATHLEEN CALVERT ....*MARCELLA MARTIN*
RHETT BUTLER ....*CLARK GABLE*

AT THE BAZAAR IN ATLANTA
AUNT "PITTYPAT" HAMILTON .*LAURA HOPE CREWS*
DOCTOR MEADE ....*HARRY DAVENPORT*
MRS. MEADE ....*LEONA ROBERTS*
MRS. MERRIWETHER ....*JANE DARWELL*
RENE PICARD ....*ALBERT MORIN*
MAYBELLE MERRIWETHER ......*MARY ANDERSON*
FANNY ELSING ....*TERRY SHERO*
OLD LEVI ....*WILLIAM McCLAIN*

IN AUNT "PITTYPATT'S" HOME
UNCLE PETER ....*EDDIE ANDERSON*

OUTSIDE THE EXAMINER OFFICE
PHIL MEADE ....*JACKIE MORAN*

A 1967 souvenir program listing of the GWTW cast. Collection of Richard Harwell.

AT THE HOSPITAL

REMINISCENT SOLDIER .... *CLIFF EDWARDS*
BELLE WATLING .... *ONA MUNSON*
THE SERGEANT .... *ED CHANDLER*
A WOUNDED SOLDIER IN PAIN ....
GEORGE HACKATHORNE
A CONVALESCENT SOLDIER .... *ROSCOE ATES*
AN AMPUTATION CASE .... *ERIC LINDEN*
A DYING SOLDIER .... *JOHN ARLEDGE*

DURING THE EVACUATION

A COMMANDING OFFICER .... *TOM TYLER*

DURING THE SIEGE

A MOUNTED OFFICER .... *WILLIAM BAKEWELL*
THE BARTENDER .... *LEE PHELPS*

GEORGIA AFTER SHERMAN

A YANKEE DESERTER .... *PAUL HURST*
THE CARPETBAGGER'S FRIEND ..*ERNEST WHITMAN*
A RETURNING VETERAN .... *WILLIAM STELLING*
A HUNGRY SOLDIER .... *LOUIS JEAN HEYDT*
EMMY SLATTERY .... *ISABEL JEWELL*

DURING RECONSTRUCTION

THE YANKEE MAJOR .... *ROBERT ELLIOTT*
HIS POKER-PLAYING CAPTAINS ....
GEORGE MEEKER, WALLIS CLARK
THE CORPORAL .... *IRVING BACON*
A CARPETBAGGER ORATOR .... *ADRIAN MORRIS*
JOHNNY GALLEGHER .... *J. M. KERRIGAN*
A YANKEE BUSINESS MAN .... *OLIN HOWLAND*
A RENEGADE .... *YAKIMA CANUTT*
HIS COMPANION .... *BLUE WASHINGTON*
TOM, A YANKEE CAPTAIN .... *WARD BOND*
BONNIE BLUE BUTLER .... *CAMMIE KING*
BEAU WILKES .... *MICKEY KUHN*
BONNIE'S NURSE .... *LILLIAN KEMBLE COOPER*

Susan Myrick caught cameraman Arthur Arling on the giant crane used to film the Confederate wounded at the Atlanta car-shed. Collection of Susan Lindsley.

This snapshot by Susan Myrick shows the gondola of the crane in mid-air, in prepara-tion for the scenes filmed 22 May 1939. Collection of Susan Lindsley.

NINE
18 May—1 June 1939

Macon Telegraph, 18 May 1939

Straight From HOLLYWOOD

Sue Finds that It Takes Long Time to Kill Man in Hollywood

HOLLYWOOD, Calif.—Vivien Leigh shot at sunrise!

Such might have been the headlines for the *Gone With the Wind* edition of the Selznick International newspaper—if we had one.

Only, of course, we didn't actually mean to shoot our Scarlett with a gun. We intended to make a shot of a scene where Scarlett is in the fields at Tara after the war. We meant to make it at sunrise.

Camera crew, hair dressers, make-up artists, directors and cast left the studio at three a.m. to drive for forty-five minutes to a location where the shot was to be made.

And the sun refused to rise!

That is, it rose but clouds piled heavily in the east hid the sun from view and the shot wasn't made.

That was one day I got a break because I was left at the studio to work with Director Sam Wood on the scene he was shooting with Belle Watling and Rhett Butler, while Vic Fleming took over the outdoor shooting.

I wish you could have seen the sad-looking crew who came in from location about eleven o'clock, sleepy-eyed and dressed in sweaters and old clothes and boots. Of course they got to go home soon and get some sleep and I worked on the rest of the day.

Ona Munson and Clark Gable played their scenes and Ona was a fascinating Belle, dressed in a bright yellow satin gown that was decorated with crimson velvet roses and black lace. Clark was wearing a fashionable 1872 model [suit] in gray broadcloth.

Between takes Clark told me about the ranch and how his alfalfa patch is the most beautiful thing he ever saw. He is as enthusiastic about that ranch as a 4-H boy who has just won first place with his pigs or corn. Clark is planting bluegrass now and he can scarcely wait for the end of the day to go home and watch green things growing.

Things are humming around the studio these days with William Wyler on hand to begin preparation for directing *Intermezzo*, on which Leslie Howard will act as associate-producer as well as play the leading male role, and with other preparations under way for casting *Rebecca*, which Selznick International will make after *Intermezzo*.

But none of the other plans can get my mind off *Gone With the Wind*, especially when I get such a kick out of the scenes like Scarlett shooting the Yankee soldier.

We shot that fellow for about two days last week and my bones ached in sympathy for the chap who took four or five tumbles down the stairs at Tara.

"Bang" went the old fashioned pistol that Vivien Leigh pointed at the Yankee deserter who had invaded her home.

And down tumbled the soldier, to sprawl at the foot of the stairs.

"Hurt you?" inquired Director Sam Wood, solicitously.

"Not a bit," answered the soldier.

Mr. Wood shook his head and muttered: "A fall like that would kill me!"

And the rest of us nodded agreement, rubbing surreptitiously the backs of our heads or legs where we felt the man must be bruised.

The past weekend was "homecoming" for me. On Saturday evening I went to dinner with Julia Lamar (Mrs. Walter) Parrish who is living at Pasadena and I spent the night and most of Sunday with Julia. Then on Sunday evening I went to dinner with Louise Hall (Mrs. Lamar) Trotti.

Julia asked the Trottis, too, and with them came Mrs. Richard Hines who insists that she be known as "Mrs. Hines of Macon, Ga., and New York."

Of course, we know her as "Miss Anne" in Macon, but since she has been living in New York City she refuses to be spoken of as from anywhere except Macon. She came out to visit Louise and Lamar for a few days before she goes to San Francisco to visit her brother-in-law and she had just spent a month in New Orleans and Shreveport.

She was looking very handsome in a blue frock at Julia's and on Sunday evening she was even lovelier in a navy-and-white striped chiffon with her white hair curled in soft waves and her dark eyes full of laughter as she talked of Macon and the friends there.

At Julia's also, were her sisters, Valieria (Mrs. T. R.) Williams and Annie Camille (Mrs. J. H.) Abramson, who lives at Long Beach.

Well, among us we kept up such a chatter of Maconites as may well have made all the ears in the city burn. And the rest of the poor guests at Julia's were flabbergasted. They never knew half of what we talked about, for the combined Southern accents were too much for Californians.

Clark Millikan,[1] instructor in aeronautics at Cal-Tech, who was one of the guests, said he'd have known what we said just as well if we had spoken Spanish or Greek!

After the party was over Julia and I talked some more about Macon and we started all over again at breakfast. Only, we were pleasantly interrupted by her two young daughters, Anne and Gail, who came in to meet the visitor.

Anne, who is four, is like all the lovely-looking Lamar girls and Gail, who is one and a few weeks, is "the spittin' image of her pa."

I could never have torn myself away from Julia's if it hadn't been I was going to the Trottis' to supper. And when I reached Louise's house I found two more Maconites, Marian and Pink Happ.

Marian is as brown as a Mexican and her hair is sun-bleached but it is very becoming. She and Pink had spent several months at Palm Springs but even there they didn't get enough sun. They have just returned from a fishing trip off the coast of Mexico.

Pink caught a marlin that weighed 224 pounds—caught him the first day out, too!

"But he was miserable," laughed Marian. "He went to catch a marlin and when he'd caught him he didn't have anything else to do. He fumed because he kept catching what he called 'little fish.' They were yellow tails and bonitas and such and not one of them weighed under fifteen pounds but Pink wasn't happy."

But Pink insisted his only unhappiness came because he got two more marlins on the hook and they got away.

All the Maconites out here look so good and so prosperous and seem so happy that it does my heart good to see them. And the folks in Macon would be happy to see the yearning look in their faces as they talk about Georgia and the people back home.

Of course, they are all interested in *Gone With the Wind*, and I felt very proud when Lamar Trotti, who has written so many excellent scripts for pictures, up and said he heard *Gone With the Wind* was going to be the finest picture ever put out.

I think he's right, too!

Macon Telegraph and News, 21 May 1939

Straight From HOLLYWOOD

Four-Year-Old Actress in GWTW Falls for Actor Clark Gable Too

HOLLYWOOD, Calif.—"Mummy, where is Clark Gable?"

Those were the first words of little Cammie King, who is playing the role of Bonnie Blue Butler in *Gone With the Wind*, when she came on the set to work the other morning.

A pretty little thing with dark hair and a faint resemblance to her mother, Scarlett O'Hara, Bonnie won the hearts of the folks on Stage 4 as she went through her scenes with Rhett, crying because of the darkness and cuddling close to her father when he comforted her.[2]

And Clark got pretty well kidded about the way all the women fall for him, young or old. Even four-year-old Cammie.

As she sat on her father's knee, Cammie rubbed her little nose against Rhett's face and several feminine visitors on the set were heard to sigh deeply and insinuate they'd not mind playing the Bonnie role.

Most mothers would have been greatly amused at the scene on the stage when Bonnie's real mother, Mrs. King, was trying to get little Cammie to cry.

"Scream, darling," she said to the four-year-old. "Cry and sob. Don't you know how you cry at home sometimes?"

But the little girl turned an angelic smile on her mother and beamed on Director Wood and shook her head.

Which tickled me immensely: for my experience with various youngsters has led me to try to stop them from crying while this mother was using all her wiles to induce tears.

Finally, Bonnie got in the mood and we made the scene while visitors and crew oohed and aahed over the winsome lass.

But in spite of the interest in scenes shot on the stage this week, I have been goggle-eyed over preparations for the big boom shot we are to make as soon as the weather report says no fog and no clouds. The scene is the one where Dr. Meade is working on the wounded at the Atlanta railroad station on the day Scarlett wants him to bring Melanie's baby.

Dr. Gilbert Stone, who is first-aid man for the Selznick lot, has worked with two other men, tearing and rolling bandages for the thirteen hundred wounded who will be in the scene.

There are eighteen hundred rolls, torn from bolts of cloth 180-feet long and the men averaged three hundred rolls per day. Twelve men are to help Doc Stone get the men bandaged and he has figured they must bandage one man every two minutes in order to get them ready in the allotted time.

O, yes, I almost forgot to tell you. The war is over! We got the word at Tara Tuesday evening. Gerald told Katie Scarlett and then Pork and Mammy were informed that they were free.

The announcement of the surrender of Lee brought forth some wisecracks from some of the standers-by who shrugged their shoulders and recalled that in the opening scenes of the picture Scarlett had told the Tarleton twins very positively "There's not going to be any war."

"How can the wah be oveh if there wasn't any wah?" they kept asking.

For the Southern accent, in various forms, pervades the set, even to calling the studio cop "de law."

Evelyn Keyes, lovely Atlanta girl, who is playing Suellen, is naturally rather Southern, of course, and half the crew was listening to her the other day as she told of her exciting trip to Omaha when the premiere of *Union Pacific* showed there.

Evelyn was looking mighty pretty, anyhow, dressed in powder blue slacks, with a beige sport coat, beige coolie shoes and with a blue bandanna over her brown hair.

She got permission from Selznick International to fly to Omaha for the show, left Los Angeles Wednesday at midnight and naturally slept very little. Arrived in Omaha, she found everything most exciting:

"It was about like welcoming Lindbergh back to America after his lone flight to Paris," she declared. "Thousands of people were on the streets and confetti was floating everywhere. We rode in carriages and soldiers lined the streets alongside us while more soldiers on horseback rode outside the marching men."

The premiere was on Friday night and at four that afternoon Evelyn got a wire telling her to be on the stage at Selznick's, ready for work, at seven the next morning.

So: immediately after the show, Evelyn and Barbara Stanwyck were escorted to the air terminal by a lot of policemen on motorcycles, and caught the plane at midnight. She was back at work next morning looking as fresh as a daisy.

We had a lot of laughs at Ann Rutherford's story of her dime bank, the other day, too. Ann, who insists that she is a frugal girl, puts her dimes in a bank she bought for a quarter. It is the sort of bank that bursts open when it gets full (five dollars).

"It looked to me as if that thing would never get full," Ann said. "I put in dimes and put in dimes and I had about given up hope.

"Yesterday I was in Magnin's shopping and the clerk gave me two dimes in change. I picked the bank out of my purse and pushed in the dimes.

"You never heard such a clatter in your life. The bank burst and the money rolled all over that store. People from all over everywhere turned and looked at me like I had hit a jack-pot!

"My mother was so embarrassed she just walked off the left me and pretended she wasn't with that silly girl. But the clerks and the customers around helped me pick up the dimes.

"I assure you I never left a one."

And that brings me to tell the funny thing that happened to Thomas Mitchell on the set one day recently. Wearing his street clothes and minus makeup, Tommy sat down beside Vivien Leigh, who was waiting for a camera set-up.

"How are you, Vivien?" he said cordially.

"How do you do?" said Vivien, as if she were speaking to a stranger.

Then she looked again at Mitchell and gasped:

"Why, Tommy, I didn't know you. This is the first time I ever saw you without your makeup and I have thought all this time you were an old man!"

Mitchell, who is young and handsome, looks quite old enough to be Scarlett's father once he is made up and in his costume so it's no wonder Vivien didn't recognize the handsome young man who sat beside her wearing an up-to-the-minute sports outfit.

There was another laugh we got on the set this week. Vivien and Olivia were sitting on the steps in Tara's hall, waiting for the lights to be arranged and they began practicing on a trick of fingers and thumbs that somebody had been showing. It is a trick that nobody can describe—a sort of worm-crawling effect you can produce by putting finger to thumb, lifting the finger, doing the same with the other hand and so on. And it is an extremely difficult coordination.

They were working earnestly at the task, watching their own hands intently. Mr. Wood turned suddenly and saw them.

"Well!" he exclaimed. "I thought this picture would drive somebody mad sooner or later but I never dreamed it would be my leading ladies!"

Then there was the conundrum pulled on us by Cecil Barker, newly appointed one of the assistant directors. Cecil went around asking everybody: "Why is a can of tomato soup like the Empire State Building?"

Nobody knew and finally he told us the answer: "Because neither of them can ride a bicycle."

I know all of this sounds as if we never work but we do. You should have seen us Tuesday night, working until 10:30.

And one evening when we stopped shooting *Gone With the Wind* at quarter to six, I encountered a stenographer on the walk and she asked:

"O, just working half a day, today, huh?"

I went around to see the daughter-in-law and the niece of Mr. A. L. Nims, Sr. the other evening. Barbara Nims has visited Art and Eddie Nims on Vista Circle and so has Mr. Nims, whose home is in Long Beach. Mr. Nims, recently returned from a trip to Africa by way of Macon, was spending the weekend with his daughter and he and I had a homecoming conversation.

He thinks, as I do, that Macon is just about the grandest place in the world.

Macon Telegraph and News, 28 May 1939

Straight From HOLLYWOOD

Gone With the Wind Crew Likes Wisecracks As Filming of Popular Novel Continues

HOLLYWOOD, Calif.—The telephone on Stage 11 lights up. Cecil Barker, one of the assistant directors, picks up the receiver:

"Butler 1868," he says into the mouthpiece.

Last week when we were still shooting on Stage 3 in the sequences at Tara after the war, Cecil answered the phone:

"Tara 1864."

Oh! they are a clever group, these fellows on the Selznick International lot. Somebody is always wisecracking. The telephone conversation is just a little example. By the way: the phone does not ring on the stages because a take would be spoiled if the bell rang at the wrong moment and even at a movie studio the operator can't tell when not to ring the telephone.

So, the red light comes on at the phone as a signal that someone is calling. It flashes once; if nobody answers it flashes again. After about nine flashes the light just stays on and on. Somebody always calls out:

"The telephone is boiling over."

"Why not answer it?" someone else will say. And the first one who observed the light will reply:

"Not in my department."

Well, nobody could notice the phone last week when Rhett Butler
was having a scene with his week-old daughter, Bonnie. Everybody
was watching the take; for somehow it struck all of us as uncommonly
amusing when we learned Clark Gable was to talk baby talk to the
infant.

Many watchers waited to grin but they all went away filled with
admiration, for Clark coo-ed and goo-gooed at his tiny child as if he
had walked through the night with a dozen of them.

Clark has been providing fun for us almost every day for the past
three or four days because he is always up to some sort of foolishness
on the set. We were shooting the scene where he gives a drink to
Mammy when she makes friends with him after Bonnie's birth and
shows him that she is wearing the red petticoat he bought for her when
he was on his honeymoon.[3]

Mammy was to walk away from Clark in the scene and he was to
hear the petticoat rustle, then he was to say:

"What is that rustling noise I hear, Mammy?"

Somehow Mammy forgot her cue and stood stock still as the
camera ground away on the take.

"What is that rustling noise I was supposed to hear if you had
walked away, Mammy?" asked Clark with a wide grin.

Clark sat down by me the other day while he waited for things to be
ready for a take and told me about the time he made *Mutiny on the
Bounty*. It took them thirty-seven weeks to make the picture he
declared (thus spoiling my idea that *Gone With the Wind* is taking the
longest time on record) and he amused me greatly by telling how he
chased the sun all over the Pacific coast.

The *Bounty* was a slow moving ship and the company had fast
boats to send out as scouts for a sunny spot, because the fog often lies
heavily over the coast here.

The speed boat would report that there was a bright sun about ten
miles away. All hands would get busy and the *Bounty* would start
heavily on her way to the latitude where the sun was bright. The speed
boat would make the distance in a few minutes but by the time the
slow-moving *Bounty* arrived at the spot designated, the fog would have
enveloped the whole place. And then they'd begin all over again.

Quite a long jump from the slow-moving *Bounty* to a flying
machine, I know, but I'll make it. Just wait. Right after I talked to

Clark about the boat, Vic Fleming came over and sat down and began to bemoan the fact that he has had to give up his pilot's license. Vic has had to work such long hours for the past year he had not had time to fly enough to get his license renewed.

"Why didn't you just go ask for a renewal and you know they wouldn't have questioned your ability to fly?" asked someone nearby who knows about renewals of licenses.

"I just didn't have the heart to lie about it," replied Vic. "You have to fill out a form that says among other things you have flown fifteen hours during the past twelve months and I couldn't say I had without lying."

Well, Vic wasn't flying a plane but he was up in the air, all right, the day we made the big boom shot. The crane on which the camera was fastened stretched eighty-six feet long and the camera rode high in the air so it might capture the scene of rows of wounded and dead near the railroad station in Atlanta. A diesel engine pulled the truck that moved the crane and as the long arm rose in the air the machine moved slowly backward, showing more and more rows of pitifully clad, crudely tended, wounded Confederates. I had a feeling that the cameraman was about as high as the Candler Building.[4]

When I saw the results of the shot, in the projection room, I got a big thrill from it. And I was not in any condition to be excited or pleased either.

For: We had just returned from a trip on location, dirty, tired and sunburned. Since one of the location shots had to be made at dawn, many of the members of the group had left the studio at 1 a.m. and everything was ready to shoot when the sun was just about to peep over the horizon.[5]

In the early morning we all shivered, drank coffee and pulled coats and sweaters tightly around us. But as the day wore on the sun shone relentlessly and all the men were working in their shirtsleeves. And before we got home we were all a bright pink; for we work indoors a great deal and long hours in a hot sun make us lobster-colored.

In spite of discomforts, however, everybody had a lot of fun and there was much laughter to keep up spirits. As a helper led two cows across the field toward the back of the shot somebody asked how come there were two cows when Scarlett had only one—the one she brought home the night she fled from Atlanta with Melanie, Prissy and the newborn Beauregard.

"O, that's the stand-in for the real cow—that other one," wise-cracked somebody.

Then just as the director had called "Roll'em" and the sound man called "Quiet! Speed!" the cow mooed a long and mournful low. Since we were shooting a dialogue scene the noise would have spoiled the take and Eric Stacey called over the loudspeaker.

"Somebody throw a herring to that cow."

A little later Vic Fleming picked up a lock of cotton from the ground (we were shooting the sequence where Scarlett and the girls are picking cotton after the war).

"Look, Susan," said Vic, "do you think if I pulled this lock of cotton to pieces I would find a mint julep inside it?"

Thus we go on being gay and foolish on the sets. We have to. If we didn't we'd get too tired of working. For make no mistake we are working early and late to get *Gone With the Wind* the finest possible picture. And from where I'm sitting I feel it will be just that.

Macon Telegraph, 1 June 1939

Straight From HOLLYWOOD

Fun Mixed with Serious Work on Selznick International Stage

HOLLYWOOD, Calif.—Things seemed so quiet and peaceful on Stage 11 at Selznick International this week after we had worked on Forty Acres and out at the forty-mile-away location. Everybody had gotten sunburned and hot on exterior work for *Gone With the Wind* and, on the stage the temperature was very pleasant. But, best of all, there was no wind blowing dirt in our eyes and stopping the progress of the scene. (For outdoors, the sensitive sound recorder often picks up the noise of the wind and spoils the dialogue.)

It was between takes on Stage 11 and Vic Fleming was sitting quietly in his chair, looking over the script he was soon to shoot. Without warning he called suddenly:

"Eric, can't you get a wind machine on this set?"

Assistant Director Eric Stacey looked puzzled, a bit embarrassed because he had overlooked something. Then he got the joke:

"Yes sir," he grinned, "I can get one ready in five minutes. If it's noise you want, I can get the public address system working too."

Then he paused a moment and added:

"I can arrange for some one to throw dirt, too, sir, if you wish."

But nobody could really throw dirt on that scene we were shooting. Vivien Leigh, wearing a green robe, trimmed in gold, sat at her dressing table in the ornate room that Rhett had built for Scarlett and she looked much too lovely for any dirt throwing.

We have been shooting for the past few days in Rhett's house in Atlanta—scenes where he quarrels with Scarlett, where she tells him she will not have any more children and where he tells her he is going to take little Bonnie and go away.[6]

Between scenes one afternoon, Clark and Vivien came along toward their dressing rooms and sat down to ask what I was looking at in the movie magazine I was reading. Vivien turned the pages idly, commenting on various lovely gals whose beauties were pictured.

And I must add, she said over and over, "What a lovely looking person she is," while I kept thinking that not one of the beauties looked half so lovely as Vivien.

As she looked at the pictures, Vivien turned a page, saw a rather dignified portrait of a movie queen and said:

"Who is she?"

"Whoa there!" said Clark. "That's my bride."

Almost at the same instant Vivien recognized Carole Lombard and exclaimed: "What a lovely picture! Isn't she beautiful?"

"It's a good thing you didn't say anything unkind about my bride," laughed Clark. Vivien said:

"But that is such a sweet picture, Clark. You ought to have it."

"I have it!" answered Clark with a wide grin. "The picture as well as the original."

About that time Vic Fleming came over and joined the group and everybody got to telling stories. Then Clark asked some questions about the next scene to be shot and Vic leaned back, closed his eyes and said nothing.

"Look at him!!" said Clark. "When he gets that *Gone With the Wind* look of worrying he looks so distressed." Then Vic laughed and we went back to work.

We have all sorts of problems to come up even at this late date with *Gone With the Wind*. For instance, the other day, Wilbur Kurtz and I were discussing the old-time ash hopper that used to be in everybody's back yard in the Southern country to make lye for home-made soap.[7]

Will Price, a dialogue coach, who hails from Mississippi, walked over and started talking about the way the ash hopper was made back in Cedarville, his grandmother's place.

Wilbur drew a picture of the way he thought the ash hopper should look and I agreed with him. Price drew the way his grandmother's ash hopper looked and though it was much the same as the one Wilbur and I preferred, we pretended we thought his was all wrong and kidded him about beng a "coarse westerner from Mississippi," even though he did go to Duke.

"Oh, well," Price remarked, "Of course, I wouldn't know how things were in the backwoods Georgia country."

You see we keep up a fine pretense of a feud between the Georgians and the Mississippians and Vic is constantly saying there is no way to settle an argument when the Southerners begin fighting their own private war.

The reason we started the ash hopper discussion was because there is to be a scene where Scarlett is making soap. There is only a brief bit that shows this scene and Wilbur and I were figuring the way it might be most typically Southern. From that we started talking about how soap was made in the back yard in a big pot and how there were earthen jars to hold the pieces of fat that always were saved on the plantation and how the good old Aunties and Mammys stirred with a wooden paddle and so on.

First thing we knew half the people working on the stage had gathered around to hear the discussion and we realized that nobody except old-timers like us knew about soap making on the plantation.

None of the crowd believed me when I said soap made on the waning moon would all go to nothing.

And, for once, Price and I agreed. He insisted that soap must be made as the moon approached the full so that there would be lots of soap and it wouldn't be all soft and mushy.

That brought Wilbur to say that the homemade soap he remembered was always soft and was kept in a jar.

"I can see it right now," Wilbur told us. "The stuff was about like a stiff jelly and there were always prints of fingers where somebody had scooped up the soap."

Well, I must leave the stage now to tell you about the beauty of a Sunday ride to Santa Barbara. The highway goes along the coast and on the left you see the broad Pacific, green and blue and gray, according to the lights on it, changing occasionally to a soft silver sheen.

The shore line is rough for the most part and the waves dash against jagged black rocks to break in a swirl of foam and a dash of wild spray.

But the lovely part is that the other side of the road is right against the mountains. Soft cloud masses lie mistily at the tops of the mountains, and float down into the deep valleys that corrugate the sides.

It looked so like the islands that I was tremendously thrilled. And I was very proud to have been to Hawaii when somebody in the car remarked on the similarity.

You see, everybody out here has been all over the world. Ned Lambert, head of wardrobe, has been around the world five times and thus it goes.

And that reminds me of a story Bill Menzies told about his arrival in Los Angeles many years ago. Bill had lived for years in New York City, had been to Europe dozens of times and he thought (he said) "the West began at Eighth avenue."

He got out here, wearing a dark overcoat, a bowler hat, a blue suit and black shoes and before he had been here two days his whole outfit was yellow from dust. For then, few streets in the small city were paved.

First thing, Bill was sent out about forty miles into the hills near the old Lasky company's property. Stopped by a cowboy, who was the first Bill had ever seen, poor Menzies almost dropped dead when the man casually inquired:

"You ain't see a lion around here nowhere, have you?"

It was not until days later that Bill learned the man was working for the movies and was searching for a moth-eaten lion who had escaped from the movie's zoo.

Well, it's a far cry from twenty years ago in Los Angeles with unpaved streets and lion hunting to now. The city is so amazingly beautiful, clean, well-kept and so widespread in its area that it seems impossible only twenty years has been required for all this.

As for the movies—well, wait until you see *Gone With the Wind* and you'll appreciate what a movie can really be!

Editor's Notes—NINE

[1]Clark Blanchard Millikan, a world-renowned physicist.

[2]"Cammie King," wrote Mrs. Kurtz in her article for the *Atlanta Constitution* on 5 June 1939, "is the most adorable little thing!—dimples in both cheeks, curly hair and eyes sparkling with fun. I saw her first in the studio cafe eating luncheon with her mother, and though I had not been told, I knew that here at last was the happy selection for little Bonnie."

[3]Gladys Hall reported this scene as of 18 May: "The scene today was in Rhett's house. Rhett and Mammy make up after a battle. . . . After Clark had kicked in the door [of Scarlett's room] and examined his big toe, or the remains of it, we all had tea. Gable had some fun with Mammy, substituting some ten-year-old Scotch for her tea when she wasn't looking." Hall, "Gone With the Wind: On the Set with Gladys Hall," p. 71.

Myrick described this scene in her 1974 recollection of the filming: "When we were shooting the scene where Rhett and Mammy were making up past differences just after the birth of Bonnie, there chanced to be a ten-minute break while electricians adjusted some lights to suit the camera's angle. Gable slipped me the key to his dressing room, asked me to fetch him the bottle of Scotch. I fetched it and he got one of the crew to empty the bottle of make-believe bourbon which he and Mammy had been sharing in their scene and replace it with real Scotch whiskey, all done furtively and unseen by the director or the cast.

"Shooting resumed, Mammy took a big swig of what she thought was tea and her discovery of the Scotch brought coughs and whoops of laughter, breaking up the scene entirely. Had anybody else pulled such a stunt as Gable had managed, the director would have hit the ceiling. As it was, he and the cast and crew had a ten-minute laugh and shooting was begun again." Myrick, "Forty Years of 'Such Interesting People'," p. 47.

[4]This boom shot was one of the big moments in the filming of *Gone With the Wind* as well as in the film. Much has been written about it. In the *Atlanta Constitution* on 5 June 1939, Mrs. Kurtz wrote: "Saturday, May 20th, will be memorable for the high point in the filming of the picture, as far as the

mechanics and the spectacular are concerned. Hitherto the camera has been mounted on rolling 'dollies,' or on mere tripods, but this time the largest crane on the West Coast was called in to do its bit. The boom, eighty-five feet in length, moved the camera from a dead level to a forty-five degree angle, the cameramen and directors on a swinging platform. Some eighteen hundred persons were there to see it and practically every one of them had a part in creating the spectacle.

"This shot was built to take care of that dramatic episode of the novel where Scarlett crosses the railroad yards, threading her devious way through the hundreds of wounded soldiers from the battle of Jonesboro. The arched facade of the car-shed closed the view on the left—the stores, offices and hotels of war-time Atlanta framed the view on the right! The multiplied horrors of war were here displayed in a manner known only to the cinema art, an unfolding expanse of misery and tragedy."

[5]The trip was to the often used movie location known as Lasky Mesa.

Mrs. Kurtz's *Atlanta Constitution* piece for 11 June 1939 described this trip. "A 1 o'clock a.m. studio call to go on location is one of the frequent variations in routine here at Selznick International Pictures. Recently we were notified to be at the studio gate at that hour of the morning. A sunrise shot being on the agenda, it required this margin of time to get ready for the cracking of dawn over the Sierra Madres. . . .

"On reaching location we found ourselves for all practical purposes, at Tara. It was the post-war Tara. Here stood the ruined cotton press, gin house, vegetable garden, cotton patch, barns, slave quarters, etc. . . .

"Throughout the long day the cameras ground out film, the principals went through their parts in the Tara settings, the 'Georgia' sun continued to beat down on the red roads and faded grass—upon paddock and the cotton fields. At 5 o'clock the welcome 'wrap it up' was sounded, and the caravan began its 31 miles of homeward journey."

[6]Gladys Hall wrote of 27 May: "Lower floor of Rhett's house. . . . I had the pleasure of watching Rhett carry Scarlett upstairs, not once, but at least a half a dozen times. . . . There was a good deal of heightened blood pressure today on the set—for this was the 'ravishment' scene!"

Then on 29 May she recorded, with some degree of inaccuracy as to the story: "Lower floor of Rhett's house again. Today I watched the scene where, after Melanie's party, Rhett comes home drunk, and Scarlett creeps downstairs to snaffle a little hooker for herself. Rhett catches her at it, seizes her forcibly, flings her into a chair and hands her as violent a tongue-lashing as the Hays office would allow. It is after this scene that, as the preceding scene shows, he grabs her and carries her upstairs screaming."

For Thursday, 1 June, she noted: "We stood very quietly today, looking into the upper hall of Rhett's house. He had just come out of Scarlett's room having told her that a cat is a better mother than she is. Then there is his scene in Bonnie's death chamber, with Melanie knocking on the door. Shot several times, this scene finally reached such a pitch of despair, in the sunken eyes, the unshaven face of Rhett Butler, and the heartfelt sympathy in Melanie's eyes, as to make all of us look the other way when Clark and Olivia came off the set. Later, Clark crept to his own bungalow via the back porch of the sound stage, slithering across the yard as though afraid that someone would see him, would speak to him. He wasn't himself for the rest of the day." Hall, "Gone With the Wind: On the Set with Gladys Hall," p. 71.

[7]"My duties," wrote Wilbur Kurtz, "brought me in contact with nearly every department in the studio—from the front office to the back end of the lot. I was on call from the scriptwriters whose task it was to interpret prose narrative into dialogue and action. I even wrote in certain lines that, by historic implication, 'gave the age and body of the time his due form and pressure.' I deleted references that were incorrect historically. . . .

"Take that scene where Scarlett is shown making soft-soap in an iron kettle over a fire—it had been originally written as showing her nailing a shoe on a horse's hoof, a highly absurd performance when horses could have been shod at Jonesboro for less than a dollar. When I called attention to this, the whole scene was dropped into my lap with instructions to design it the way I thought it ought to be—with the result that Scarlett wields a paddle in a kettle of soft-soap instead of wrestling with a horse that might have taken exception to feminine blundering!" Kurtz, "Technical Adviser," p. 25.

TEN
4 June—2 July 1939

Straight From HOLLYWOOD

Scarlett's Home Shows Opulence but Poor Taste in Furnishings

HOLLYWOOD, Calif.—All the ornate, over-decorated, scroll-designed doo-dad effects that can be imagined are to be seen in the home of Rhett and Scarlett, as the designers have built it on the stage of Selznick's for *Gone With the Wind.* There is the feeling about the whole thing that follows faithfully the description given in Miss Mitchell's novel, showing the bad taste of Scarlett, who tried to outdo everybody who had built in the style of that period when architecture had sunk so low.[1]

Somebody on the set remarked the other day that the house was so terrible it was fascinating and almost beautiful.

The dining room where we shot the scene with Rhett and Scarlett drinking brandy the night after Melanie's party, is paneled with ornately carved oak and the scenes painted on the walls are typical of that era. The heavy arm chairs beside the dining table are walnut, highbacked and upholstered in red plush. On the sideboard is a magnificent silver service, and opulent silver candelabra stand on table and mantel and sideboard.

Scarlett's bedroom is a honey, itself! There is pink tufted satin for femininity and the dressing table is a clutter of silver-backed hair brush, hair receivers, perfume bottles, candle sticks with many clinky prisms and other gadgets. Opulence and poor taste are rampant.

It was in the dining room scene that we got a good laugh the other day. The camera was making a close up of Rhett, looking a little drunk and saying to Scarlett "Sit down."

Just as Clark Gable spoke his lines there came a sound of whistling. Some workman at the other end of the stage had failed to hear the bell for quiet and was merrily tuneful.

Clark looked up, laughed and asked, "How're we doing?"

Eric Stacey called out, "Quiet! What's the matter? Don't you know this is a take?"

Then Clark said, "Once again, without music, if you please."

We had much pleasure again this week with that cute little Cammie King, who is playing Bonnie Butler. When she came on the stage with her mother to get ready for her role, she was wearing a white dress trimmed in soft blue and over it she wore a little white piqué coat with Irish lace on the collar and cuffs. Over her dark curls she had a kerchief tied in the fashion of the out-door adult of today and she held the eyes of everybody around.

Her mother, too, wore white, a wash silk shirtwaist dress with a pleated skirt, white shoes and a white mesh turban.

Little Cammie is descended from both American Revolution and War Between the States fighters and while the Kurtzes and I declare she is definitely a Southerner and a Daughter of the Confederacy, the Yankees claim her for their side. Cammie has many Mississippi and Louisiana relatives.

An amazing thing happened down on Forty Acres the day we made the big boom shot. I had forgotten to tell you about it before. Vic Fleming was a stand-in!

As you probably know, all stars have stand-ins, persons who stand or sit while the lights are properly placed and so on; then the star comes in to take the place of the stand-in and the scene is shot.

Well, Vic stood in for—of all things—a lamp post!

Ernie Haller, head cameraman, was figuring on the set-up and he said maybe it would be better if a certain lamp post were moved over a little. Vic moved over a few feet, raised his arms high over his head and said:

"How would this be, Ernie?"

"Move over a foot to your left, Vic," smiled Ernie; "no, a little bit forward."

Thus, with the six-foot-two Vic as a stand-in for the lamp post, the scene was planned.

Visitors from Georgia on the stage this week included Mrs. Frances Gordon-Smith, formerly of Atlanta, now of Augusta, who is the daughter of Gen. John B. Gordon, and Mrs. William P. Duvall, the former Maria Lamar of Augusta. Mrs. Duvall who has lived almost everywhere in the United States, is descended from the Georgia and Carolina Lamars. She is the daughter of Derosset Lamar and is now living in Hollywood.

Mrs. Gordon-Smith has been in California for about six weeks and is returning to Georgia soon. She is a friend of Mrs. Ross Chambers of Macon and Madison.

Like the other Georgia visitors who have had an opportunity to see Vivien Leigh, Mrs. Gordon-Smith and Mrs. Duvall were delighted with the little actress. And like all the rest of the women in the world, they were excited over seeing Clark Gable.

Clark, by the way, gave us a big laugh on the stage the day we shot the scene where he takes Scarlett up the stairs in his arms. The lighting and the camera angles were being figured and rehearsals were going on. Vic Fleming was undecided whether Clark should go one way or another up the long flight of stairs to get the best camera angle and so on.

Clark said, "Well, watch me, Vic, and see how you like it." And he walked upstairs one way came down again and once more walked very fast up the steps.

Arrived the second time at the top of the stairs, he turned to start down, grinned at Vic and said, "I am exhausted!" Then he put his leg over the banister rail and made as if he would slide down.

We all laughed and Vic said, "O.K. Clark, we'll take it the first way."

Then he turned to the cameraman and said, "Roll 'em."

"No, you don't," said Clark. "Give me a minute to rest before I tote that Scarlett up these steps."

"Pshaw! Clark" returned Fleming. "Our Scarlett doesn't weigh but ninety pounds."

"Yes," answered Clark, "but boy, that elegant robe she wears with trains and embroideries weighs more than she does and I have to carry it too."

Such a beautiful day Sunday was. The sun shone brightly and the air was balmy and I had Sunday dinner at 1:30 with some friends who served the meal on the terrace. And later in the afternoon I went to tea with Harry Davenport, whom I really know better as Dr. Meade.

Harry lives in a cool, quiet modest home and his garden is his great pride. He isn't like most Hollywood stars about his garden, either. For Harry digs and hoes and spades and waters and he never makes a trip without bringing home some plant for his garden. If he goes to the desert, he digs up some pretty cactus plant and tenderly transplants it to his own garden. If he goes to visit a friend he wrangles the friend out of some shrub or plant to bring back.

The things he plants seem to grow every time and Harry smiles proudly when he admits he has "green fingers" (which we would call, back in Macon, "a growing hand").

We are making progress on *Gone With the Wind*. Sam Wood is back from a short vacation in New York and has taken over a second first unit again. There are a lot of scenes in which Gable works and Vivien doesn't and vice versa. So Vic is directing with one of the stars and Sam Wood with the other. And William Cameron Menzies is directing a third unit shooting montage sequences (I'll tell you what they are soon) and atmospheric shots.

Straight From HOLLYWOOD

Macon Lays Claim to Tiny Actor in Gone With the Wind Cast

HOLLYWOOD, Calif.—A Macon child is playing in *Gone With the Wind*.

At least, he is the grandson of a Macon man and the son of a former Macon man and Macon woman.

Little Ricky Holt, who plays Beauregard Wilkes at the age of eleven months, is the son of Mr. and Mrs. L. E. Holt and Mrs. Holt is the former Martha Massey, daughter of Mr. and Mrs. G. I. Massey on the Milledgeville road.

Mrs. Holt came over to me on Forty Acres when we were shooting the sequence that showed little Beauregard with Melanie, as she talks to the returning Confederate soldiers who stop for food at Tara, and told me she was from Macon and we almost embraced each other right there.

Little Ricky was adorable with fat cheeks, big blue eyes, fringed by long curling lashes and blondish-brown hair. He played with the spoon that the soldier had for eating his food and enjoyed the rehearsal immensely. When Olivia de Havilland picked him up and cuddled him in her lap he beamed on her.

Everything was ready for the take and still Ricky beamed. But when the camera started to turn and Olivia picked up the youngster he started crying.

Four times the scene was tried and Ricky cried each time.

"He seems to think he gets a cue to cry," said Vic Fleming and he sat down on the steps and cooed and chuckled at the child until the smiles were restored. Then Mrs. Holt gave Ricky a drink of orange juice and the scene was tried again. This time with vast success.

Mrs. Holt and I looked upon the child with equal pride for I felt as if Macon had showed itself in a favorable light, and she was just naturally a proud mother.

Mrs. Holt's sister, Mrs. S. B. Driggers, is bookkeeping at Burden-Smith's and Mrs. Holt is a cousin of Evelyn Stripling of Macon.

Well besides the fun of seeing the Macon grandson perform with much credit I had a fine time that same day with the props. I ate them. Not all of them but a good bit.

I went to see what the chef had brought to serve for the Confederate soldiers on the porch at Tara and when I saw the turnip greens, black-eyed peas (cooked with side meat) and the cornbread I just had to have some. The chef, a Negro who used to live in Texas, was so tickled at my approval of his food and my understanding of what Southerners eat that he volunteered to give me a serving.

And when he offered me some melted butter in which I might dip my baked potato we were friends for life.

Though it was only 9:15 in the morning I turned in and ate greens, peas, potatoes and cornbread as if I had been hunting quail for four hours and had stopped for dinner at Mr. Tom Wagner's over in Baldwin County.

I tried to get Vivien Leigh to try the Southern cooking but she said it did not appeal to her at such an hour. However, I noticed that almost everybody on the set did try a piece of watermelon when we had finished shooting the scene.

We had fun about the watermelons, too. They were small melons and Wilbur Kurtz said the crop at Tara was poor that year because there was so little time to tend it with so few hands. Both of us vowed that a melon so small as those would be fed to the hogs in Georgia nowadays. Nobody believed us so we continued to tell about the forty- and fifty-pound melons that are just medium-sized down in Georgia.

But in spite of their small size those melons certainly were good.

Well, after eating the props and finishing the scene we moved indoors and kept working on various scenes. During the last few days we have finished up the sequences where Rhett is so repentant over Scarlett's illness and the ones where Scarlett gets the idea of marrying Frank Kennedy after Rhett has refused to lend her the $300 to pay off the taxes on Tara.

The Atlanta streets are a mess, I can tell you, with mud all over the place, free issue Negroes and scalawags and carpetbaggers and Yankee women walking about, and the rebuilding of the burned city in progress.

But one of the most interesting of all the shots we have made was the one where Mammy tells Melanie about Mr. Rhett and the way he is behaving since Bonnie's death. It so happened that the conversation between Melly and Mammy took place on the stairs at Scarlett's house and that made a boom shot necessary. The boom was not half so big as the one we used at Forty Acres, of course, but it was no snide boom at that; for it measured about twenty feet in length and as Mammy and Melly climbed the stairs the camera climbed right along beside them.

Of course the microphone has to follow closely on the steps of the persons speaking in order to get conversation recorded in a clear fashion, so the mike had to climb the stairs, too. Just a step ahead of the characters and the camera the sound man walked up the stairs, holding the mike on the end of the long pole and managing by the skin of his teeth to stay out of sight of the camera's lens and at the same time to stay well within sound of the voices.

I never shall cease to marvel at the way movie folks do anything they want to do. There is no such word as impossible in their vocabulary. That shot proved to me they can do anything!

Then when a shot seemed fairly easy, as did the one we made of Melly going into the room where Rhett sat beside the body of his dead child, we encountered the most unexpected difficulties. The floor squeaked as the dolly was pulled forward. Of all things! Well, that seemed to give nobody any trouble for a few minutes and everybody thought we would be ready to shoot as soon as Fred Williams' workers got some pieces of composition material nailed down for the dolly track. But the thing still squeaked.

Then it appeared the fault was not in the floor but in the dolly so Fred's men went out and got a dolly that had pneumatic wheels and ran on the floor instead of on iron wheels and in a grooved track.

Well, that squeaked, too!

I don't know what they finally did but Fred Williams (who is head man about moving things and managing cameras and such) got it fixed.

By that time, however, we had got to feeling sort of gay and talkative and when Vic was ready to shoot, Clark Gable was in one of his fun-making moods.

To make the shot the camera was trained on the closed door to Rhett's room, Melly knocked at the door and Rhett admitted her and closed the door.

Well, I was listening for accent on the side of the room where Clark sat with the door closed. There were about four of us there—make-up man, electricians, and so on. And every time Melly knocked Clark would make horrible faces and carry on mightily so that we could scarcely keep from laughing and spoiling the take.

Then after Melly came into the room and closed the door Clark would break into a light tap dance or pretend to be an old man with a catch in his back or do some other ridiculous thing. Olivia, catching the spirit of the thing, grabbed up a chair, turned it and put it over her head so it looked as if she were behind bars or in a cage as the legs and rounds of the chair partly shielded her face. Softly, she would make little noises like a puppy growling and we almost burst with laughter.

As Vic would call "cut" and the take was over we would laugh like high school kids. Then Vic would open the door and come in to talk about how the scene went and make suggestions for the repeat of the scene.

Well, Olivia and Clark would be as grave and sober as if they had never cracked a smile but it was almost too much for us who watched.

Macon Telegraph and News, 11 June 1939

Straight From HOLLYWOOD

GWTW Shooting May Be Finished in Another Month, Myrick Says

HOLLYWOOD, Calif.—Remember way back when I said in this column that I was jealous of those who went on location? Well, I am about past that stage now. For location on *Gone With the Wind* yesterday kept us from before dawn until almost sunset, and though there are various songs of praise on sunrises, I belong to the school which believes in sleeping peacefully and letting the dawn go ahead and break without any watching.

But we did have fun laughing about how tired we were and pretending to be quite dead from lack of sleep and kidding about the dangers of the great outdoors. We were at a spot known as Agoura (somehow it is all I can do to keep from calling the place Angostura; maybe it is because of the association with bitters, for it is rather bitter to get up before the dawn breaks), and it is remote from the highway and way up in them thar hills.

It wasn't long after sun-up that one of the men killed a rattlesnake and everybody began pretending to see snakes and watching for the mate of the dead rattler. One of the men working on the *Gone With the Wind* set would sneak up behind another one, touch him on the ankle with a switch and yell. Then everybody would pretend to see a snake and we managed to get wide awake and full of cheer with the foolery.

The sun rises in Southern California about four o'clock at this time of year. That's why we got such an early start. Anyway, we got some beautiful shots that you'll see in *Gone With the Wind*.

Victor Jory, who plays Jonas Wilkerson in the picture, was on location with us and I spent some time chatting with him about the stage and his work. He played in stock for ten years and has played in almost every one of the Shakespearean dramas. And he declared he was quite happy over the fact that he didn't have to have any lessons in Southern accent because Jonas was a Yankee overseer.

But his mother was a Virginian and he could have gone Southern with little trouble if it had been necessary.

As we returned to town we passed a sub-division called Sherman Oaks and Wilbur Kurtz and I said "O-oh! don't look!" The others in the car had no notion about what we meant, but Victor knew at once and recalled the time his mother refused to speak to him when he brought home a copy of the memoirs of Gen. Ulysses S. Grant.

The scene we shot with Jonas was one in which he rode along the red clay road and looked over to see Tara in the distance and vowed he would own it some day, and you should have seen the red road we made.[2] Tons of red dust flew over the place, for the wind blew hard and dust swept off the road with each gust so that the stand-by effects man had to keep putting more red on.

But the movies don't seem to mind anything. The boy who works with effects told me he used ten thousand gallons of water to break up the ground and get it in condition for a garden patch so we could shoot a scene with Scarlett in the garden at Tara.

One laugh I got from the day at Agoura came from Harve Foster, who was assistant director on the location unit. The camera was about to turn and three property men were still working at something on the scene, where bearded, ragged Confederate soldiers limped along the road.

"We're about to roll 'em, boys!" called Harve to the prop men. "You better get off the set—or put on beards."

Fortunately for us who work pretty long hours, somebody is always being funny on the sets. Clark Gable, for instance, entertained us greatly the other day when he had a scene with Pork. Director Vic Fleming told Clark he must bump into Pork as he came from his room to go rapidly across the hall.

"Bump him hard. Be in a hurry," said Vic.

"But, Vic, Pork is almost as big as Jack Dempsey. Why pick out a chap that size for me to bump into?"

Then as Clark walked onto the stage he added, "And Pork with gray hair looking like an old man, too; my public will say it is just like Gable, picking on an old man."

Pork and the rest of us grinned and the scene started. Clark rushed out of his room. Pork rushed toward the room, and Clark gave Pork such a bump that Pork fell right down on the floor.

Clark apologized and everybody, including Pork, yelled with laughter.

Oscar Polk, who plays Pork, is a good actor and is most conscientious about his work. The other day he had only one line to say in a scene, and we saw him rehearsing for dear life. He was partly shielded by a screen and unaware of observers, and he watched himself in a mirror as he repeated his line over and over with varying inflections and expressions.

You're going to love Pork in *Gone With the Wind*.

But the person who is going to steal your heart is little Cammie King, who is playing Bonnie Blue Butler at the age of four. We shot the scenes where Bonnie rides her little pony, calls to her mother and father that she is going to take the high jump and rides away in spite of her mother's protest. Bonnie was wearing a blue velvet riding habit, like the one described in *Gone With the Wind*, and she wore little red gloves and riding boots and sat on her horse like a veteran, though she had only been practicing on a side saddle for about a week. She learned to ride several years ago but the side saddle was new for her. She was such a darling that everybody on the stage went into ecstasies over her as she trotted that little pony up to the terrace where Scarlett and Rhett were sitting, told them to watch her jump and rode off at a fast pace.

Everybody enjoyed, too, the little boy who trained the pony to carry a rider on a side saddle. He is little Dick Smith, son of the man who owns the pony. He is a red-headed child of seven years, and has been riding ever since he can remember. His father says he put Dick on a horse the first time when the baby was only four months old, and that at a year-and-a-half the child could ride a gentle horse without any help at all.[3]

Dick and Cammie hit it off well, and Cammie's mother says the little girl has been having a wonderful time riding on a big circus horse that Mr. Smith owns. Cammie and Dick stand on the broad back of the horse and pretend they are members of a circus troupe.

And speaking of circuses, I had a regular circus last weekend with Lee Hutchins, formerly of Fort Valley, now of—well, almost anywhere. For: Lee's field headquarters are Brownwood, Tex., but he skitters about the United States looking after all sorts of virus diseases of fruit trees.

Lee is staying several weeks at Riverside, Cal., about fifty miles from Hollywood, and he spent a weekend here. We visited Earl Carroll's night club, and took in the La Conga and a few other night spots Saturday night. Strangely enough, I had the good luck to be off from work early (I call seven p.m. "early"), and we had a fine evening talking about folks back in Macon and Fort Valley and other Georgia places.

Sunday, we called on the Lamar Trottis and had a second reunion, for Lamar and Louise know many friends of Lee's and there was much chatter about Helen Harrold Fredericks and Beth Hiley Strother, and the John Bairds and the John Allens, and—oh, everybody in Middle Georgia.

We took time to congratulate Lamar on the production: *The Young Mr. Lincoln*, which has recently opened here. Lamar wrote the script and John Ford directed the picture, and critics are acclaiming it as a fine piece of work. Lamar, with his usual modesty, would not talk about the picture, but we managed to get the news from Louise that he does think it is a good picture. Which seems to make it unanimous.

But, of course, I think *Gone With the Wind* is going to be the picture of all time, and it looks from where I now sit that we shall not be much longer at the filming—maybe about a month. Of course I am not quite sure, but, anyway, we are rushing toward the finish, with two units shooting much of the time and some days with three. But with editing and all, I am told it will probably be November or December before the premiere.

Macon Telegraph, 22 June 1939

Straight From HOLLYWOOD

Miss Myrick, Clark Gable, and Hattie McDaniel Suffer Colds

HOLLYWOOD, Calif.—Clark Gable, Hattie McDaniel and I have colds. Naturally I feel happier about a cold when I am in such good company, but the thing that really pleased me was Hattie's bringing me a bottle of home-made cough syrup. I think Hattie has played Mammy so long in the picture *Gone With the Wind* that she is being Mammy in real life, for she worried about my coughing and insisted that I take a swallow of cough syrup every time I felt a cough coming on.

The prescription is made up according to an old formula which Hattie got from her mother and the medicine contains, among other things, linseed oil, lemon juice and "some of the best bourbon."

In spite of his cold Clark has been working right along at Selznick International and he spent all of one day on a big black horse in the sequence where he is teaching little Bonnie Butler how to ride and how to take her pony over a jump.

Cammie King is still the darling of the lot and the way that five-year-old rides her pony and is not afraid of anything is evoking vast admiration from all of us.

As Clark, riding his horse, led the pony over the jump, Cammie jumped higher than the little animal and when he told her she could take the jump the child was as thrilled as you are when the Peaches win a baseball game.

Several times Cammie took the jump without trouble, but one time the pony was going pretty fast and as he jumped Cammie was unseated and rolled easily to the ground. All of us started toward her, but Vic Fleming reached her first, picked her up in his arms and asked if she was all right.

Cammie pushed her dark curls back from her face, managed a tremulous smile and said:

"I didn't even cry, did I?"[4]

Everybody breathed again and then we turned to look at Mrs. King, Cammie's mother, who sat near. She hadn't moved a muscle. Though she was scared half to death she managed to sit quietly and not rush into the scene. So—we decided it was no wonder Cammie was the child she is—what with that sort of mother who can control herself in the face of excitement.

Cammie insisted that she was not afraid and got right back on the pony to finish the scene. We held our breaths every time she took the jump but she never missed again.

There is another child on the Selznick lot who is attractive, too—Douglas Scott is playing in *Intermezzo*, which is being directed by Gregory Ratoff, and in which Leslie Howard is playing the leading role.

Douglas is fair-haired and pink-cheeked and he is the sort of boy whom you just know looks like his mother. Aged only thirteen he is a senior in high school and his mother told me the other day that Douglas could read before he was three. At the age of four he was reading books that second and third grade children usually read.

Douglas and I started an acquaintance because of a mutual interest in Kodaking—for making pictures is his hobby right now.

Pretty soon we are meeting another youngster—for little Phyllis Callow, daughter of Reggie Callow (who is assistant to Eric Stacey) is to play a bit as Bonnie Butler at the age of two-and-a-half.

You see, we have Bonnie in various stages of growth in this picture, so we have a number of children. I never shall know how the casting director manages to find children that resemble each other for the various ages. A six-months-old Bonnie was on the set today. She is named Julia Ann Tuck and is a darling to look at. She has not acted her role yet. Tell you more about her when I have seen her before the camera.

The Technicolor camera, expensive and fine as it is, has grown sort of commonplace to me after these months of close association and right now my admiration has switched from Ernie Haller, and his wonderful ability to light scenes and make them look their best and his artistic pictures, over to Lee Zavitz, special effects man.

Lee does things that make my brain reel in an effort to comprehend how he does them. For instance—we took some pictures of Scarlett walking through a foggy dawn toward her home after the death of Melly. Remember in the book? Well, it was Lee's job to make fog.

Which is of itself amusing—for we have the foggiest fogs on the Forty Acres in Culver City that can be found outside of London or maybe Nova Scotia. But it seems real fog doesn't photograph well (just as rain and snow do not photograph properly. Remember I wrote once of Eric Stacey's remark that if he were going to photograph a scene in Alaska the first prop he would plan to take would be artificial snow?).

Well, Lee puts some mineral oil and some chemicals in a bucket and sprays them over dry ice and the effect produced is far more like a fog than a real fog would be.

When we shot scenes filled with smoke from the fire as Atlanta burned, Lee made magnificent smoke for the camera. He ought to wear a pennant bearing the words "Watch my Smoke."

And Lee makes beautiful sounds of exploding shells and guns firing and any other sort of noise that is desired. My advice to boys looking for a vocation is learn how to be a special effects man.

Lee even knows how to make an ice-skating rink for your back yard at a cost of sixteen cents a square foot and the artificial ice (it isn't really ice at all but it looks like ice and skates like ice) doesn't melt unless the temperature in your back yard gets to 120 degrees F.

We didn't need Lee for any effects, however, the day we made shots at Reuss's Ranch. The place is so green and lovely and the day was just sunny enough (I don't think Lee can make sunlight) and all of us felt rested and fine when evening came. Someone found a king snake and one of the crew put it in his pocket and let it wrap itself around his neck and wore it for a bracelet and I felt like I had been on a picnic with the high school set.

Except that I talked to Tommy Mitchell for quite a long time and you'd never think of Tommy as a high school boy. He is much too bright and successful as an actor and playwright.

Tommy (who is Gerald O'Hara) wrote *Little Accident* and played the lead in it, some years ago, when the play was a great success and ran for months on Broadway.

During the next few days we'll be working on Forty Acres again and before many more weeks the production schedule on *Gone With the Wind* will be closed. If you are half as anxious to see the picture as I am I don't know how we'll wait!

Macon Telegraph and News, 25 June 1939

Straight From HOLLYWOOD

More Interesting Scenes Are Filmed for Gone With the Wind

HOLLYWOOD, Calif.—Frank Kennedy's business has certainly grown since Scarlett bought the saw-mill and took over the management of the store. We worked at Forty Acres the other day on the *Gone With the Wind* set, making scenes that show the development of the business and the way in which Scarlett works hand in glove with carpetbaggers and scalawags.

It was hot on the Forty, too, and all of us hunted the shade. But such are the vagaries of the California climate that as soon as I sat in the shade I wanted my coat. Imagine—if you can—wanting a coat at midday in June! I have yet to see a day on the Forty that does not bring cool breezes and often those breezes are so cold everybody hunts the sunshine and shivers even then.

Annie Laurie Kurtz was the funniest thing I ever saw the other evening at the Forty. You know she is assisting her husband, Wilbur, who is technical director for *Gone With the Wind*. Annie Laurie was so cold she wrapped up in two of the shawls that had been provided for the extras in the scene. Then to protect her hair from the red dust that was blowing on Atlanta's streets, she put a cornshuck bonnet on her head. She looked so quaint and funny that Wilbur took a picture of her and half of us stopped working to laugh.

But I have left the Frank Kennedy business and I meant to tell you how well the set decorator did his stuff on that store. Eddie Boyle is the man and he certainly did a marvelous job of making it look like a combination general store and builders' supply business. In front of the entrance are horse collars, churns with dashers, demijohns, well-windlasses, big saws and split baskets. The place looks so much like the little old store my father used to have on the plantation that I got homesick. There was plenty of red dust all over the place, too, to add to the effect of a Georgia town.

I liked that scene but I reckon the most fascinating sequence I have seen was the one we made that showed Rhett and Scarlett wheeling little Bonnie in the baby carriage. Vivien looked so pert and smart in her bustle-gown of pink, trimmed in black and pink striped ruffles, and Clark was so elegant in his morning clothes and top hat.[5]

And that little Julia Ann Tuck was a darling! She smiled and seemed so happy about the whole thing. Maybe I ought not to tell you the secret of her smiles, but I can't resist it. Vic Fleming walked backward just out of sight of the camera and waved his handkerchief and smiled at the seven-months-old baby so that she cooed and laughed at him. For that matter, I laughed too—though I didn't coo!

For that shot we had a three hundred-foot-dolly track. To see the men lay the track was about like watching the construction of a railroad. They put down planks so fast and finished the job so quickly it made me marvel all over again at the efficiency of people who work in the movies.

It required twelve men to push the carriage on which the camera and the boom rode, for a fifteen-foot steel boom is not a lightweight even when it rides on pneumatic tires. And the dolly must move with exactly the right speed and it must stop and start at just the right places.

On the boom and on the dolly the camera has three movements at the same time. The dolly moves forward along the track, the boom moves up or down and the camera turns left or right angles high or low as the cameraman cranks it.

So, you see, the possibilities for error are great and when the dolly moves three hundred feet along a track it is quite a stunt to make everything move in perfect coordination.

We made a boom and dolly shot, too, on the scene with Ashley and Scarlett and Frank Kennedy in the sawmill. It was fun to have Leslie Howard on the set again for he has been absent for weeks. His work in

Gone With the Wind is about finished and for several weeks he has been working on *Intermezzo*, a Selznick production, in which Howard plays the role of a violinist.

Intermezzo is being filmed on the stage next door to our *Gone With the Wind* scene and Gregory Ratoff is directing it. Ingrid Bergman and Edna Best are playing in the production and so is the young Douglas Scott about whom I wrote last week.

I am getting almost blasé about famous persons since there are so many of them around from time to time, but I did get a kick out of seeing Ben Bernie when he visited our set the other day.

And speaking of the famous, I found my first visit to the Field and Turf Club most fascinating. This club is at the Ambassador Hotel, the same building that houses the Cocoanut Grove about which you have read, I am sure—the spot where movie stars are often reported dancing—you know in the gossip columns.

The cocktail bar at the club is decorated with caricatures of movie and stage stars, with a border about three feet below the ceiling and the painting continues on the ceiling. There is a bit of surrealism in the drawing; for on the head of Maurice Chevalier is a real straw hat; Mary Pickford's figure is practically swathed in real hair; Mae West's jewels are lighted with electric light bulbs; Jimmie Durante has a plaster nose of enormous proportions and Eddie Cantor has plaster eyes that are bulgingly enormous.

Below the mural border the walls are cream-colored and on them are good wishes, wisecracks and poems written and signed by the great and near-great. On one wall are the signatures of famous fliers. There is Richard Byrd's name and there too are the signatures of Wiley Post and Lincoln Ellsworth.

A Ben Bernie looks over the transom of the door and takes cracks at Walter Winchell, who has his ear to the keyhole.

It is a fascinating place, the club. It brought to my mind the room at Aaron Bernd's country house, Teeter-on-the-Jitters, where his Macon friends used to sign their names on the beaver-board walls.

In fact, many things here remind me of Georgia. I suppose it is partly because *Gone With the Wind* is a Georgia story.

I wish I could say that the trees, flowers and markets here remind me of Georgia. Never have I seen anything so beautiful as the markets in this city! Vegetables and fruits are displayed with the artistry a painter would use for his finest work. The yellow-gold of carrots, squash and canteloupe, the soft green of watercress, escarole, water-melon, chicory; the tender pale green of lettuce and endive; the bright color that is radishes. The effect is like a gigantic canvas splashed with color.

And the flowers out here are positively indecent in their size and plenitude. Roses are as big as breakfast plates!

Everybody has a garden and a gardener. A family may not be able to afford a cook or a maid but they always have a gardener. And when anybody plans to build a house out here, they first figure the cost of landscaping and of putting in an irrigation system. It makes for a town of great beauty.

And it gives me a great enthusiasm for the effort of the Marshal-lville committee, headed by John Wade, who plan to make a beauty spot of the highway from Macon to Andersonville Prison Park.

Not more beautiful, of course, than the camellias and the crape myrtles that have been planted on Georgia's roads are the strangely fascinating trees here. But there is a certain sort of tree that I drive five blocks out of my way to see every morning.

Somebody told me it is a type of mimosa, but it is really a jacaranda tree. The foliage is the same feathery sort that we have on the lovely trees in Coleman Hill Park and in Baconsfield Park. But the blossoms are a deep lavender color and the trees are fairly dripping with bloom. Looking down the street that is bordered with the trees, one sees a misty purple that looks like a mountain shadow and fades away into the distant hills in a manner to warm the heart and uplift the soul.

Well, enough of California! I'm pretty soon "gwine back to Dixie" and for the next three weeks or so, I shall continue to live in the atmosphere of Georgia on the *Gone With the Wind* set at Selznick International Pictures.

Straight From HOLLYWOOD

Work Nears End on GWTW and Sue Will Be Back Home Next Month

HOLLYWOOD, Calif.—Vivien Leigh hid under a bridge a night or two ago, shivering with dread while the Yankee troops passed overhead, and dust and trash sifted through the cracks between the planks. The poor girl has eaten so much red dust in the making of *Gone With the Wind* that I think Georgians should adopt her as a native daughter.

But nothing seems to bother our Vivien. Men stand off and pour dust into a wind machine so it blows all over her; cavalry horses almost run into her, cannons pass within a few inches of her, a wagon tries to run away with her as she makes her escape on the Shantytown road. Vivien takes it all as calmly as Scarlett O'Hara should.

We have been shooting all sorts of scenes the past few days, trying to finish up odds and ends that have been omitted as we went along and there is every indication that we have "jes' a few mo' days fer to tote de weary load."

In spite of working early and late I found time to shift the weary load for one night and with Lee Hutchins, former Fort Valley resident, I had quite an evening.

Gather 'round girls. If you've heard this, don't stop me. I want to hear it again myself.

At long last I went to the Trocadero Saturday night.

The spot is all it is reported, an atmosphere that is delightful, with beautiful decorations, with two good orchestras, with plenty of handsome men dancing and with the most beautiful women I ever saw,— 'scusin' none.

Concealed lighting provides a soft glow over the room with its pale pink walls, its deep blue drapes, its pale blue and silver ceiling. The place was packed and if Lee hadn't been smart enough to make a reservation we'd have been left standing by the silver ropes at the door, waiting for a table, as many other disappointed couples were standing.

As it was, we had a grand table, along the wall, on a little raised platform where we could see everything and everybody. We had scarcely sat down when a familiar voice called to me and I looked up to see Pink and Marian Happ dancing. They came over and talked to us and both of them looked gay and sunburned and happy. They've been having guests from Miami and enjoying a fine summer at Bel Air, on the edge of Los Angeles.

But I scarcely had time to notice how ravishing Marian looked in her flowered chiffon gown when Lee excitedly showed me a tall, dark man and asked who he was.

You'd have died laughing at us; for neither of us is any good at recognizing faces. We spent the evening asking each other excitedly: "Now who IS that person with the face that is so familiar?"

If it had not been for the gentleman at the table next to us we'd have recognized only about two faces. As it was, everytime we asked each other, "Who is that?" the gentleman at the next table would tell us.

But even I recognized Caesar Romero, the slender, dark chap who was dancing like a professional, gliding as smoothly as the best rhumba dancer in all Spain.

Then I sighted another tall, slender fellow, this time a somewhat blondish chap.

"Look! Robert Montgomery," I whispered to Lee.

"Robert Montgomery, your grandmother!" said the gentleman at the next table. (How he heard me I don't know!) "That's Robert Young."

And he was right.

And in case any of you girls want to get thrilled over it I may tell you that Robert bumped against me when Lee and I were dancing.

Little by little (with the aid of the helpful gentleman next to us) we discovered various celebrities. Most beautiful of all the women in the room was Norma Shearer, who was dancing with a tall fellow whom we failed to recognize. The gentleman-next-door was dancing and didn't hear us talking about Norma, so we never found out who her partner was.

No movie yet made shows how lovely that Shearer woman looks. You'd vow she was not a day over twenty and her skin is so flawlessly smooth and soft and pinky-white that all other skins in the world look muddy. She was wearing a slinky dark evening gown with a huge shawl collar of dark blue, cherry and white.

Alice Faye's gown was of chiffon, the color that fashion editors used to call "off-white," but we of the Technicolor movies know the shade as White No. 4. I tried to remember the names of a dozen Macon men who wanted me to bring back Alice as a present for them but Art Nims was the only one I could think of at the moment. I decided I didn't blame Art and I should have been happy to bring Alice except she looked so happy with her husband as she danced with him I didn't have the heart to interfere.

As for what one of the technical advisers of *Gone With the Wind* was wearing, I shall say little—only that it was not the old gray suit she wore when she left home. But Lee Hutchins, now, he was the pattern for the well-dressed young man with a double-breasted Tuxedo and a maroon tie and cummerbund.

Later, we did Slapsie Maxie's and then had scrambled eggs and I felt like I was a high school senior celebrating Little Commencement.

I had time to recover from gaiety and late hours on Sunday and it was fortunate for me because Monday we worked until midnight.

The reason for such late hours is the finishing of the first unit work on *Gone With the Wind*. Vivien Leigh is all through and has gone for a vacation and the rest of our shooting will be finished this week.

Shortly after that I shall start on a brief trip about Southern California, then I'm selling my little puddle-jumper, packing up and starting toward Georgia. But I am taking a vacation trip, so don't look for me until about the middle of August.

I'll write from time to time and when I get back I'll promise to tell you all you want to know about *Gone With the Wind*. I hope you will forgive me if I constantly rave about what a marvelous picture it is going to be.

Our work may be nearly done, but our producer, David O. Selznick, is only half through with his task. They tell me that all motion pictures are a long time editing after the last scenes are filmed on the set. Takes just as long to edit as it does to shoot. So the inside dope is that *Gone With the Wind* probably will be ready for the theaters about the first of the year.

Editor's Notes—Ten

[1]Gladys Hall described the "dream house" of Scarlett's Reconstruction days in her record of studio activities for 27 May: "Rhett's house, by the way, is a fearful and wonderful accumulation of architectural and interior-decoration modes and styles. There are Ionic columns at the doorway, medieval tapestry on the walls, a Byzantine fireplace, a Chinese bronze statue, life-sized, Gothic furniture, Georgian silverware, mammoth cloisonné vases, red plush carpets. The whole, of course, was deliberately designed to fulfill Scarlett's desire to have something 'elegant' with which to impress her old friends who had snubbed her when she took up with scalawags, made money off carpetbaggers and was responsible, because of her carelessness, for the death of her husband, Frank Kennedy." Hall, "Gone With the Wind: On the Set with Gladys Hall," p. 71.

[2]This scene was dropped from the picture during its editing.

[3]Richard Smith was Cammie King's riding double in the scene in which the horse throws Bonnie.

[4]In her entry for 13 June, Gladys Hall told of this incident differently (or was it a different incident?): "I had a comfortable chair in one corner of Rhett's garden today, while I watched Rhett teach his small daughter, Bonnie, to ride horseback and jump rose bushes. On the first jump, Cammie fell off her pony. Clark rushed over to her, inquiring anxiously, 'Are you hurt?' She laughed up at him and said, 'Not now!' " Hall, "Gone With the Wind: On the Set with Gladys Hall," p. 72.

[5]Hall described this as of 21 June: "Today they shot the scene where Rhett and Scarlett promenade with little Bonnie in her trick baby carriage, Rhett being very sweet to the society ladies of Atlanta, Scarlett uncompromisingly resentful. Rhett tells her that if she'd thought of her social position before, they wouldn't have to go through this gauntlett now. Gable was really Something to See today. He wore a black broadcloth suit, a gray hat, the ensemble relieved by a pink Ascot tie and a pink rose boutonnierre [sic]. According to wardrobe figures, Clark told me, disgustedly, he now has more wardrobe changes than any male actor in cinema history has ever had—thirty-six in all.

Previous record was held by Freddie March in *Anthony Adverse*, with a total of thirty-two." Hall, "Gone With the Wind: On the Set with Gladys Hall," p. 72.

ELEVEN
9 July—13 July 1939

Goodbye HOLLYWOOD

Sue Finishes Work on GWTW and Plans to Rest for Short Time

HOLLYWOOD, Calif.—The wind stopped blowing (for me) Saturday night and I walked off the lot at Selznick International Pictures a free woman once more. The tornado had gradually subsided to a gentle breeze and I was no longer needed for the slight wafting of air that must go on. For the company will continue to shoot battle scenes and montages for weeks and then there is editing to do and there will be probable retakes to make when Vivien Leigh returns from her vacation in about six weeks.[1]

The night that Vivien completed her work (after some five months of almost daily enacting the role of Scarlett O'Hara) we had a party. I mean, Vivien Leigh, Clark Gable, David O. Selznick, Olivia de Havilland and Victor Fleming gave a party for the company.[2]

And what a party! There was a dance floor laid on Stage 5 and tables arranged around the huge room and we danced until a late hour. A buffet supper was served us and there was much gaiety served up along with the aperitifs.

A dance contest narrowed down to three couples and there seemed to be some trouble among the judges about which couple was winner so the announcer said the three judges would be invited to dance and let the company see if they were competent judges. Then he insisted that I should ask Mr. Daniel T. O'Shea to dance with me to prove his ability. So I did. The other judges danced, too, and the crowd applauded vigorously.

Finally, the crowd yelled that the judges would do all right, the announcer sent the three contesting couples back to the floor and the prize was awarded.

The biggest thrill I got from the party, I think, was meeting Carole Lombard, who came to the party with her husband, Clark Gable. Carole looked so svelte and lovely with her blond hair swirling about her shoulders, wearing a wine-colored frock and a silver-fox coat that would make her the envy of any woman in the world. She was gracious and smiling, too, and when Clark introduced me to her she said:

"Oh yes, I've heard about you. You are the woman who has made my life miserable because I've had to listen to Clark going Southern."

But she admitted, later, she was proud of his ability to sound like he came from the Deep South.

But I must jump away from the Selznick International lot, because I am really not even near to it, in the flesh. I came up to Santa Barbara to stay several days at the Samarkand, a hotel that is the most fascinating place I ever saw.

The hotel building sits high on a hill, looking down on the southeast, to the Pacific. (I know it doesn't make sense for the Pacific Ocean to be on the southeast. I was taught in geography that the Pacific was on the west. But on the S.E. it is!) Across the town of Santa Barbara, looking to the north and the west, the mountain ranges brood in their dark purple shadows and where their high peaks come through the fog, they shine in yellow, tan lights.

Don't ever tell a Californian I said so, but I miss the green trees that grow on Georgia's mountains. The covering for these mountains is low brush and grass and when the summer comes the grasses and shrubs are brown with dryness because it doesn't rain here after the first of March.

Still, I must say the mountains have a beauty of their own—the shimmering of the brown grasses when the sun strikes them and the strange fantastic shapes that erosion brings to the sides and the sharp pyramidal peaks that break the lines of the ranges.

It is difficult, at the Samarkand, to look off as far as the mountains, however. For the gardens are so lovely your eye can scarcely bear to leave the riot of color that is here.

At the rear of the tall hotel building is a long courtyard flanked on each side by garden villas where guests live. Mine is a sitting room, decorated in Swedish modern, and a bedroom, attractive and comfortable. Right now, I have shut all the windows, for it is too cold to write unless I wear a coat.

From time to time I must stop writing to walk to my little front porch and look out at the garden again. Directly in front of my doorway is a mirror pool in which wades a sculptured flamingo, looking disdainfully at the lovely yellow water lilies that grow near him.

Down the flagged walk that leads through the garden the eye follows to the lapis color that is the swimming pool, backed by gay and colorful dressing rooms, bright (though I have no idea it ever gets hot enough for one to sit under a parasol) and still further backed by a high wall that guards the tennis courts and badminton courts.

Masses of bright yellow flowers glow in the sunlight; purple and lavender petunias; bright red geraniums; a tall purple lily of some sort, in great numbers; flowering magnolias and many colorful flowers which are strangers to my Georgia eye make the garden as gay as a bright corner in the ten-cent store at Christmas time.

It is difficult to tear myself long enough from the garden to write but I must tell you about having dinner with Marian and Pink Happ the other evening. They have taken a house in the Bel Air estates, a Los Angeles residential district where the swank live. They are next door to Bob Burns and often see him walking about his garden playing with his dogs.

Pink and Marian asked me many questions about Maconites, though they actually knew more news from home than I did. Marian says somebody is always sending them clippings and then, too, Morris Michael Jr. and his wife, Helen, have recently visited the Happs, bringing more news from home.

Another interesting day for me recently was the one on which I met Paul Osborne, playwright. I had gone to the office to see Mr. Selznick and was waiting in the anteroom when Mr. Selznick's secretary came in and introduced Mr. Osborne.

For once in my life I said the right thing:

"Mr. Paul Osborne, the playwright?" I asked.

He admitted that he was and I said: "O yes, I know, *On Borrowed Time* and *The Vinegar Tree*."

"You have a good memory," said he, and looked pleased.

"Not at all," I answered. "You write good plays."

I reckon that "Fannie Squeersed" him for he asked me to go to lunch with him.

Of course I told him that Macon's Little Theater had produced *The Vinegar Tree* and he appeared greatly interested in Mrs. Piercy Chestney's ideas about the Little Theater and asked many questions about our progress.

With Lee Hutchins (who is still stationed at Riverside, Calif.) I went to see the Pacific fleet, anchored off Long Beach, and it was a sight to arouse the patriotism in one's breast.

Huge gray battleships, trim cruisers, giant airplane carriers rocked ever so proudly on the broad blue waters of the Pacific with their turrets reaching grimly into the air and their big guns, sleek and dangerous, pointing upward.

We "water-taxied" out to the *California* and were guided over it from quarters of the enlisted men to quarterdeck, to gun turrets to life boats and so on. Hundreds of visitors milled about; fresh-looking, sunburned young sailors grinned and ushered visitors; occasional young ladies sat in obscure corners holding hands with gobs and there was a gala air over the fleet.

I felt like announcing proudly to the whole outfit that I came from Georgia and what was more, from the Sixth District that sent Carl Vinson to Congress. There was born in me a great patriotic feeling of admiration for the Navy and I was more proud than ever that Macon has given to the United States five admirals.

We tried to find A. L. Nims Sr. in Long Beach but did not succeed. Seems he was taking a trip somewhere, though he has so recently returned from Africa and from Macon, where he visited his son, Art Nims Jr.

I am vacationing around Southern California for a while and shall gradually work my way back to Macon. Meanwhile, I wish all the folks in Georgia could see this wonderful Samarkand Hotel; for it is unique in its beauty. I may just stay here the rest of my life.

Macon Telegraph, 13 July 1939

Goodbye HOLLYWOOD

Sue Sees More of California and Plans to Go to Canada Next

By THE TIME you read this I shall be in Victoria, eating Devonshire cream and strawberries and sipping a dish of tea, if Olivia de Havilland is to be believed—and I think she is. For Olivia says no place in America is so English as Victoria and she has told me the spots to visit and just where to find the best Devonshire cream. She adds that the cream is so good one does not mind gaining the inevitable pounds.

For that matter I put on a few pounds, I fear, at the Samarkand in Santa Barbara, for eating on the American plan always induces over-eating. You know how it is: lots of good things on the menu and you are paying for the food whether you eat it or not—so!

The drive to Santa Barbara from Los Angeles is a magnificent panorama of scenery with mountains on one side and ocean on the other. The road curves and twists along the shore, darting behind an enormous boulder that makes you feel all hemmed in, then emerging upon a view of the Pacific that makes you hold your breath.

Santa Barbara itself, is a town of enchantment with its wide streets, its quiet air, its Spanish tiles, colorful and bright, its houses of Mediterranean influence and its flowering trees and shrubs.

The vine called Cup of Gold was in flower when I was there. The blossom is all the name implies, pure gold in color and shaped like an enormous teacup. The vine grows so rapidly that in four or five years it will cover the side of a two-story building. In fact, I fear it is somewhat like our kudzu for rapid growth and I can see, in fancy, the Santa Barbara housewives employing a man whose sole duty it is to prune the Cup of Gold lest it take possession of the place and drive the householders into the street.

Bougainvillea in flame and purple colors was blossoming, too, at Santa Barbara. Of course it doesn't make sense for that vine to be blooming now: for in Florida it puts forth flowers in February. But nothing here has any season. At the Samarkand, for instance, it was so cold we had a fire in our living room fireplace every night. And the swimming pool in the patio garden is heated to 80 degrees so the guests will be able to go swimming in the cool breezes.

In Santa Barbara is the only Spanish courthouse in the world. (At least that is what the guide told me.) And it is a building well suited to the surroundings and planned with attention to detail that makes it a show place of charm and beauty and old world atmosphere.

The interior of the courthouse is so colorful with its superb archways, its bright Spanish tiles, its balconies and its unexpected windows that I could not imagine the ordinary, the tax receiver, the county commissioners at work here. I kept expecting a Spanish don to step from back of the curtains and bow, or looking for senoritas with combs in their hair to click heels in a Spanish dance.

The sashes of the windows with their wrought iron grills are painted a vivid blue; curtains of terra cotta red hang against the white balconies and match the tile roof and hundreds of gay potted plants rim outdoor staircases, loggias and window ledges.

The assembly room on the second floor is magnificent; I don't know how county commissioners (they call them supervisors here) can attend to prosaic business in such a place. Superb murals on three of the walls represent Santa Barbara's history.

There is the arrival of Juan Rodriguez Cabrillo in 1542 pictured on the seventy-foot wall. His two staunch galleons ride at anchor on the sunlit bay and friendly Indians give him welcome.

Another wall shows the Santa Barbara mission beginning and a third mural shows the coming of Colonel Fremont and his soldiers to announce the new sovereignty of California.

The furniture is of Spanish and Moorish influence, made of heavy hand-carved oak and studded with large brass nails.

Throughout the halls there are richly tinted tiles and mosaics and the staircase, with its cathedral-like circular windows, is gay with the blue terra cotta and yellow tiles that form the lifts of the steps.

Amazing as the building was for a courthouse, I got a bigger thrill from the fact that Helen Hayes, Ben Hecht and Charles McArthur were in Santa Barbara, staying at the Samarkand, right under the same roof with us.

Helen Hayes and Herbert Marshall were opening in a new play, written by Hecht and McArthur and the premiere was to be held at Santa Barbara several nights after we left.

Marcella Rabwin, private secretary to David O. Selznick, told me excitedly that she was in the play. Not in the flesh but in the lines. Ben Hecht had told her she was in his play and she had sent a scout to find out just how she was used.

The play was all about the movies and in one scene the producer was calling his office on the phone. He kept asking questions and at intervals he would say:

"Well, ask Marcella, she knows."

Which, of course, made Marcella very proud and happy, though the critics did not acclaim the play as any world-beater.

Saturday night I drove with some friends up to Mount Wilson to the famous observatory. The mountain is six thousand feet high and the drive was a continuous scene of far-flung magnificence, with the setting sun making distant shadows glow rosy-purple and with jagged peaks lifting their heads high out of the low hanging mist.

We ate picnic supper in the park that surrounds the observatory and a deer came up and ate out of my hand. There is a herd of a hundred and fifty deer in the park and they are tame. No dogs are allowed on the reservation and—for that matter—no smoking is permitted on the drive of twenty miles up the mountain. Fire wardens ride the road as speed cops ride the streets in cities and if you are caught smoking it means a $50 fine and no excuses accepted.

As one of about a thousand people I got in line to look through the sixty-inch telescope that was trained on a bit of nebulae in the Milky Way. And miraculously, there appeared what seemed to be a thousand twinkling stars in the heavens at the spot where my eye had beheld only a shadowy whiteness.

It was exciting to see the dome of the great building roll back so the telescope could be trained on the stars but even more exciting, I think, was the view of Los Angeles miles below us where millions of lights made stars in a velvety sky that was mysteriously below us instead of above us.

Glowing neon signs, great searchlights and clusters of brightness that were advertising signs shone like major constellations and Mars in his red beauty in the sky above us was pale beside the Sirius and the Betelgeuse which the lights formed below us.

And now, if I may leap nimbly back to prosaic things, I should like to tell you of seeing Bette Davis, in disguise at Marcel's, where I went to dance one evening. I should never have recognized her if the waiter had not obligingly told me who she was for she wore her hair pinned back tightly under a black hat with a black wimple and her heavy-lensed glasses changed her appearance completely. She wore a black blouse and a short black-and-white plaid skirt and she was dancing with her husband (Or, so the waiter said—I wouldn't know).

Well; that's all for this time. See you in Canada.

Editor's Notes—ELEVEN

[1]Myrick wrote Margaret Mitchell on 28 May: "Our production schedule that came to us yesterday is meant to show us through to the finish and with two directors working first unit we are scheduled to be through on June 22. Sam Wood is going to shoot on one stage while Vic shoots on the other and I am to dash madly between here and there. And besides those, Bill Menzies has a third unit working at things where doubles are used and making Montages and so on. . . . On the 22, if we are really closed by that time, Vivien is to have a five weeks holiday and the stuff we have made is to be re-cut and reviewed and previewed and cut some more and plans made for some scenes and so on."

[2]This was a few days later than had been projected on 28 May. The call sheet for 27 June is actually an invitation to a studio wrap-up party. It reads: "In gratitude for your unfailing efforts and courtesy during the long Siege of Atlanta, and in celebration of the conclusion of the damned thing, we request the pleasure of your company at a little party to be given on Stage 5 immediately after Tuesday's shooting, June 27th." It was signed in the mimeograph template by the four principal players, each identified by his or her part; and then by Victor Fleming, identified as Big Sam; and David O. Selznick, identified as Jonas Wilkerson.

SELECTED BIBLIOGRAPHY

Canutt, Yakima, with Oliver Drake. *Stunt Man: the Autobiography of Yakima Canutt*. New York: Walker and Company, 1979.

Clarens, Carlos. *George Cukor*. Cinema One Series, 28. London: Secker and Warburg, in association with the British Film Institute, 1976.

Edwards, Anne. *Vivien Leigh: a Biography*. New York: Simon and Schuster, 1977.

Flamini, Roland. *Scarlett, Rhett, and a Cast of Thousands: the Filming of Gone With the Wind*. New York: Macmillan Publishing Co., Inc.; London: Collier Macmillan Publishers, 1975.

Hall, Gladys. "Gone With the Wind: On the Set with Gladys Hall." *Screen Romances* 18:128 (January 1940): 16-18, 68-72.

Haver, Ronald. *David O. Selznick's Hollywood*. New York: Alfred A. Knopf, 1980.

Howard, Leslie Ruth. *A Quite Remarkable Father*. London: Longmans, 1960.

Howard, Sidney Coe. *GWTW, the Screenplay*. Based on the novel by Margaret Mitchell; edited by Richard Harwell. New York: Macmillan Publishing Co., Inc., 1980.

Kurtz, Wilbur George. "Technical Adviser: the Making of *Gone With the Wind*—the Hollywood Journals of Wilbur G. Kurtz." Edited by Richard Harwell. *Atlanta Historical Journal* 22:2 (Summer 1978): 7-131.

Lambert, Gavin. *GWTW: The Making of Gone With the Wind*. Boston, Toronto: Little, Brown and Company, 1973.

Mitchell, Margaret. *Gone With the Wind*. New York: The Macmillan Company, 1936.

_____ . *Margaret Mitchell's "Gone With the Wind" Letters, 1936-1949.* Edited by Richard Harwell. New York: Macmillan Publishing Co., Inc.; London: Collier Macmillan Publishers, 1976.

Myrick, Susan. "Forty Years of 'Such Interesting People.' " *Atlanta Journal and Constitution Magazine* (8 September 1974): 8, 10, 42-44, 47.

_____ . "Memoir of GWTW." *Georgia* 16:9 (April 1973): 35-37, 47, 49.

_____ . "My Friends Have Gone With the Wind." *Southern Living* 2:9 (October 1967): 30-33, 46.

_____ . "Pardon My Un-Southern Accent." *Collier's* 104:25 (16 December 1939): 20, 31-32.

_____ . "Vivien Leigh IS Scarlett." *The Atlanta Journal Sunday Magazine* (19 November 1939): 1-2.

Pratt, William. *Scarlett Fever: the Ultimate Pictorial Treasury of Gone With the Wind.* New York: Macmillan Publishing Co., Inc.; London: Collier Macmillan Publishers, 1977.

Selznick, David O. *Memo from David O. Selznick.* Selected and edited by Rudy Behlmer, with an introduction by S. N. Behrman. New York: Viking Press, 1972.

Selznick International Pictures, Inc. Call sheets. Culver City, California, 1939. Various dates, January-July 1939.

Vance, Malcolm. *Tara Revisited.* New York: Award Books, 1976.

Manuscript Sources

Susan Myrick's letters to Margaret Mitchell are included in the Margaret Mitchell Marsh Collection of the University of Georgia Libraries. There is a much larger collection of her own papers, many of them relating to *Gone With the Wind*, filed as Susan Myrick Papers in the Robert W. Woodruff Research Library of Emory University. This collection was presented to Emory by Susan Lindsley, a niece of Miss Myrick. Miss Lindsley still has in her possession a remarkable collection of photographs, studio memos, and other items relating to the filming of *Gone With the Wind*, and an extensive collection of general correspondence retained by Susan Myrick in her personal file over the years of her long life.

The Margaret Mitchell Marsh Papers at the University of Georgia Libraries comprise the retained files of the author of *Gone With the Wind*, about sixty thousand items of correspondence, clippings, photographs, and so forth.

The Sidney Coe Howard Collection of the Bancroft Library of the University of California, Berkeley, comprises the literary archive of that distinguished playwright and screenwriter. In addition to manuscripts of his plays and screenplays, the collection includes a generous amount of letters from his business and personal correspondence files.

A NOTE ON THE ENDPAPERS

SUSAN MYRICK kept two copies of *Gone With the Wind* with her during the making of the film. One was a working copy in which she marked passages relating to the work scheduled for a day's shooting. The other was a very special copy, the one Margaret Mitchell had inscribed and in which the technical adviser later invited the *GWTW* stars and staff members to sign their names.

The novelist's inscription appears on the book's front flyleaf. It reads: "To Sue Myrick who has charm and gumption and gallantry—and totes her own load. Margaret Mitchell. Atlanta, Ga. Jan. 22, 1937."

Signatures and inscriptions inside the front cover are "Alicia Rhett"; "To Sue From Frederic 'Screwy' Crane"; "To my own Sue from George Bessolo [George Reeves]"; "All my best, Always, Rand Brooks"; "Leona Roberts 'Mrs. Meade' "; "Happy daze from your copy editor Neville Reay"; "Jane Darwell—Mrs. Merriweather [Merriwether], the old buffalo"; "Diane King"; "[a scribble representing Cammie] Eleanore King"; "Victor Jory, Jonas Wilkerson."

In the upper left corner of the flyleaf, Susan Myrick wrote her own last name. Above the novelist's inscription is "Thank you for Georgia, Sue—love Vivien [Leigh]." Along the left margin appears "To Susan Myrick—My affection, always, Olivia de Havilland." Below, the inscriptions are: "Laura Hope Crews"; "Thomas Mitchell"; "Leslie Howard"; "Carroll Nye"; "To Lovely Miss Myrick whom I have been so happy to know. I trust we can get our Southern Dinner before she says adieu—'Mammy'—Hattie McDaniel." On the lower left half of the page are: "Clark Gable"; "Victor Fleming"; and "Reggie Callow—To one who appreciates the value of laughter."

The signatures and messages on the back flyleaf are "Hazel O. Rogers, 'scalp doily artist?' "; "Naomi 'Dillie' Thompson—Script-Heelair!"; "Fred A. Parrish 'World's greatest bald headed photographer' "; "Jim Potevin Just Plain light headed"; "Mozelle Miller—'Quiet Sue' "; "Arthur Roland Tovey—'a stand-in!' "; "Needles and pins so glad to have met you on 'Gone with the Wind'—Helene Henley"; "John Flinn—'Our Girl' "; "Bill McGarry"; " 'To My Sue'—Stanley Campbell"; "E. G. Boyle"; "Luck—To A lovely little 'lady' I have enjoyed working with—The Green Man [Roy] McLaughlin"; "To the Sweetest Girl I have ever met from Macon, Georgia—Doc Gil Stone"; "Lydia Schiller"; "G. C. Barker"; "Connie Earle"; "Martha Acker—'Hair pin Hattie' "; "To Sue Sincerely Monty G. Westmore 'let's you and I make up.' "

Inside the back cover Susan Myrick again wrote her name in the upper left corner. Along the left margin is "To Sue—A person I am delighted to have been associated with—Love—Ann Robinson." Opposite, along the right margin is "To a nice Southern Lady—Antonio Samamiego (sound)." From top to bottom and left to right other signatures and messages are: "Annie Laurie Fuller Kurtz"; "Wilbur G. Kurtz"; "Ray Rennahan"; "Ernie Haller"; "Lee Zavitz"; "William Cameron Menzies"; "Al Cline"; "Paul Hill"; "For Flat-foot—Susie—'She may tote her own load but she's really 'too po to tote it'—All my love Will Price"; "Arthur Arling"; "To Susie—that nice gal from Macon—Bobby (Keon) P.S. Love & Kisses"; "Thanks to Miss Mitchell for creating 'Prissy' Thanks to Miss Myrick for helping her. Butterfly McQueen"; "Elmer Ellsworth"; " 'Rollem' Frank Maher Sound"; and "The South has given you something I missed. That gift—combined with your own personality—I both admire—and envy—Highest regards Marian Dabney."

The original of this unique copy of *Gone With the Wind* is in the collection of Susan Lindsley, and the endpapers are reproduced with her permission. The photographs of them were taken by Tom Fletcher of the Medical Illustration Department of Emory University School of Medicine.

INDEX

MP   WHITE COLUMNS IN HOLLYWOOD

Designed by Haywood Ellis
    additional art by Margaret Brown
Composition by Omni Composition Services
    interior design by Margaret Brown
    additional typesetting design by Edd Rowell and Haywood Ellis
    typeset on an A/M Comp/Set 5404 Phototypesetter
    and paginated on an A/M Comp/Set 4510
    text typeface—Times Roman (11 on 13); display type—Souvenir
    and Souvenir italic

Production specifications:
    text paper—60 pound Warren's Olde Style
    end papers—80 pound Natural Sunray Opaque, printed PMS 490 brown
    cover (on .088 boards)—Holliston Roxite B 53501, foil
    (Kurz-Hastings Colorit 929 P) and blind stamped
    dust jacket—100 pound offset enamel, printed two colors
    (PMS 178 peach and PMS 490 brown) and varnished

Printing (offset lithography) by Omnipress of Macon, Inc., Macon, Georgia
Binding by John H. Dekker and Sons, Inc., Grand Rapids, Michigan

Hazel C. Rogers. Scalp oiling artist

Naomi "Tillie" Thompson — Scalp-heel- ace

Fred A. Parrish "Worlds greatest bald headed

Jim Blevin Just light headed Photographer"

"Mozelle Miller — Quiet Sue"

Arthur Roland Tovey — a stand-in!

Needles and pins so glad to have met ya
on "Gone with the Wind" — Helene Hurley.

John Flinn — "Our Girl"

if Bill McGarry

To my Suzy

Stanley

Luck To a lovely little
"Lady" I have enjoyed
working with The snow man
McLaughlin

To the Sweetest Girl
I've ever met from Macon George

Lydia Schell Ce Barker Joe Gil Stone

Connie Earle

Martha Acker
hair pin setter you

To Sue Sunday
Monty Westmore
"Let's you + I"

Eddie Allen